FIRST CERTIFICATE SKILLS

Use of English

Mark Harrison

With Answers

OXFORD
UNIVERSITY PRESS

Contents

Unit 1
The present

Grammar
1.1 The present
1.2 Habits & normality

Vocabulary
1.3 Frequency
1.4 Word focus

1.1 The present

Stop & check

You meet a visitor to your country. Tick the correct questions and correct the errors.

1 Are you enjoying your visit here? ✔
2 ~~Do you stay~~ in a hotel? Are you staying
3 ~~Are you liking~~ the food here? Do you like
4 Do you know much about this country? ✔
5 Are you travelling alone? ✔
6 ~~Do you have~~ an interesting holiday? Are you having
7 Do you go to other countries very often? ✔
8 ~~Are you understanding~~ much of our language? Do you understand

Present tenses

Use	Example
Use the present simple for • facts of life, things that are generally true • things people do or things that happen in general or habitually • permanent situations that won't change or are unlikely to change	*People who have jobs earn money.* *I read a lot of books.* *All matches start at 3.* *Jack lives alone because he prefers it.*
Use the present continuous for • actions at exactly this moment • actions during this period of time • temporary situations that will or may change	*You're reading this sentence.* *This country is changing a lot.* *Robert's working in a bar this summer.*

Verbs that have no continuous form

Many verbs which are connected with the idea of thinking or having a feeling are not usually used in the present continuous form, for example:

like want hate mind prefer care need know understand realize

It is not correct to say ~~*I'm not knowing his name*~~ or ~~*Are you wanting something to eat?*~~ Instead say *I don't know his name* and *Do you want something to eat?*

▶ note: The continuous form of *be* is used to talk about someone's temporary behaviour.
You're being stupid. (at this moment, not that you are a stupid person)

→ ExA p5

Have (got)

Use	Example
• Use **the present simple** if *have* refers to possessing something ▶ note: Do not ask ***Have you*** with this meaning.	*They have/They've got a nice house.* *Does he have/Has he got a well-paid job?* NOT ~~*Has he a well-paid job?*~~
• Use **the present simple** and **the present continuous** if ***have*** is part of a phrase that refers to an action ▶ note: Forms of ***have got*** are not correct with this meaning.	*I have a shower every morning.* *She's having a shower at the moment.* NOT ~~*I have got a shower every morning*~~.

→ ExB p5

A Put the verbs in brackets in the correct present tense form.

1 The trains to London ....leave......... from platform 5 every half an hour. (leave)
2 Leave me alone. I ...am/'m trying... to concentrate. (try)
3 People in Italy ....eat.......... a lot of pasta. (eat)
4 .Do you understand. how to fill in this form? (you understand)
5 As part of her job, she ....goes......... to a lot of conferences. (go)
6 ....Do you like.... this kind of music? (you like)
7 Cars like that ....cost......... a lot of money. (cost)
8 I ....don't know..... what to do at the moment, I'm very confused. (not know)
9 Don't shout at me. I ...am/'m doing... my best. (do)
10 The fans are unhappy because the team ...is/are playing.. very badly at the moment. (play)
11 Brian ....wears........ a suit for work when he has to look smart. (wear)
12 Why ..are you being.. so rude to me today? Have I done something to upset you? (you be)
13 'I ....don't want..... this sandwich.' 'OK, I'll have it.' (not want)
14 I ..am/'m waiting.. for a letter from my friend in San Francisco. (wait)
15 'Is anyone using. this chair?' 'No, it's free, you can take it.' (anyone use)

B Decide whether these sentences are correct or not. Correct those which are incorrect.

1 Julie hasn't got much money at the moment. correct..........
2 They ~~haven't got~~ a lot of fun at work. don't have/aren't having..........
3 Terry is having a lot of problems at the moment. correct..........
4 Helena has two brothers and a sister. correct..........
5 Tom is having a rest in the bedroom. correct..........
6 Have you got a pen I could borrow? correct..........
7 We ~~'ve got~~ lunch at about 1pm every day. have..........
8 Have they any children? got..........

1.2 Habits & normality

Use	Example
Expressions + *-ing*/noun • Use ***be used to* + *-ing*/noun** to talk about situations which are familiar to or normal for someone and which they therefore do not find strange or difficult • Use ***get used to* + *-ing*/noun** to talk about situations becoming familiar or normal after at first being strange or difficult • Use ***be*/*get accustomed to* + *-ing*/noun** with the same meanings as *be*/*get used to* but used in a more formal context	*I'm used to getting up early so I don't find it difficult.* *Keith wasn't used to living in a hot country so he had a few problems at first.* *In Japan Maddy got used to different kinds of food.* *Don't worry, you'll get used to travelling long distances soon.* *Eventually they got accustomed to working for a large organization.*
Expressions + *-ing* • Use ***have a habit of* + *-ing*** to talk about things that people often do, especially when these things are considered bad • Use ***be always* + *-ing*** as an emphatic exclamation to describe habits causing annoyance or surprise	*I'm afraid I have a habit of forgetting people's names.* *You're always complaining! Please stop.* *Dave was always talking about very strange things!*
Expressions + infinitive (with *to*) • Use ***tend* + infinitive (with *to*)** to talk about things that people usually do or that usually happen or are true • Use ***have a tendency* + infinitive (with *to*)** with the same meaning as *tend*; often used when the speaker disapproves of or dislikes something	*The weather tends to be quite mild at this time of year.* *We tend to have dinner at about 7.* *Tom has a tendency to blame other people for his own mistakes.*
Expressions + infinitive (without *to*) • Use ***would* + infinitive** (**without *to***) to talk about things that happened repeatedly in the past ▶ note: *used to* also expresses this idea.	*When I was young, my father would tell me stories before I went to sleep.* *... my father used to tell me stories ...*

➔ ExA p7

Adjectives used to talk about habits and normality

typical being a very good example of something because of having its most usual qualities	*What's a **typical** dish from this country?*
everyday happening regularly or every day and therefore not unusual or special	*I want to find out what **everyday** life in that country is like.*
frequent/regular happening or done often	*He makes **frequent** visits to the doctor.* *Are you a **regular** visitor to this country?*
common usual or familiar; happening or found often and in many places	*Hats like that are quite **common** in this region.*
usual that happens or is true on most occasions	*Lessons will start at the **usual** time.*
average normal statistically	*What's the **average** income for people in this country?*
normal being what people expect or consider usual; not strange	*Although she's a star, she says that she leads a **normal** life.*

ordinary not unusual, special or different	*I'm going to buy an* ***ordinary*** *CD player that doesn't cost very much.*
unusual not happening, done or true usually; different from what is normal and therefore strange	*He has an* ***unusual*** *approach to his work.*
rare = *very unusual*	*Snow is* ***rare*** *in this country.*
▶ note: You can use ***it*** **+** ***be*** **+ adjective +** ***for*** **+ object + infinitive (with** ***to*****)** with *usual, unusual, common, normal* and *rare.*	*It's* ***usual for*** *rain to fall in April.* *It's very* ***unusual for*** *Joe to be late.* *It's* ***common for*** *families to eat together.* *Is it* ***normal for*** *trains to run on time here?* *It's* ***rare for*** *me to have a lot of free time.*
In this pattern, do not use ~~*typical for*~~. Instead, say *typical of.*	*It's* ***typical of*** *him to get angry if he loses a game.*

→ ExB+C p8

A Rewrite these sentences using the word in brackets.

1 I usually have more energy in the morning. (tend)
I tend to have more energy in the morning.

2 You criticize other people too often! (always)
You're always criticizing other people!

3 My mother worries too much. (tendency)
My mother has a tendency to worry too much.

4 She used to feel exhausted at the end of every day. (would)
She would feel exhausted at the end of every day.

5 Ken found it strange to be so poor. (used)
Ken wasn't used to being so poor.

6 I haven't driven this kind of car before. (accustomed)
I'm not accustomed to driving this kind of car.

7 Frank doesn't usually tell lies. (tends)
Frank tends not/doesn't tend to tell lies.

8 Ian finds it normal now to sort out other people's problems for them. (used)
Ian is used to sorting out other people's problems for them.

9 As a child, he played some kind of sport every day. (would)
As a child, he would play some kind of sport every day.

10 Zoe often makes jokes about her problems. (habit)
Zoe has a habit of making jokes about her problems.

B **Read this beginning of a novel and underline the correct word for 1–10.**

My Neighbourhood

Remarkable events are not a 1 regular/ordinary occurrence in my neighbourhood. It's full of 2 usual/ordinary people doing the 3 normal/general things that people do – getting up, going to work, and then going home again. They talk about 4 average/everyday things like the weather and their illnesses, and the government is another 5 typical/average subject of conversation. If someone has a problem, it's very 6 ordinary/usual for their neighbours to help them out. Serious arguments are rare and strong friendships are very 7 common/average. In the 8 average/ordinary year, there's very little crime and visits from the police are not very 9 frequent/everyday. But nothing lasts forever, as we were about to find out. It started as a 10 normal/common day but then something truly remarkable did happen.

C **Complete the second sentence so that it means the same as the first, using the word given.**

1 People quite often arrive late. (common)
It is ......(quite) common for people to...... arrive late.

2 Harriet often says things that annoy other people. (habit)
Harriet ....has a habit of saying.......... things that annoy other people.

3 I don't find it strange to travel all the time any more. (got)
I .have/'ve got used/accustomed to travelling.. all the time.

4 Tell me, do people usually wait patiently in queues in Britain? (usual)
Tell me, ...is it usual for people.......... to wait patiently in queues in Britain?

5 I think she'll always find it strange to work as part of a team. (get)
I don't think she'll ....(ever) get used to working....... as part of a team.

6 In fact, I don't usually get as many presents as this. (normal)
In fact, it's ....not normal for me............ to get as many presents as this.

7 In my experience, Noel doesn't usually lose his temper like that. (rare)
In my experience, ...it is rare for Noel............ to lose his temper like that.

8 Hard work is a new experience for George. (used)
George ....is not/isn't used to working....... hard.

9 Reg often panics when there's a problem of any kind. (tendency)
Reg ....has a tendency to panic......... when there's a problem of any kind.

10 Judy always found it difficult to give people the sack in her job. (used)
Judy couldn't ....get used to giving............ people the sack in her job.

→ Glossary p209

1.3 Frequency

A Put the adverbs and phrases below in the correct place in the table.

invariably, over and over again, time and again, now and again, from time to time, once in a while, time after time, seldom

always	(too) many times	sometimes	almost never
invariably	over and over again	now and again	seldom
	time and again	from time to time	
	time after time	once in a while	

B Read this information sheet and underline the correct word for 1–10.

Join The School Orchestra!

- Rehearsals are on Tuesdays and Thursdays every week.
- Rehearsals 1 **periodically/normally** begin at 6.30 but one or two may have to be held earlier.
- 2 **Time after time/As a rule**, rehearsals last for one hour, although some may be longer.
- Auditions for new members are held 3 **periodically/invariably**, usually about every two months.
- Members are encouraged to practise as 4 **usually/frequently** as possible and extra lessons are available.
- These 5 **generally/constantly** take place at weekends, although they may be available on weekday evenings.
- We 6 **constantly/seldom** need new musicians so it is always possible to join.
- We 7 **regularly/time after time** put on our own concerts here and 8 **seldom/occasionally** we also play at other venues.
- We are 9 **all the time/continually** trying to improve and we 10 **rarely/in a while** get bad reviews!

C Fill the gaps in this report with one of the words or phrases given.

every then hardly often most all

TV VIEWING HABITS IN BRITAIN

TWENTY YEARS AGO, families in Britain used to watch the same programmes on TV together 1 ....all.......... the time. Certain well-known programmes were national events and it was common for people to discuss them excitedly at school and at work the next day. This kind of thing 2 ....hardly.......... ever happens these days. With the arrival of new technology, people have got used to having more and more channels to choose from. Nowadays, as 3 ....often.......... as not families watch different programmes in different rooms. Now and 4 ....then.......... they might watch something together, but 5 ....most.......... of the time they don't. However, 6 ....every.......... so often a programme is made that appeals to people of all ages.

→ Glossary p209

1.4 Word focus

Phrasal verbs: *be* & *do*

A Complete the phrasal verbs with *be* using the particles below.

up out of over away up to on

1 I couldn't buy anything else because I **was** ....out of.... money.
2 It's ....up to.... you which film we see, I have no particular preference.
3 When the match **was** ....over.... , we went home and celebrated.
4 Julia **is** ....away.... on holiday until the end of next week.
5 Hurry up – your favourite programme **is** ....on.... in two minutes.
6 You look angry – **is** something ....up.... ?

B Choose the correct meaning, A or B, for the phrasal verbs with *do* in these sentences.

1 I could ***do with*** a holiday, I'm getting very tired.
A need **B** am able to have
2 They ***did up*** the house before moving into it.
A built **B** redecorated
3 Suzanne can't ***do without*** her home comforts.
A find better **B** manage without
4 They should ***do away with*** that ridiculous law.
A get rid of **B** copy

Word formation: adjective suffixes

C Complete the text by forming adjectives using the word in capitals at the end of each line and the suffixes below. You may need to make more than one change to each word.

-al -ic -ful -able -ing -ous

The holiday of a lifetime!

If you want a truly 1 ..memorable.. holiday, book with us now! We can MEMORY
offer you a 2 ..personal.. service that no other company can. Our expert PERSON
staff will provide you with very 3 ..useful.. information about all of USE
the 4 ..historic.. buildings and areas that you can visit. On some excursions, HISTORY
for a small 5 ..additional.. charge, we can even provide you with your own ADD
individual guide. A trip with us will give you an insight into the 6 ..cultural.. CULTURE
life of the region. We try to make sure that nothing is 7 ..missing.. in order to MISS
make your trip a 8 ..marvellous.. one that you will talk about for ages. MARVEL
We have something to offer both those looking for a 9 ..peaceful.. time taking PEACE
it easy, and more 10 ..energetic.. people looking for the adventure of a lifetime. ENERGY

→ Glossary p209–10

Collocations

D Fill the gaps in this text with the correct form of one of the verbs below.

do have make take cause

How to be a Good Manager

Being a good manager is not just about how you 1 ...do... your own work, it's much more about your attitude. Here are some tips to keep in mind:

- remember that everyone in the company has an important contribution to 2 make
- try to 3 .have. a good relationship with the people working for you
- if a member of staff has a problem, always 4 .take.. the time to listen to them – they will appreciate it if you show that you 5 .have. sympathy for them
- if you 6 .have. the feeling that someone who works for you is 7 .causing/(having)/(making). trouble, speak to that person directly and listen to any comments they wish to 8 make
- your job involves 9 making/(taking) decisions and sometimes you are bound to 10 make mistakes when you do this; if so, be honest about it, don't 11 make excuses
- equally, if someone working for you 12 makes a bit of a mess, don't 13 make the assumption that they don't care – they may be very upset about it
- when important meetings with staff 14 .take. place, 15 make certain that you're fully prepared for them; 16 make clear statements on policy so that you don't 17 cause/have any confusion
- if members of staff 18 make suggestions, listen to them carefully and 19 .take.. them seriously – nobody likes to have their ideas ignored
- the company is there to 20 make a profit and if this happens, praise the rest of the staff – it's their company too!

Word sets

E Complete each sentence with one of the words given.

contains consists involves includes

1 The cost of the trip ...includes... all accommodation and meals.
2 Her job ....involves... a lot of travel overseas.
3 This parcel ...contains... all the books I ordered.
4 The course ...consists... of lectures and practical work.

particular single unique individual

1 I like all of her novels but this ..particular.. one is my favourite.
2 He did the whole job without making one .....single..... mistake.
3 Each .individual. member of the group makes an important contribution.
4 It was a totally ...unique.... experience, which could never be repeated.

win gain earn achieve

1 Jobs were scarce and he found it hard to .....earn...... a living.
2 As she became more successful, she began to ......gain...... confidence.
3 It is unlikely that she will ever ....achieve.... that aim.
4 He always gets angry if he doesn't ....win....... at games.

ECCE Practice 1

Grammar

1 Sarah __c__ in the Accounts Department.
- a to work
- b working
- **c** works
- d been working

2 It's unusual __d__ me to go out on a Monday night.
- a of
- b with
- c to
- **d** for

3 When I was young, I __a__ always walk to school in the mornings.
- **a** would
- b could
- c will
- d did

4 I __d__ a cooked meal every evening.
- a has
- b have got
- c am having
- **d** have

5 'Oh no! I forgot my keys!' 'You're always __c__ your keys!'
- a forget
- b forgot
- **c** forgetting
- d leaving

6 Rita __c__ getting up early. She finds it difficult.
- a is used to
- b has a habit of
- **c** isn't used to
- d is always

7 'I think you __c__ silly – just tell the truth!'
- a being
- b 've being
- **c** 're being
- d been

8 Phil has a __c__ to lie to his friends when it comes to his relationship.
- a habit
- b custom
- **c** tendency
- d mind

Vocabulary

9 It's so wet here – it __b__ rains non-stop for several days.
- a seldom
- **b** frequently
- c periodically
- d all the time

10 Jenny is __a__ on holiday for a week.
- **a** away
- b out
- c in
- d to

11 Please will you just tidy your room, and stop __c__ excuses!
- a taking
- b having
- **c** making
- d doing

12 When the party was __d__ we helped them clear up the room.
- a up
- b off
- c out
- **d** over

13 They __c__ their living by selling fruits and vegetables.
- a gain
- b have
- **c** earn
- d win

14 'I'm afraid there's no more milk left in the fridge.' 'Don't worry we'll __d__ it.'
- a manage
- b do with
- c do away with
- **d** do without

15 This job __a__ working very long hours.
- **a** involves
- b consists
- c includes
- d contains

16 'Let's go to the cinema!' 'Which __a__ film did you have in mind?'
- **a** particular
- b individual
- c single
- d unique

Exam techniques
→ p223

FCE Practice 1

Part 4

For Questions **1–15**, read the text below and look carefully at each line. Some of the lines are correct and some have a word which should not be there. If a line is correct, put a tick (✔) in the space next to the number of the line. If a line has a word which should **not** be there, put that word in the space next to the number of the line.

MY FAVOURITE FILM

1 ....a.... I'm really ~~a~~ keen on going to the cinema, so I've got lots of favourite

2 ...as... films. But the best one ~~as~~ I've seen lately is called *Pressure*. In some

3 ...✔... ways, I suppose that you could regard it as a detective film but it's

4 ..one.. different from most films of that ~~one~~ kind because the characters are

5 ..they.. ~~they~~ such unusual people. The detective in it, for example, is a computer

6 ...✔... expert who solves crimes on her computer using information given to

7 ...to... her by her assistants, who go out and interview ~~to~~ people. The case in

8 .about. the film concerns ~~about~~ the wife of a millionaire, who has gone missing.

9 ...✔... Sometimes the plot gets a bit complicated but it isn't too hard to keep

10 ...✔... up with it. There are a lot of strange characters in it, such as a man

11 ...on... who always wears two hats ~~on~~, and some of the scenes really made me

12 ..you.. laugh. Also, there is a big surprise at the end but I won't say ~~you~~ what

13 ...the... that is in ~~the~~ case you go to see it. It's very well acted and I also like

14 ...do... the music in it. But what ~~do~~ I really like most about the film is that

15 ...✔... it's so original – I've certainly never seen another film quite like that.

Unit **2**

The past

Grammar
2.1 The past
2.2 First & last
2.3 Time adverbs & prepositions 1
2.4 Periods of time 1

Vocabulary
2.5 Periods of time 2
2.6 Word focus

2.1 The past

Stop & check

You are talking to a visitor to your country. Tick the correct sentences and correct the errors.

1 When did you arrive in this country? ✔
2 What ~~have you done~~ yesterday? did you do
3 Did you go to that concert last week? ✔
4 How long have you been here? ✔
5 Have you been to many other countries? ✔
6 I ~~was used to~~ live in a different city. used to
7 We ~~have moved~~ to this city when I was nine. moved
8 I ~~supported~~ this football team since I was a child. have supported
9 I ~~'ve always been enjoying~~ football. 've always enjoyed
10 Before this trip, I hadn't heard of your town. ✔

Use	Example
Use the past simple to talk about	
• a specific time in the past and say exactly when something happened	*I arrived at 2.*
• a specific time in the past but not say exactly when, because that is understood and has been established by what was previously said	*'What did you do last night?' – 'I met some friends and we went to see a film.'*
• something that happened for a period of time in the past but is not happening in the present	*I lived there for three years.*
Use *used to* + infinitive to talk about	
• something that happened or was true for a period of time in the past, but does not happen or is not true now	*People used to think the world was flat.*
Use the past continuous to talk about	
• something that continued for a period in the past	*My tooth was hurting all day yesterday.*
• two things that happened in the past; one of them happened for a period of time (past continuous), the other happened during that period of time (past simple)	*They were waiting for me, so I called to say I would be late.*
• use *while* or *when* before the past continuous and *when* before the past simple	*While / When I was walking to the shop, I met a friend.* *I was walking to the shop when I met a friend.*
Use the present perfect to talk about	
• something that happened in the past without saying when it happened, because you don't know when or because it is not important when	*Helen has travelled all over the world.*
• something that happened at an unspecified time in the past and has a result now	*I've lost my keys. (= I haven't got them now)*
• something that has happened very recently	*They've just scored a goal. Hurray!*
• use *gone* if the subject is still at the place mentioned; use *been* if they have now returned	*My dad's gone to work – he won't be back until 6pm.* *Her cousin's been to China – she brought back some really unusual things.*

Compare

used to and the past simple

- the length of the period of time is not stated with *used to*
  I used to live there.
- if you say how long the period of time was, use the past simple
  I lived there for ten years.

the present perfect simple and the past simple

- the time is not stated with the present perfect simple
  I've seen this film.
- if you say when something happened, use the past simple
  I saw this film when I was on holiday last year.

→ ExA+B p16

Use	Example
Use the present perfect continuous to talk about	
• something that started in the past, continued for a period and is still happening now	*They've been learning English for three years.*
• *for* and *since* are used with this meaning, *for* before the period of time and *since* before the point in time when it started	*I've been feeling ill since I got up this morning.*
• something that happens repeatedly during a period starting in the past and continuing until now; *lately* and *recently* are often used with this meaning	*She's been having a lot of problems lately.* *I've been reading some interesting books recently.*
▶ note: If the verb refers to a continuing state or situation rather than an action, the present perfect simple can also be used.	*I've lived / I've been living here for three years.*
▶ note: With negative verbs, the present perfect simple (NOT the present perfect continuous) is usually used with *for* or *since*.	*I haven't read a newspaper since Monday.* *She hasn't phoned me for weeks.*
Use the past perfect simple to talk about	
• two things that happened in the past which are connected in some way. One thing happened before the other.	*She got promoted because she'd done a lot of good work.*
• use the past perfect for what happened before and the past simple for what happened after that	*I hadn't met her before so I didn't know who she was.*
Use the past perfect continuous to talk about	
• something that happened for a period of time in the past before something else in the past happened • *for* and *since* can be used	*I was tired when I got home because I'd been working hard (for hours/since early in the morning).*

Compare

the past perfect continuous and the past continuous

- with the past continuous, a period of time is not mentioned
- if the period of time is mentioned, use the past perfect continuous
  I was waiting when they arrived. I had been waiting for half an hour when they arrived.

Verbs that have no continuous form

Many verbs which are connected with the idea of thinking or having a feeling are not usually used in continuous tenses, for example:

like want hate mind prefer care need know understand realize

It is not correct to say ~~*I've been knowing her for years*~~. Instead say *I've known her for years.*

▶ note: The continuous form of *be* is only used to talk about someone's temporary behaviour.
I told him that he was being stupid (at that moment, not that he was a stupid person).

→ ExC p17

A **Read this text and underline the correct word for 1–15.**

Louis Armstrong

Louis Armstrong, who 1 **was/has been** born in 1900 and 2 **had died/died** in 1971, was a very famous jazz musician and bandleader. He 3 **used to be/had** known as 'Satchmo', and this nickname 4 **was staying/stayed** with him all his life. As a child in New Orleans, he learned to play the trumpet while he 5 **was living/lived** in a special home for children who 6 **had got/have got** into trouble with the police. When he 7 **used to finish/had finished** his stay in the home, he joined various bands and then he 8 **formed/used to form** his own. Between 1925 and 1928 he 9 **made/was making** about sixty records as the leader of two small groups called the *Hot Fives* and the *Hot Sevens*. These records 10 **were making/made** him one of the first solo stars in the history of popular music. When he died, he 11 **had been making/was making** records and he 12 **was touring/had been touring** all over the world for more than forty years, and he 13 **was/was being** just as popular as he 14 **had been/has been** before. He even 15 **was having/had** a number one pop record – *What A Wonderful World* – in the 1960s.

B **Complete this text by forming the correct tenses of the verbs in brackets.**

Manchester United

MANCHESTER UNITED is a football club that these days 1 ....has become.......... (become) one of the most well-known in the world. It 2 ....started.......... (start) in 1902 and it 3 ....has won.......... (win) the FA Cup, a famous competition in English football, more times than any other club. In 1958, many of its players 4 ....died.......... (die) when their plane crashed in Germany. Ten years later, the club 5 ....won.......... (win) the European Cup, with famous players like George Best and Bobby Charlton. In the early 1990s, the club 6 ....became.......... (become) a public company, with shares on the Stock Exchange. Since then, it 7 ....has started.......... (start) its own TV channel and it 8 ....has become.......... (become) even more famous world-wide, with all kinds of publicity and many different kinds of goods related to the club. In 1999, the team 9 ....won.......... (win) the European Champions League. They 10 ....were losing.......... (lose) the match against Bayern Munich 1–0 but right at the end of the match they 11 ....scored.......... (score) two goals.

The club has millions of supporters both in Britain and abroad – although many of them 12 ....have never been.......... (never go) to Manchester in their lives!

C **Complete this text by filling gaps 1–20 with the correct verb form, A, B, C or D.**

Karen & Dave

Karen sat at her desk. She couldn't concentrate on her work because she 1 ....C....... about Dave. They 2 ....B....... together for three years and she 3 ....D....... him more than any of her other colleagues. They 4 ....B....... an argument. They 5 ....A....... talk about anything together – work matters or things that 6 ....C....... their private lives at the time. But now, everything 7 ....D....... . She felt that Dave 8 ....A....... very strange. 9 ....B....... some terrible secret? She decided to speak to him about it.

Dave 10 ....C....... a coffee in the canteen when she found him. She got straight to the point. 'Dave,' she said, 'I 11 ....A....... you for years. We 12 ....C....... working here at the same time and we 13 ....A....... well together. But you 14 ....B....... very strangely. 15 ....D.......?

16 ....A....... something to upset you?' Dave said nothing at first. He 17 ....D....... there in silence. Then he leaned forward and whispered, 'No, you 18 ....A....... anything wrong. It's me. For the past couple of months, I 19 ....C....... something I shouldn't. But I can't tell you about it now.' And then he got up and left. As he disappeared, Karen 20 ....B....... what on earth it could be.

1	A thought	B used to think	**C** was thinking	D has thought
2	A have worked	**B** had been working	C were working	D used to work
3	A was always liking	B had always been liking	C has always liked	**D** had always liked
4	A were never having	**B** had never had	C never used to have	D had never been having
5	**A** used to be able to	B were being able to	C have been able to	D have been being able to
6	A was affecting	B have affected	**C** were affecting	D has affected
7	A has changed	B changed	C used to change	**D** had changed
8	**A** was being	B used to be	C has been	D had been being
9	A Had he	**B** Did he have	C Was he having	D Did he used to have
10	A had	B has been having	**C** was having	D has had
11	**A** 've known	B knew	C used to know	D was knowing
12	A used to start	B have started	**C** started	D were starting
13	**A** 've always got on	B were always getting on	C 've always been getting on	D 'd always been getting on
14	A had behaved	**B** 've been behaving	C used to behave	D were behaving
15	A What used to happen?	B What was happening?	C What happened?	**D** What's happened?
16	**A** Have I done	B Had I done	C Was I doing	D Did I used to do
17	A had sat	B has been sitting	C used to sit	**D** sat
18	**A** haven't done	B hadn't done	C weren't doing	D used not to do
19	A had done	B used to be doing	**C** 've been doing	D was doing
20	A used to wonder	**B** wondered	C had wondered	D had been wondering

2.2 First & last

The first time

Use	Example
be **(present/future) +** ***the first time*** **(+** ***ever*****) + present perfect** • to talk about the first time something happens in the present or future ▶ note: *ever* = in the whole of someone's life; in the whole of history	*If they lose, it will be the first time they've lost a match this season.* *This is the first time I've (ever) been to this place.*
be **(past) +** ***the first time*** **(+** ***ever*****) + past perfect** • to talk about the first time something happened in the past	*It was the first time she'd ever travelled on a plane.*

▶ note: *The second time*, *the third time*, etc. can be used in the above patterns
This is the third time I've told you this.

▶ note: Any noun can be used instead of *time* in the same patterns.
This is the first job I've (ever) had.

▶ note: Any superlative adjective and any noun can be used in the same patterns.
This is the best meal I've ever eaten.

The last time

Use	Example
be **(present) +** ***the last time*** **(+** ***ever*****) + present simple /** ***will*** **/** ***going to*** • to talk about the last time something happens in the present	*This is the last time I (ever) come here / I will (ever) come here / I'm (ever) going to come here.*
be **(future) +** ***the last time*** **+ present simple** • to talk about the last time something happens in the future	*It will be the last time I (ever) travel to work in that place.*
be **(past) +** ***the last time*** **+ past simple** • to talk about the last time something happened in the past	*That was the last time I (ever) saw her.*
it is **/** ***has been*** **+ period +** ***since*** **+ subject (+** ***last*****) + past simple** • to talk about the period of time between when something happened and now • *last* can be used when talking about something that used to happen regularly • often used to talk about the period of time between an important event and now	*It's more than three years since I last saw her.* *It's been months since I last read a good book.* *It's five years since she left university.*

▶ note: Any noun can be used instead of *time* in the same patterns:
It will be the last exam I ever take.

A Complete the second sentence so that it means the same as the first.

1 I'm asking you this question for the third time.
This is ......the third time I've asked you...... this question.

2 Tomorrow, she'll be driving a car for the first time.
Tomorrow will be the first time ......she has (ever) driven...... a car.

3 After those words, he never said anything to me again.
Those ...were the last words/words were the last he (ever) said... to me.

4 Before then, she had never had to earn her own money.
That was the first time ......she had (ever) had...... to earn her own money.

5 After that, she never mentioned the subject again.
That was the ......last time she (ever) mentioned...... the subject.

6 After next week, I'll never have to work with her again.
Next week will be ...the last time I (ever)/I'll ever/I'm ever going to have to... work with her.

B Complete the second sentence so that it means the same as the first.

1 They've never made a record better than this one, in my opinion.
This is the best ......record they've (ever) made,...... in my opinion.

2 I haven't been to a football match for years.
It's ......(been) years since I (last) went...... to a football match.

3 I've already written two letters to them before this one.
This will be the third letter ......I've written...... to them.

4 I've never met anyone like her before.
This is the first ......time I've (ever) met...... anyone like her.

5 Not again! I've already had chicken three times this week.
This is the fourth ......time I've had...... chicken this week.

6 I never trusted them again after that.
That was the last time ......I (ever) trusted...... them.

7 She last got in touch with me about two months ago.
It is about two months ......since she (last) got...... in touch with me.

8 I've never seen a worse film than this one, to be honest.
This is the worst ......film I've (ever) seen,...... to be honest.

9 Fiona went on a trip around the US two years ago.
It is ......two years since Fiona went...... on a trip around the US.

10 I've never met a person as unpleasant as him before, I must say.
He is the most unpleasant ......person I've (ever) met,...... I must say.

11 We moved into this flat three years ago.
It is three years ......since we moved...... into this flat.

12 My dad will never lend me money again after this.
This is the last time ......my dad will ever lend...... me money.

2.3 Time adverbs and prepositions 1

already • to say that something has happened before now, or before the moment you are referring to • to show surprise in questions	*I* ***already*** *know how to do this.* *I knew the end of the story because I'd* ***already*** *heard it.* *Have you* ***already*** *finished this?* *Have you finished* ***already****?*
yet to say that something has not happened but it is expected that it will happen	*Have you paid the bill* ***yet****?* *I haven't finished this* ***yet****.*
still to say that a situation or action continues and has not changed or ended	*He was* ***still*** *working when I left.* *I* ***still*** *don't know what you're talking about.* *Are you* ***still*** *waiting?*
any more / any longer with negative verbs to say that something that was true or happened in the past doesn't continue to be true or to happen ▸ note: Remember to use *any*.	*Jackie doesn't live here* ***any more****.* *I don't work for that company* ***any longer****.* NOT ~~*She doesn't live here more.*~~
***just* + present perfect / present perfect continuous** • in this pattern, *just* = a short time ago • use with *only* to emphasize a **very** short time ago	*I've* ***just*** *finished work and now I want to take it easy.* *I've* ***only just*** *arrived so I don't know what's happening.*
***just* + past perfect / past perfect continuous** in this pattern, *just* = a short time before	*I'd* ***just*** *been talking about Graham when he phoned me.*
***just* + present continuous / past continuous** • to say that someone is in the middle of doing something • in this pattern, *just* = in the process of • often used with *when*	*I'm* ***just*** *getting ready, so can you wait for me?* *I was* ***just*** *leaving my house* ***when*** *some friends arrived.*
***just* + present simple / past simple / future tenses** in these patterns, *just* = simply	*I don't know why, I* ***just*** *don't like him.*
***hardly* + past perfect** • in this pattern, *hardly* = only a short time before • often used with *when*	*I'd* ***hardly*** *met him* ***when*** *he started asking me personal questions.*
***lately* + present perfect / present perfect continuous** to talk about a period of time beginning not long ago and continuing until now	*I've been working hard* ***lately****.* ***Lately*** *I haven't been sleeping well.*
***recently* + present perfect / present perfect continuous** same meaning as *lately*	*I haven't seen her* ***recently****.* ***Recently****, I haven't been sleeping well.* *I've* ***recently*** *been working rather hard.*
***recently* + past simple** = at a point in time not long ago	*I spoke to her* ***recently****.* *They* ***recently*** *got married.*
***so far* + present perfect** = until now but the situation might/will change	*I've enjoyed my visit* ***so far****.* ***So far****, they've won all the games they've played*
currently • to talk about something that is happening now but which may not continue • = during this period of time	*I'm* ***currently*** *looking for another job.* ***Currently****, I'm working very hard.* *She's having a lot of problems* ***currently****.*
nowadays / these days • to talk about present situations or facts, especially in comparison with the past • both used at the beginning of a sentence and between two clauses	*There's a lot of technology* ***nowadays*** *to make people's lives easier.* ***These days*** *I don't go to the cinema as often as I used to.*
***in the last / past* + period** to talk about a period of time before and until now	*His health has improved* ***in the last few weeks****.* ***In the past week*** *we've visited lots of places.*

A Complete this letter to a friend by deciding which word or phrase (A, B, C or D) fits into each gap.

Dear Dina,

As it's a couple of months since you came to stay with us here in the UK, I thought I'd send you some news about what's been happening here 1 ....D....... . Carol has 2 ....B....... got back from a trip to Germany but she hasn't told me much about it 3 ....C....... . I expect she'll give me the full story later. Tim is 4 ....A....... working in a bar to support himself in his studies – I suppose you know that 5 ....B....... students in the UK often have to have a job as well as studying. So he studies and then he goes to work in the evenings – I 6 ....C....... don't know where he gets the energy from! Rob is 7 ....D....... playing in his band – he's quite excited because they've 8 ....D....... been booked to play at a very well-known club. And me? Well, I've 9 ....C....... had three job interviews but I haven't had any luck 10 ....B....... . The problem is that 11 ....A....... you need more qualifications than you used to if you want to do what I want to do. So I've been thinking of doing another course, although I haven't decided which one 12 ....A....... . Please keep in touch with us and tell us your news.

George

1	A any longer	B still	C any more	**D** recently
2	A so far	**B** only just	C nowadays	D currently
3	A already	B still	**C** yet	D hardly
4	**A** currently	B so far	C lately	D recently
5	A recently	**B** these days	C just	D lately
6	A hardly	B yet	**C** just	D already
7	A yet	B any longer	C any more	**D** still
8	A hardly	B nowadays	C these days	**D** just
9	A yet	B any more	**C** already	D so far
10	A already	**B** so far	C only just	D any more
11	**A** nowadays	B any more	C so far	D yet
12	**A** yet	B still	C already	D just

B **These sentences are all incorrect. Rewrite them correctly.**

1 Nothing interesting has happened in past couple of weeks.
Nothing interesting has happened in the past couple of weeks.

2 Young people don't want that kind of thing more.
Young people don't want that kind of thing any more.

3 I saw Elaine at a party lately.
I saw Elaine at a party recently./I recently saw Elaine at a party.

4 I knew his name because we'd met already each other.
I knew his name because we'd already met each other.

5 She's lately been having a lot of problems.
She's been having a lot of problems lately./Lately she's been having a lot of problems.

6 I just was writing a letter to him when he rang me.
I was just writing a letter to him when he rang me.

7 Are still you working for the same company?
Are you still working for the same company?

8 Have you finished already your work?
Have you already finished your work?/Have you finished your work already?

9 They live still in the same place.
They still live in the same place.

10 I contacted them last week but they yet haven't replied.
I contacted them last week but they haven't replied yet.

11 Have you yet had anything to eat?
Have you had anything to eat yet?

12 I'd solved one problem hardly before another one came up.
I'd hardly solved one problem before another one came up.

13 I don't still understand what happened.
I still don't understand what happened.

14 I just fell asleep when a noise outside woke me up.
I had just fallen asleep when a noise outside woke me up.

C **Read this letter to a newspaper and fill the gaps using one of the words or phrases below.**

any longer yet past nowadays already still

The Transport System

Dear Sir/Madam

The transport system in this country certainly hasn't improved in the 1 ....past............ few years. People have been complaining about the railways for years and they're 2 ....still............ as bad as ever. Nobody has been able to come up with a solution to that problem 3 ....yet............ . More people than ever are travelling to work by train 4 ......nowadays...... but the number of trains has not increased. So trains that were 5 ....already.......... overcrowded are now even worse. People who have to use them every day to get to and from work have decided that they can't stand it 6 ......any longer...... and have started going by car. Of course, that makes the situation on the roads worse. Surely something can be done!

Yours faithfully

Sam Jones

D **Complete this article by deciding which word or phrase (A, B, C or D) fits into each gap.**

New Music Venue

A new music venue has 1 ......C...... opened in the town. It's called *The Blue Note* and it's 2 ......D...... proving to be a major success. 3 ......A...... , every event held there has sold out, with people queuing down the street to get in. The club's owners 4 ......A...... announced that they have reached an agreement for The Factors to appear there next month. This group is 5 ......B...... beginning to achieve nationwide fame, so tickets will probably be hard to come by. They're not on sale 6 ......C...... but they will be soon. So, if you feel that you haven't had a great night out 7 ......D...... , *The Blue Note* could be just the place for you. Certainly, people who like live music can't complain 8 ......B...... that there isn't anything to do in this town.

1	A lately	B so far	**C** recently	D these days
2	A yet	B recently	C hardly	**D** already
3	**A** So far	B Last week	C Only just	D Nowadays
4	**A** recently	B currently	C lately	D hardly
5	A lately	**B** just	C hardly	D yet
6	A just	B still	**C** yet	D nowadays
7	A nowadays	B these days	C currently	**D** lately
8	A so far	**B** any more	C already	D still

2.4 Periods of time 1

take to talk about the amount of time an action requires **subject + *take* + period** ***it* + *take* + period + *for* + object + infinitive with *to*** ***it* + *take* + object + period + infinitive with *to***	 *The journey will take five hours.* *It will take five hours for us to get there.* *It will take us five hours to get there.*
last to talk about how long an event continues from the beginning to the end **subject + *last* (+ *for*) + period**	 *A football match lasts (for) 90 minutes.*
spend to talk about the amount of time someone uses for a particular activity ***spend* + period + *-ing***	 *She spent an hour doing her homework.*
waste to talk about the amount of time someone uses doing something unnecessary or useless ***waste* + period + *-ing***	 *We've wasted an hour talking about this silly subject.*
pass **period + *pass*** to talk about a period of time being completed ***pass* + period / *the time* + *-ing*** to talk about doing something for a period of time because you have nothing else to do or because you are waiting for something	 *Three weeks passed before I heard from her again.* *I passed a pleasant hour looking out of the window.* *I passed the time reading magazines while I was waiting for my appointment.*

A Complete the second sentence so that it means the same as the first, using the word given.

1 After only five minutes the interview was over and I left. (lasted)
The interview ......only lasted (for) five minutes...... and then I left.

2 In fact, it was three years before I had saved enough money. (took)
In fact, it ......took me three years to/took three years for me to...... save enough money.

3 Yesterday I cleaned the flat for three hours and then I went out. (spent)
Yesterday I ......spent three hours cleaning...... the flat and then I went out.

4 They didn't reply to my letter for two months. (passed)
Two ......months passed before...... they replied to my letter.

5 I'm angry with myself because all I've done this afternoon is watch silly TV programmes. (wasted)
I'm angry with myself because ......I've wasted this/the afternoon...... watching silly TV programmes.

6 The doctors say that she will recover from the illness in about three weeks. (take)
The doctors say that it ......will take (her) about...... three weeks to recover from the illness.

7 I took the train and, during the journey, I chatted with the person sitting next to me. (passed)
I took the train and ......(I) passed the journey chatting with...... the person sitting next to me.

8 How long will it be before you've finished that work? (take)
How long ......will it take (for) you...... to finish that work?

→ Glossary p210

2.5 Periods of time 2

A **Complete this article by deciding which word or phrase (A, B, C or D) fills each gap.**

Snackbite Sandwich Bars

WENDY GRANGER used to spend her 1 ......B....... lunch hour looking for something to eat, but there was nowhere near her office where she could find anything she liked. After a 2 ......D....... , she realized that there must be a lot of other people like her. So she decided to start her own sandwich and take-away business. It took her 3 ......A....... to find a suitable location, but eventually she found a small shop close to the city centre. It's not perfect, but Wendy says that it will do for the 4 ......C....... being. 'I don't intend to stay here 5 ......D.......,' she says, 'I've got much bigger plans. In the long 6 ......A....... I aim to have five shops in the city, but at this 7 ......B....... I'm happy that the one that I have opened is so successful.' Wendy is looking for new products to introduce all the 8 ......C....... . 'Variety is the important thing,' she says. 'In this business, you won't survive for 9 ......A....... if you keep selling the same old things.' She knows that it might take 10 ......C....... , but she's determined to become the Sandwich Queen of the city!

1	A all	**B** whole	C long-term	D forever
2	A term	B stage	C era	**D** while
3	**A** ages	B long	C while	D short-term
4	A while	B period	**C** time	D years
5	A in good time	B some time	C in advance	**D** forever
6	**A** run	B era	C period	D while
7	A term	**B** stage	C while	D era
8	A forever	B ages	**C** time	D period
9	**A** long	B permanently	C some time	D long-term
10	A in good time	B long-term	**C** years	D while

B **Fill each of the gaps using one of the words below. Some of these words do not fit into any of the gaps.**

notice stage time term advance era run

The College Film Club

During the next 1 ......term...... our theme will be '*Cinema during the silent* 2 ......era...... ', and we'll be showing some of the great films of the 1920s. Tickets can be purchased in 3 ......advance...... by contacting the Club secretary. Make sure that you get your tickets in good 4 ......time...... because they are likely to sell out very quickly. Performance times are shown below, but if we have to change any of these at short 5 ......notice...... , ticket-holders will be informed.

C **Decide whether these sentences are correct or not. Correct those which are incorrect.**

1 I arrived not long ~~time~~ before the game started. ....long before....
2 The rescuers got there in ~~the~~ time to save them. ....in time....
3 Please try to get here in ~~some~~ time for dinner. ....in time....
4 The new job will make her happier in the short term. correct........

→ Glossary p210–11

2.6 Word focus

Phrasal verbs: *bring* & *take*

A Fill the gaps with the correct form of *bring* or *take* and decide which word or phrase, A or B, could replace the phrasal verb.

1 He ....took.......... off his coat and hung it on the door.

A removed **B** opened

2 I ....took.......... to him immediately and we've been friends ever since.

A noticed **B** liked

3 In terms of looks, she certainly ....takes.......... after her mother.

A tries to copy **B** is similar to

4 The company is going to ....bring.......... out a number of new products next year.

A stop making **B** produce

5 The bed ....takes.......... up almost the whole of the room.

A fills **B** improves

6 The new law was ....brought.......... in two years ago.

A introduced **B** considered

7 I was born and ....brought.......... up in this city.

A raised **B** changed

8 Bigger companies often ....take.......... over smaller ones.

A take control of **B** compete with

9 They are trying to find out what ....brought.......... about the disaster.

A resulted from **B** caused

10 Lots of people ....take.......... up a hobby as a way of relaxing.

A start doing **B** think about

Word formation: *noun suffixes*

B Complete this article by forming nouns using the words in capitals at the end of each line and the suffixes below. You may need to make more than one change to the word given to form the correct noun.

-tion -ety -ment -ity -iour -dom -ence -ition -er

Reality TV shows

A new kind of television 1 ....entertainment.......... has become a talking point in ENTERTAIN
millions of houses – reality TV shows. These came into 2 ....existence.......... EXIST
a few years ago and have achieved enormous 3 ....popularity.......... . These POPULAR
programmes show the 4 ....behaviour.......... of ordinary members of the public BEHAVE
in a 5 ....variety.......... of different situations – doing their jobs, trying to VARIOUS
win talent 6 ....competitions.......... , being faced with challenges so that their COMPETE
7 ....reactions.......... can be observed and spending a period of time living in REACT
a house with 8 ....strangers.......... . Some of these programmes attract a great STRANGE
deal of 9 ....publicity.......... in newspapers and magazines and some of the PUBLIC
people who appear in them achieve a kind of 10 ....stardom.......... for a time. STAR

→ Glossary p211

Collocations

C Complete the second sentence so that it means the same as the first, using one of the verbs below and the noun given.

do have make take lose

1 I can't understand his behaviour.

sense

His behaviour ......makes no sense to/doesn't make (any) sense to...... me.

2 She's finding it difficult to get all her work done on time.

problems

She's ......having problems getting...... all her work done on time.

3 He didn't say anything about his new job when I last spoke to him.

reference

He ......made no/didn't make any reference to...... his new job when I last spoke to him.

4 If you don't look after your belongings, you'll lose them.

care

If you don't ......take care of your belongings...... , you'll lose them.

5 Last year, the industry was damaged by problems in the world economy.

damage

Problems in the world economy ......did damage to the industry...... last year.

6 Jim suddenly became angry and started shouting.

temper

Jim ......(suddenly) lost his temper...... and started shouting.

7 There is a reason why I'm annoyed.

reason

I ......have a reason for being...... annoyed.

8 She ignored the warnings from her friends.

notice

She ......took no notice of/didn't take any notice of...... the warnings from her friends.

Prepositional phrases: *preposition* + *noun*

D Fill the gap in each sentence using *in* or *on*.

1 I was looking forward to the film but ......in...... fact it was rather disappointing.
2 All sorts of interesting things were ......on...... sale at the market.
3 I've just been ......on...... a trip to Scandinavia.
4 ......On...... the whole, I'm quite pleased with the way things are at the moment.
5 If you help me, I'll do something for you ......in...... return.
6 My room is ......in...... a terrible state, I must clean it up.
7 If you have a complaint, put it ......in...... writing and send it to us.
8 I've had arguments with him ......on...... several occasions.
9 Is there anything ......in...... particular you'd like to do tonight?
10 The building was ......on...... fire and firemen were rushing to it.

ECCE Practice 2

Grammar

1 I visited Alaska __c__ and I thought it was beautiful.
  a just
  b currently
  c recently
  d lately

2 I'd __d__ known Jim for three months, when he moved abroad.
  a often
  b always
  c then
  d hardly

3 'I __d__ play sport when I was younger.' 'Why did you stop?'
  a would
  b never
  c seldom
  d used to

4 'Have you seen Legally Blonde 2?' 'No, not __c__ – I'm going on Friday.'
  a ever
  b still
  c yet
  d since

5 'Bobby is getting married.' 'Really! The __a__ time I heard from him he was single.'
  a last
  b first
  c previous
  d right

6 'Have you tried pesto?' 'Once, but I __c__ didn't like it.'
  a only
  b only just
  c just
  d always

7 'I __b__ my leg. Can you help me?'
  a hurt
  b 've hurt
  c 'd hurt
  d 'm hurting

8 Last year we went to New York and we __d__ at the Plaza Hotel for two weeks.
  a used to stay
  b were staying
  c 've stayed
  d stayed

Vocabulary

9 Please __b__ off your shoes when you come in the house.
  a bring
  b take
  c remove
  d put

10 His new CD will be __c__ sale in January.
  a in
  b of
  c on
  d to

11 She __a__ no notice of his behavior towards her.
  a took
  b paid
  c made
  d gave

12 It took her __d__ to find the building she was looking for.
  a time
  b money
  c while
  d ages

13 Thanks for helping me. I'll do the same for you in __b__ sometime.
  a grateful
  b return
  c favor
  d appreciate

14 '__a__ care of that necklace – it's very valuable.'
  a Take
  b Make
  c Have
  d Keep

15 My father thinks the late sixties and early seventies was the greatest __d__ for popular music.
  a term
  b stage
  c run
  d era

16 I thought he was small but in __c__ he's rather tall, isn't he?
  a actual
  b deed
  c fact
  d particular

Exam techniques
→ p223

FCE Practice 2

Part 2

For Questions **1–15**, read the text below and think of the word which best fits each space.
Use only **one** word in each space.

THE YOUNGEST ROUND-THE-WORLD SAILOR

An 18-year-old returned to a hero's welcome in Australia yesterday after becoming the youngest person **(1)** ......to...... sail round the world non-stop. David Dawson sailed into Freemantle, Western Australia, anxious to enjoy a cold beer **(2)** .....and..... warm shower for the first time in nine months. 'I could do it another four times,' he joked as he stepped ashore to **(3)** ......be...... greeted by his family in front **(4)** ......of...... 15,000 spectators crowding the quayside. His 14-metre boat, *Sea flight*, had to be towed into the port **(5)** ..because.. of strong winds and obstruction from the 300 boats that **(6)** .....had..... gathered to escort him in. Sailing club officials said that he passed **(7)** .....the...... finishing line five kilometres out to sea late on Friday.

Mr Dawson had covered **(8)** ....more.... than 50,000 kilometres since leaving Freemantle, but it was anything but **(9)** ......an...... easy trip. His radio flooded, his boat lost her mast and the generator broke down, threatening to end the voyage prematurely. **(10)** ......At...... one point, he **(11)** .....was..... forced to accept a bolt from the British Royal Navy to repair his damaged mast and **(12)** ......as...... a result he could not claim to **(13)** ....have.... made the journey 'unassisted'.

(14) ...During... his 264 days at sea, the teenager became the youngest person to sail single-handedly around Cape Horn, **(15)** ...which.... he did in winter, with a damaged sail. He said he had missed his girlfriend, real food, beer and surfing.

Unit 3 The future

Grammar
3.1 The future
3.2 Time conjunctions
3.3 Time adverbs & prepositions 2

Vocabulary
3.4 Time adverbs & prepositions 3
3.5 Word focus

3.1 The future

Stop & check

Read the situations and decide which is the correct thing to say, A or B.

1 You have got a ticket for a football match tomorrow.
A I'll go to the match tomorrow. **B** I'm going to the match tomorrow.
2 You have arranged a holiday.
A I will go on holiday next week. **B** I'll be going on holiday next week.
3 You want to apologize for something.
A It won't happen again. B It doesn't happen again.
4 You are starting to feel ill.
A I think I'll be ill. **B** I think I'm going to be ill.
5 You can see that someone needs help.
A Will I help you? **B** Shall I help you?
6 You have organized a party.
A I will have a party next week. **B** I'm having a party next week.

Use	Example
Use *will* for	
• decisions, plans & intentions made at the moment of speaking	*I think I'll go home now, it's getting late.*
• predictions & facts about the future	*Mark will be 14 next month.*
• offers made to another person	*Sit down, I'll do the washing-up.*
• informal requests made to someone you know well	*Will you give me a hand?*
• promises	*I won't make that mistake again.*
• threats to warn people you may do something bad to them	*Don't say that again or I'll get very angry with you!*
• refusals/to say firmly you're not willing to do something	*We won't accept such terrible service. Get me the manager!*
Use *going to* for	
• decisions, plans & intentions made some time before speaking	*I've decided that I'm not going to continue with my course.*
• predictions & facts about the future	*Mark's going to be 14 next month.*
• predictions about things we can see are going to happen	*Just a second – I'm going to sneeze.*
• threats to warn people you may do something bad to them	*Don't say that again or I'm going to get very angry with you!*
• refusals / to say firmly you're not willing to do something	*We're not going to accept such terrible service. Get me the manager!*
Use *was / were going to* for	
• talking about plans and intentions in the past that did not happen	*I was going to go out last night but I changed my mind.*
Use the present simple for	
• things that are fixed or planned for the future as part of a timetable	*The next bus leaves in 20 minutes.*

Use	Example
Use the **present continuous** for • plans that have been fixed and arrangements (e.g. the time, the place, tickets, etc.) that have been made	*We're leaving on the 4 o'clock flight.*
Use the **future continuous** for • things that have been arranged for a specific time in the future • things that have been arranged and will happen for a period of time in the future • actions starting before and continuing at a specified point in the future	*I'm going away for a week and I'll be coming back / I'm going to be coming back on the 25th.* *She's going to be staying in Italy for a week and then she'll be visiting friends in Spain.* *Meet me at the café at 6. I'll be sitting at a table outside.*
Use the **future perfect** for • talking about actions that will be completed before or at a specified point in the future	*When you arrive, I will have left.*
Use the **future perfect continuous** for • talking about how long an action or situation has been continuing at a specified point in the future	*On the 15th, we'll have been going out together for exactly three months.*
Use ***shall*** for • offering to do something for someone • asking for advice • making suggestions ▶ note: usually used only with *I* and *we* and most commonly in question form	*Shall I carry that bag for you?* *Shall I call her or wait for her to call me?* *It's boring here. Shall we leave?*

➔ ExA–C p32–3

Other structures used to express the future

be about to

be intending to do sth in a very short time — *Could you phone back later? I'm about to eat?*

be just about to

be intending to do sth almost immediately — *Don't tell me again, I'm just about to do it.*

be on the point of + -ing

= be just about to do — *I was on the point of explaining when she suddenly left the room.*

am/is/are* + infinitive with *to

• to give or describe instructions about what someone should do in the future — *In their letter they said that I'm to phone them when I get to the airport.*
• also used in formal announcements concerning future arrangements — *The conference is to take place on 25th March.*

was/were* + infinitive with *to

• to talk about past arrangements that did not happen — *We arranged that I was to meet them at the concert but I couldn't find them.*
• to talk about something that proved to be true in the future but was not predicted or could not have been known at the time — *Nobody imagined that years later he was to become a star.*

be due* + infinitive with *to

to talk about future arrangements that are expected to happen at a specific time — *I'm due to get a pay rise next month.*

➔ ExD p34

A Read this extract from a novel and underline the correct future forms for 1–10.

Lynn's Decision

Steve and Stuart took their coffees to a table at the far end of the café and sat down. Steve spoke first. 'Have you heard that Lynn 1 gives up/is giving up her job next week? She's already handed in her notice and she says that she 2 's going to do/'s doing something more interesting.'

Stuart tutted and sighed with disapproval. 'Well, I 3 'll tell/'m telling you what I think. I think she 4 's regretting/'s going to regret it because she 5 won't get/doesn't get a better job.'

Steve was more sympathetic. 'I don't know about that,' he said. 'She thinks that she 6 's finding/'ll find something she prefers. She reckons it 7 'll be/'s being easy. As a matter of fact, she 8 's going/'ll go somewhere for an interview next week.'

Stuart was not convinced. 'The way things are at the moment, I'm sure it 9 's going to take/'s taking her a long time to get what she wants. In fact, I wouldn't be surprised to find out that she 10 'll look/'s looking six months from now.'

B Read this letter and underline the correct future forms for 1–10.

Dear Eddie,

There isn't much news from here except that the local festival 1 starts/will start tomorrow. I 2 'm not taking part/don't take part myself, but some of my friends, who have a group, 3 play/are playing in it.

There 4 's being/'ll be a concert in the square in the evening and that's where they 5 'll be performing/perform. Most of the local people, especially the young ones, 6 go/will be going there and I'm really looking forward to it because I think it 7 's going to be/'s being great fun.

I 8 'm letting/'ll let you know how it went and maybe I 9 'll send/'m going to send you some photos.

I 10 'm writing/'ll write to you again soon,

Claudia

C **Complete this conversation from a novel by putting the verbs in the correct tenses. There is sometimes more than one correct answer.**

Meeting Up

Ruth was sitting at her desk trying to sort the problem out when the phone rang. She answered it nervously, expecting more trouble.

'Hi, it's Pete,' a friendly voice said. She was relieved. 'Listen, 1 ....are you doing.......... (you do) anything tonight?' he asked.

'Yeah,' she said, trying to focus on her social life, 'I 2 ...'m meeting/'m going to meet... (meet) some friends in a bar after work.'

'Well, what about one evening next week? We haven't seen each other for weeks,' said Pete. She reached for her diary. 'Hang on a minute. I 3 ....'ll look.......... (look) in my diary.' She turned some pages, had a quick look and then said, 'Well, I 4 ....won't be able to.......... (not be able to) see you on Monday because I've got a meeting that always 5 ....goes on.......... (go on) until quite late.'

'Well, what about after the meeting? Say, around 8.30?'

'I'm afraid not,' said Ruth. 'At 8.30 I 6 .I'll be sitting/I'm going to be sitting. (sit) in traffic on my way home from the meeting. It's out of town and it usually 7 ....doesn't end.......... (not end) until after 8.'

'OK, what about Tuesday?'

'Well, you 8 .won't believe/'re not going to believe. (not believe) this, but I've taken up fitness training and the classes are on Tuesday evenings. You see, I've decided that I 9 ....'m going to start.......... (start) getting fit.'

'Good for you,' said Pete. 'So, is Wednesday any good?'

'Let me see,' she said, looking at her diary again. 'Well, I 10 ....'m seeing.......... (see) a client from 2 till 5 but I 11 ...'m not doing/won't be doing... (not do) anything after that. 12 ....Shall we fix up.......... (we fix up) something for Wednesday, then?'

'At last!' said Pete, laughing. '13 ....Shall we meet.......... (we meet) in The Shangri-La at 7?'

'Fine,' said Ruth. I 14 ....'ll see.......... (see) you there.'

D **Complete the second sentence so that it means the same as the first, using *was/were going to*, *be about to*, *be on the point of*, *be* + infinitive with *to*, or *be due to* and including the word in bold.**

1 According to the timetable, their plane arrives at 4.55.
due
Their plane ....is due to arrive.................................... at 4.55.

2 The programme you want to watch starts in one minute, so come in and sit down.
about
The programme you want to watch ....is about to start.................................... , so come in and sit down.

3 The annual meeting will be held next month.
is
The annual meeting ....is to be held.................................... next month.

4 My intention was to phone you last night but I forgot.
going
I ....was going to phone.................................... you last night but I forgot.

5 On the instructions it says that you should call this number if the computer stops working.
are
On the instructions, it says that ....you are to call.................................... this number if the computer stops working.

6 If you'll listen to me, I'm going to explain what happened in a few seconds.
just
If you'll listen to me ....I'm just about to.................................... explain what happened.

7 They had arranged to get married last month but they had to cancel it.
going
They ....were due to/going to get.................................... married last month but they had to cancel it.

8 This bill should have been paid two weeks ago.
due
This bill ....was due to be paid.................................... two weeks ago.

9 He didn't know at the time that it would be his last visit to the place.
was
He didn't know at the time that ....it was to be/it was going to be.................................... his last visit to the place.

10 I thought that he would lose his temper in a few seconds.
about
I thought that ....he was about to lose.................................... his temper.

11 He regretted his decision years later.
was
Years later, ...he was to regret.................................... his decision.

12 If he hadn't arrived at that moment, I would have gone home a few seconds later.
point
I was ....on the point of going.................................... home when he arrived.

3.2 Time conjunctions

	Use	Example	Other conjunctions used with this tense with a change in meaning
when / as soon as / once / the moment / immediately **+ present simple**	to talk about two things happening at the same time in the future ▶ note: Do not use these conjunctions with a future form to talk about the future.	*The moment I see Ian tonight, I'll tell him to call you.* NOT *The moment I ~~will see ...~~*	until/till *Until I go there, I won't know what it's like.* before *Before she begins the race, she'll do some warm-up exercises.*
when / as soon as / once / the moment / immediately **+ present perfect**	to talk about one thing happening before another in the future	*Once you've seen him, will you call me?*	until/till *Until they've moved house, they won't have any free time.* before/after *After we've been on holiday, we'll feel much better.*
when / as soon as / once / the moment / immediately **+ past simple**	to talk about two things happening at the same time in the past	*When I saw Ian last night, I said hello.*	until/till *Until I saw it for myself, I didn't believe it.* before *Before she left the office, she closed all the windows.*
when / as soon as / once / the moment / immediately **+ past perfect**	to talk about one thing happening before another in the past	*As soon as I'd spoken to him, I understood the situation better.*	until/till *Until you'd worked there for a while, it was hard to make friends.* before/after *After they'd been to the zoo, they went home to bed.*

after + *-ing*

- used to talk about the past, present or future and to say that one thing happens and then another thing happens
- can only be used if the subject of both verbs is the same
  After arriving at the hotel, guests will be invited to a special welcome party.

▶ note: If the verbs have different subjects, the second subject and the appropriate verb tense must be used.
  After guests have arrived at the hotel, a special welcome party will be held.

then/afterwards/after that

- *after* cannot be used alone as a linking word to join one thing that happens with another thing that happens after it. Instead, use (*and*) *then*, (*and*) *afterwards*, or (*and*) *after that*:
  We went to a party and then/afterwards/after that we went to a club.

▶ note: NOT ~~We went to a restaurant and after we went to a nightclub.~~

before + *-ing*

- to talk about the past, present or future
- can only be used if the subjects of both verbs are the same
  I finished all my work before leaving.

▶ note: If the verbs have different subjects, the second subject and the appropriate verb tense must be used.
  I finished all my work before she got back.

A Complete the second sentence so that it means the same as the first, using the word given.

1 Make up your mind and then tell me what your decision is.
once
Tell me what your decision is ....once you've made up..................... your mind.

2 The judges will hear all the evidence and then they will decide.
after
The judges will decide ....after hearing/after they have heard......... all the evidence.

3 Answer all the questions and then check your answers.
before
Don't check your answers .before answering/before you have answered. all the questions.

4 I'm going to her party next week but I won't see her before then.
until
I ....won't see her until...................... I go to her party next week.

5 I made sure she wasn't badly injured and then I called a doctor.
after
I called a doctor ....after making sure/after I had made sure..... she wasn't badly injured.

6 I'm going to think about this carefully and then give an opinion.
before
I won't give an opinion ....before thinking/before I have thought....... about this carefully.

7 I'm going to save enough money and then I'll be able to have a holiday.
until
I won't be able to have a holiday ....until I have saved/I save................ enough money.

8 He said that he had worked extremely hard and he hoped he would be successful.
after
He said that .after working/after he had worked extremely hard. , he hoped that he would be successful.

9 She spoke to me and then I found out that she had an accent.
until
I didn't find out that she had ......an accent until she spoke/had spoken...... to me.

10 The train was still moving when he opened the door.
before
He opened the door ....before the train (had) stopped............ moving.

B **Decide whether these sentences are correct or not. Correct those which are incorrect.**

1 I had something to eat and then I began to feel better. correct

2 When he told me the truth, I was amazed. correct

3 After ~~going~~ to bed, the phone rang and I had to get up again. I had gone

4 Guests must return room keys before leaving the hotel. correct

5 He had a shock ~~afterwards~~ he was upset for a long time. and afterwards/then/after that

6 I couldn't get the job I wanted until I had gained more experience. correct

7 Think about your own faults before criticizing other people. correct

8 I posted the form and ~~after~~ I realized that I hadn't filled it in properly. afterwards/then/after that

9 I knew it was a mistake immediately I'd said it. correct

10 I ran out of the room the moment I ~~hear~~ a noise outside. heard

11 After listening to what he had to say, I realized that he was right. correct

12 The boss was nice to me and after that I felt better about the job. correct

C **Join these pairs of sentences using the word(s) given to begin the sentence.**

1 You're going to see Alan tonight. Give him my regards.
When you see Alan tonight, give him my regards.

2 I'm going to tell you this secret. Then you're going to be upset.
After I've told you this secret, you're going to be upset.

3 He dressed and shaved. Then he went out.
After he had dressed and shaved/dressing and shaving, he went out.

4 You're going to meet her. You'll find out how nice she is.
As soon as you meet her, you'll find out how nice she is.

5 They're going to visit me. They're going to phone me first.
Before they visit me/visiting me, they're going to phone (first).

6 I'm going to the bank. Then I'm going to the supermarket.
When I've been to the bank, I'm going to the supermarket.

7 She rang to say goodbye. Then she left the country.
Before leaving the country/she left the country, she rang to say goodbye.

8 I finished all my work. Then I went home.
When I had finished all my work, I went home.

3.3 Time adverbs & prepositions 2

***during* + noun** throughout or within a specified period of time ▶ note: Do not use *during* + subject + verb, etc.	*I had a job during my school holidays.* NOT ~~*during I was on holiday*~~.
***while* + subject + verb, etc.** • happening throughout or within a specified period of time • = during the time that • to talk about something that happens during a period of time • to talk about two things that were happening during the same period of time ▶ note: After *while*, use a present tense to talk about the future.	*I had a job while I was on holiday from school.* *I met her while we were both working at the same place.* *While I was working hard, my friends were having fun.* *While I'm travelling next month, I'll send you a postcard.*
***as* + subject + verb, etc.** • happening throughout or within a specified period of time • = at exactly the same time as; during exactly the same period as	*As I got nearer, the noise got louder.* *As I was walking down the street, I heard someone call my name.*
***just as* + subject + verb, etc.** to emphasize that two things happen at exactly the same time	*Just as I was leaving, the phone rang.*
***over* + noun/period of time** to talk about something that happens while a period of time continues	*Over the next few weeks, they became very good friends.*
***throughout* + noun/period of time** = during all of; during the whole period of	*He played very well throughout the game.*
***for* + period of time** to say how long something continues	*We're going to stay there for three weeks.*
***since* + point in time** to say at what point in time a situation started	*I've been living here since January.*
***ever since* + point in time** to emphasize that something has really continued from a particular point in time in the past	*I've liked her ever since I first met her.*
past simple + period of time + *ago* to say how long in the past something happened	*I posted the letter three days ago.*
past perfect + *before* to say that something had happened before another thing happened in the past	*I knew him because I'd met him before.*
past perfect + period of time + *before* to say how long one thing in the past happened before another thing in the past happened	*I knew him because I'd met him three days before.*
present perfect + *before* to say that something happened before now	*I've been here before.*
beforehand = before a particular point in time	*I wasn't nervous because I'd prepared my speech beforehand.*
previously = before this/that time	*Have you done this kind of work previously?*
later (on) • = at a time in the future • = at a time after the time being referred to	*I'll do the washing-up later (on).* *I found out later (on) that the story wasn't true.*

A Complete this text by deciding which word or phrase (A, B, C or D) fits into each gap.

James Dean

JAMES DEAN was a Hollywood film star 1 ....C....... the 1950s, but his name and his face have remained well known 2 ....A....... since. He made three highly successful films 3 ....D....... a two-year period, including *Rebel Without a Cause*. 4 ....B....... he was appearing in these films, the idea of teenagers as a social group was beginning in the US – 5 ....D....... , teenagers had not been regarded as a special group. James Dean played a rebellious teenager in *Rebel Without a Cause* and he became associated with the image of teenagers arguing with authority and rebelling against society. 6 ....A....... he was at the height of his fame, he died in a car accident. However, 7 ....C....... the next few years, he became even more famous and he was a cult figure 8 ....B....... the 1960s and 1970s. Teenagers still rebel and young people still buy posters of James Dean. It seems likely that his face will continue to be well known for many more years.

1	A as	B since	**C** during	D while
2	**A** ever	B just	C over	D as
3	A while	B as	C just	**D** over
4	A During	**B** While	C Over	D Throughout
5	A ever since	B throughout	C just as	**D** previously
6	**A** Just as	B During	C Later	D Ever since
7	A later on	B as	**C** over	D while
8	A while	**B** throughout	C as	D ever since

B Decide whether these sentences are correct or not. Correct those which are incorrect.

1 Have you ever seen anything like that before? ....correct.......
2 I can post this letter while I ~~'ll be~~ at the shops this afternoon. ....am/'m.......
3 Something amusing happened while I was waiting to get on the plane. ....correct.......
4 I recognized the place as I had been there a few days ~~ago~~. ....before/previously.......

C Complete this text by filling the gaps with a word below.

as ago during beforehand since later for before

The Woodstock Festival

POP AND ROCK music festivals have been taking place 1 ....for....... many years, but probably the most famous one of them all took place over thirty years 2 ....ago....... . It is known as Woodstock because it was held near a place of that name in New York State in the US. It took place in August 1969 and nothing like it had ever happened 3 ....before....... . About half a million young people came from all over the US – 4 ....as....... the festival was going on, more and more people heard about it and decided to go there. 5 ....Beforehand....... , the organizers had not been expecting so many people and both the field where the festival was happening and the roads around it became very crowded. Lots of famous singers and bands performed. It rained a lot 6 ....during....... the festival but people were having such a good time that they didn't care. When it was over, it become a legendary event in the history of popular culture and a film of the event was 7 ....later....... released. 8 ....Since....... then, there have been lots of other big festivals all over the world.

→ Glossary p211

3.4 Time adverbs & prepositions 3

A **Decide whether these sentences are correct or not. Correct those which are incorrect.**

1 You can get in touch with me between 9 am ‸ ~~until~~ 5 pm tomorrow. ..and..........
2 Will you still be working here ‸ ~~by~~ two years' time? ..in..........
3 I won't make that mistake in future. ..correct..........
4 He went on to become the world champion ‸ following year. ..the..........
5 This product should be consumed within seven days. ..correct..........
6 She works very hard from Monday to Friday. ..correct..........
7 They should have received my letter by now. ..correct..........
8 It was getting dark by the time we finally got home. ..correct..........
9 I'm going to meet up with some friends ~~the~~ next Tuesday. ..... friends next ....
10 I'd like to visit Africa some time. ..correct..........
11 I was a student there from 1990 until 1995. ..correct..........
12 He got a part in a film and ‸ ~~by~~ then on his career was a big success. ..from..........

B **Complete this extract from a novel by deciding which word or phrase (A, B or C) fits into each gap.**

The Job That Wasn't

Kate and Lucy found a table and sat down. 'So what happened about that part-time job you told me you were going to get at the theatre?' Lucy asked.

Kate sighed. 'Well, it all came to nothing 1 ....B....... week,' she said. 'I thought you'd been told you'd be starting 2 ....D........ two weeks,' said Lucy.

'Yes, that's true,' said Kate. 'So, I phoned them on Tuesday to find out exactly when I'd be starting and I spoke to the same person I'd been interviewed by. He said he'd call me back 3 ....B........ the end of the day, but he didn't.'

'What happened then?' asked Lucy.

'Well,' said Kate, 'I phoned him again 4 ....C....... day. He didn't seem to remember talking to me 5 ....A....... day!'

'What a mess!' said Lucy sympathetically.

'I know,' said Kate. 'Of course, 6 ....B........ I'd realized that I wasn't going to get the job after all. In fact, I'm not sure there really was a job at all.'

'Well, I'm sure you'll find something else like that 7 ....B....... ,' said Lucy.

'Maybe,' said Kate, 'but 8 ....A....... I'm not going to believe that something is going to happen until it actually happens!'

1	A the last	**B** last	C in last	D since last
2	A by	B from	C over	**D** in
3	A between	**B** by	C in	D from
4	A following	B by	**C** the next	D over the
5	**A** the previous	B the last	C previous	D last
6	A some time	**B** by then	C within	D during
7	A in some time	**B** one day	C from now on	D by now
8	**A** from now on	B by now	C the following	D ever since

→ Glossary p211–12

3.5 Word focus

Phrasal verbs: *come* & *go*

A Complete the second sentence so that it means the same as the first, using the correct form of one of the phrasal verbs below.

come about come across come out come up come up with

1 I found this book by chance in a shop yesterday.
I ....came across.......... this book in a shop yesterday.

2 George thought of a brilliant plan.
George ....came up with.......... a brilliant plan.

3 What caused the problem?
How did the problem ....come about..........?

4 I can't see you tonight because something has happened unexpectedly.
I can't see you tonight because something ....has come up.......... .

5 Is this magazine published every week?
Does this magazine ....come out.......... every week?

B Complete the phrasal verbs with *go* using the particles below.

away off on out through

1 Tina **went** .through. a terrible time last year, with lots of personal problems.
2 I'**m going** ...away... for a few days and I'll be back next Friday.
3 I'**ve gone** .....off..... this programme, it's not as good as it used to be.
4 I always read a newspaper to find out what'**s going** .....on..... in the world.
5 Robert **went** .....out..... last night and got home very late.

Collocations

C Fill the gaps in this article with the correct forms of the verbs below. You will need to use some of the verbs more than once.

do come give keep make put tell

A Teenage Phenomenon

The highly successful author of teenage fiction, Helen Morris, has 1 ...given... pleasure to readers all over the world and her books have 2 ...done... well in many countries. She certainly knows how to 3 .....tell..... a story so that it keeps teenagers interested, and she seems to be able to 4 .....put..... into words many of the feelings of young people today. She is currently 5 ..making.. slow progress on the latest of her series of novels about the adventures of teenage musician Rob Grange. 'I haven't 6 ...made... up my mind yet whether this will be the last in the series,' says Helen. 'The success of the books has 7 ...come... as a big surprise to me and I'm 8 ...doing... my best to provide what my readers want. I said that there would be another book in the series and I'm going to 9 ...keep.... that promise, but after that I think it's time for the series to 10 ...come... to an end.' I asked her what will be happening to Rob in the latest book but she wouldn't 11 ....give.... me an answer. She's 12 ..keeping.. that a secret so that her readers find out first.

➔ Glossary p212

Word formation: adverb suffixes

D Complete the text by using the word in capitals at the end of each line to form an adjective that fits in the space in the same line. Use the endings below. You may need to make more than one change to each word.

-fully -ably -ally -ly -ingly

Local Youth Put On A Show!

This production was 1 ..originally.. created as a project for schools — ORIGIN
in the region and is funded 2 ....jointly.... by the local authority and — JOIN
some local businesses. It is 3 .musically. very ambitious, with over — MUSIC
100 young people playing at various times. 4 Fortunately , on the — FORTUNATE
opening night nothing went wrong and it was a 5 ....truly.... — TRUE
successful event. It was clear that everyone had been 6 ...carefully... — CARE
rehearsing and the quality of all the performances was 7 .remarkably. — REMARK
high. 8 .Surprisingly. , some of these young people had never performed — SURPRISE
in public before – they looked confident. The audience was 9 ...suitably... — SUIT
impressed and 10 ...hopefully... this will be just the first of many events — HOPE
like this.

Word sets

E The underlined words are all used incorrectly. Choose the correct one from the word set for each sentence.

bit part piece share

1 It's important that everyone works together as <u>share</u> of the team. part...................
2 I had a <u>piece</u> of help but I cooked most of the meal myself. bit...................
3 I bought some bread and a large <u>part</u> of cheese. piece...................
4 They all have an equal <u>bit</u> in the company. share...................

advantage benefit profit reward

1 Many people will get the <u>advantage</u> of this new medical discovery. benefit...................
2 She was given a present as a <u>profit</u> for all her hard work. reward...................
3 They managed to sell their apartment at a considerable <u>reward</u>. profit...................
4 I'm going to take <u>benefit</u> of this opportunity to relax. advantage...................

aspect case matter point

1 It was only a <u>point</u> of time before something went seriously wrong. matter...................
2 I know that this is true of most people but it's not true in my <u>aspect</u>. case...................
3 You did the right thing but the <u>matter</u> is that you should have done it earlier. point...................
4 Let's concentrate on the most important <u>case</u> of the problem. aspect...................

ECCE Practice 3

Grammar

1 'It's hot in here.' '__b__ I open the window?'
a Do
b Shall
c Will
d Would

2 'What are you going to do?' 'Well, __a__ I've had a shower, I'm going to go out.'
a as soon as
b before
c while
d during

3 They've finally announced that the elections are __b__ on 21 June.
a due
b to take place
c happening
d probably

4 I didn't understand the problem __b__ she explained it to me.
a as soon as
b until
c before
d at once

5 I __c__ with my aunt when I go to Mexico next summer.
a stay
b staying
c 'll be staying
d 'll have been staying

6 The crowd are getting very excited. The race __a__ start.
a is about to
b is due to
c is to
d is just

7 We often go to Florida __c__ the winter.
a while
b until
c during
d since

8 John moved away three weeks __c__ .
a since
b before
c ago
d over

Vocabulary

9 Do you think she can __a__ a promise?
a keep
b preserve
c tell
d do

10 I'll give you ten minutes to come __d__ with a better idea.
a out
b in
c through
d up

11 Lucy found the missing dog. She was given $100 as a __c__ .
a profit
b benefit
c reward
d bonus

12 'Have they arrested the criminals yet?' 'It's only a __b__ of time.'
a period
b matter
c length
d waste

13 Just think, __d__ two years' time, we'll be 18!
a under
b over
c after
d in

14 I'll give them a call – they should be back home __c__ now.
a for
b until
c by
d from

15 It's been a really difficult time. I don't want to go __b__ another week like that.
a over
b through
c back
d off

16 The Rolling Stones have __d__ pleasure to millions of fans for more than 40 years.
a made
b done
c put
d given

Exam techniques
→ p223

FCE Practice 3

Part 1

For Questions **1–15**, read the text below and decide which answer **A**, **B**, **C** or **D** best fits each space.

THE EXECUTIVE WIFE WHO DECIDED TO TAKE OFF

It was a routine problem for an executive wife. Jennifer Murray's husband had **(1)** .B. himself to an expensive new toy but did not have the time to use it. So she decided to **(2)** .D. a go herself. It was a helicopter. Today, the 56-year-old grandmother **(3)** .B. off to try to become the first woman to fly a small helicopter around the world. She admits: 'It's crazy.'

Mrs Murray plans to stop in 26 countries in 97 days, **(4)** .A. desert sandstorms and tropical monsoons on the 40,000-kilometre **(5)** .C. . With her co-pilot, she took a survival course in which they **(6)** .B. through a practice crash-landing in water.

Aboard their four-seater helicopter, two seats have **(7)** .D. way for an extra fuel tank which will slow them **(8)** .C. but ensure that they can go up to 1250 kilometres on a single stretch. They are also carrying special equipment to enable them to survive in freezing conditions in the **(9)** .A. of a mechanical breakdown.

Mrs Murray said of her husband: 'It's all his **(10)** .D. . He bought a helicopter but he didn't have time to learn to fly it, so he **(11)** .A. I learn. Now I really have the bug.' After flying for three years, she said as a joke that she should try a trip around the world. She was **(12)** .B. seriously and planning began. Mr Murray can now fly but he is too busy to make the global trip and will **(13)** .A. meet her on several stopovers.

The trip is costing hundreds of thousands of pounds but they have succeeded in **(14)** .D. about half the cost through sponsorship from various companies. They hope to **(15)** .C. about £500,000 for charity.

1	**A** purchased	**B** treated	**C** allowed	**D** entertained
2	**A** hold	**B** do	**C** get	**D** have
3	**A** comes	**B** sets	**C** leaves	**D** turns
4	**A** risking	**B** gambling	**C** endangering	**D** daring
5	**A** way	**B** travel	**C** route	**D** path
6	**A** fell	**B** went	**C** saw	**D** put
7	**A** moved	**B** changed	**C** let	**D** made
8	**A** off	**B** out	**C** down	**D** through
9	**A** event	**B** happening	**C** matter	**D** occasion
10	**A** lack	**B** blame	**C** guilt	**D** fault
11	**A** suggested	**B** indicated	**C** warned	**D** persuaded
12	**A** caught	**B** taken	**C** considered	**D** given
13	**A** instead	**B** rather than	**C** aside	**D** other than
14	**A** fulfilling	**B** satisfying	**C** matching	**D** meeting
15	**A** mass	**B** pile	**C** raise	**D** grow

Unit 4

Linking words & phrases

Grammar
4.1 Contrasts
4.2 Causes & results
4.3 Alternatives
4.4 Exceptions & additions
4.5 Intentions

Vocabulary
4.6 Intention & purpose
4.7 Word focus

4.1 Contrasts

Stop & check

Look at the sentence in italics. In what other ways could you say the same thing? Tick (✓) the correct sentences and underline the errors.

I usually like their music but I don't like this particular song.

1 Although I usually like their music, I don't like this particular song. ..✓..

2 I usually like their music. I don't like this particular song, though. ..✓..

3 Even though I usually like their music, I don't like this particular song. ..✓..

4 ~~However~~ I usually like their music, [however] I don't like this particular song. ..✗..

5 Despite [usually liking] ~~I usually like~~ their music, I don't like this particular song. ..✗..

6 In spite of [the fact that] I usually like their music, I don't like this particular song. ..✗..

Use	Example
Use *although / though / even though* • at the beginning of a sentence or between two clauses • all have a similar meaning; *though* is more formal at the beginning of a sentence, but a little more informal when used between two clauses; *even though* is more emphatic	***Although / Though / Even though*** *her job is hard, her salary is low.* *Her salary is low,* ***although / though / even though*** *her job is hard.*
Use *however* • at the beginning of a second sentence	*Her job is hard.* ***However,*** *her salary is low.*
Use *however / though* • at the end of a second sentence, or between two clauses of a second sentence	*Her job is hard. Her salary is low* ***though / however****.* *Her job is hard. Her salary is low,* ***though / however****, so she's leaving.*
Use *yet* • between two clauses in the same way as *but* • it is emphatic, for surprising or unusual contrasts	*Her job is hard* ***yet*** *her salary is low.*

▶ note: You cannot use *although* in a second sentence in the way that you can use *though* and *however*.
It is not correct to say ~~*Her job is hard. Although, her salary is low*~~ or ~~*Her job is hard. Her salary is low, although*~~.

→ ExA p46

Use ***in spite of / despite*** • at the beginning of the sentence or between two clauses	
in spite of / despite **+ noun / pronoun**	***In spite of / Despite*** *her qualifications, she can't find a job.*
Use ***in spite of / despite* + *-ing*** • when the subject of both clauses is the same	***In spite of / Despite*** *leaving early, I arrived late. (I left early; I was late)*
Use ***in spite of / despite the fact that*** **+ subject + verb** • if the clauses of the sentence have different subjects	***In spite of the fact that*** *they live near me, I don't see them very often.* NOT ~~*In spite of / Despite living near me, I don't often see them*~~.

▸ note: do not use *in spite of / despite* + subject + verb, etc.
It is not correct to say ~~*in spite of she has qualifications*~~ ... ~~*Despite I left early*~~ ..., ~~*despite they live near me*~~

Use ***while*** • to compare and contrast facts • before a statement that is true but is not as important as the statement that follows it	*My brother is good at sciences* ***while*** *I'm good at languages.* ***While*** *I understand your problem, there is nothing I can do to help you.*
Use ***whereas*** • to compare and contrast facts and emphasize the contrast between these facts, in the same way as *while*	***Whereas*** *I like sport, my friends hate it.* *I like sport,* ***whereas*** *my friends hate it.*
Use ***even so / nevertheless*** • in a second sentence, at the beginning or end, with the meaning 'although that is true' or 'in spite of that' • for emphasizing that the first statement is true but it does not prevent the second statement from also being true	*I know he has some bad habits.* ***Nevertheless*** *you shouldn't be so rude to him.* *I know he has some bad habits. You shouldn't be so rude to him,* ***even so****.*
Use ***on the other hand*** • to introduce a fact or opinion that contrasts with the fact or opinion before it	*It's a nice place to visit.* ***On the other hand****, it's rather expensive.*

Compare

even so and *even though*

- *even though* forms part of a single sentence
  Even though I explained carefully, she didn't understand me.
- *even so* forms part of a second sentence
  I explained carefully. Even so, she didn't understand me.

➔ ExB–E p47–8

A Decide whether the following are correct or not. Correct those which are incorrect.

1 Sarah lost her job recently. However, she soon found another one. ..correct..
2 I saw a jacket that I liked. It was very expensive, ~~although~~, so I didn't buy it. ..though..
3 ~~Yet~~ they were the better team, they lost the match. ..Athough..
4 This kind of music is very popular. I don't like it, though. ..correct..
5 I was looking forward to the party. I felt ill, however, so I couldn't go. ..correct..
6 Ruth has a very difficult life yet she never complains. ..correct..
7 I tried to speak to the manager. ~~Although~~, he was in a meeting and couldn't speak to me. ..However..
8 I want to contact John. I've lost his address, ~~although~~. ..though..

B **Rewrite the sentences using the words in brackets. There may be more than one way of doing this correctly.**

1 The weather wasn't very good but we enjoyed the holiday. (although)
Although the weather wasn't very good, we enjoyed the holiday. OR We enjoyed the holiday, although the weather ...

2 Your success was due to hard work. However, mine was due to good luck. (whereas)
Your success was due to hard work whereas mine was due to good luck. OR Whereas your success was ...

3 It's very disappointing for you but it's not the end of the world. (though)
It's very disappointing for you though it's not the end of the world. OR Though it's very disappointing ...

4 She has no real problems. However, she's always complaining. (yet)
She has no real problems, yet she's always complaining.

5 There were protests from the public but the law was passed. (even)
Even though there were protests from the public, the law was passed. OR The law was passed even though ...

6 You're right in some ways. On the other hand, you're wrong in other ways. (while)
While you're right in some ways, you're wrong in other ways.

7 I was very angry but I said nothing. (though)
Though I was very angry, I said nothing.

8 I've known her for years but I don't really understand her. (even)
Even though I've known her for years I don't really understand her.

9 We have little in common but we get on very well. (although)
Although we have little in common, we get on very well. OR We get on very well, although we ...

10 My sister is very patient. However, I often lose my temper. (whereas)
My sister is very patient whereas I often lose my temper. OR Whereas my sister is very patient, I ...

11 Even though they've lived here for years, they don't know the place very well. (yet)
They've lived there for years, yet they don't know the place very well.

12 I can understand how you feel. Even so, I don't think you should get so upset. (while)
While I can understand how you feel, I don't think you should get upset.

C **Rewrite the sentences using *despite* or *in spite of*. There is more than one way of doing this correctly.**

1 Although she played poorly, she won the match.
Despite/In spite of playing poorly, she won the match.
Despite/Inspite of the fact that she played poorly, she won the match.

2 The trip was enjoyable even though the weather was bad.
The trip was enjoyable despite/in spite of the (bad) weather.
The trip was enjoyable despite/in spite of the weather being bad.

3 I apologized to him but he remained angry with me.
Despite/In spite of apologizing to him he remained angry with me.
Despite/In spite of the fact that I apologized to him, he remained angry with me.

4 Even though he has little money, he enjoys life.
Despite/In spite of having little money, he enjoys life.
Despite/In spite of the fact that he has little money, he enjoys life.

5 She worked as hard as she could but she didn't finish on time.
Despite/In spite of working as hard as she could, she didn't finish on time.
Despite/In spite of the fact that she worked as hard as she could, she didn't finish on time.

D **Read this story and decide which word or phrase (A, B, C or D) fits into each gap.**

The Wrong Word

For the first time in my life I was alone in a foreign country. 1 ......C........ , I wasn't worried. 2 ......A...... I couldn't speak the language very well, I could make myself understood fairly well. So I decided to be confident, and 3 ......B....... the things I said probably weren't totally correct, it didn't matter. 4 ....D........ , there were some difficult moments and this was one of them. I walked into a café, wanting to buy a pineapple juice. 5 ......A...... I wasn't completely sure of the word for 'pineapple', I thought I could remember it. I asked for my drink. The waiter simply looked at me. 6 ......A...... that, I tried again, this time saying the same word in a slightly different accent. Later I found out what a stupid mistake I had made. 7 ......D...... the word I used was similar to the word for 'pineapple', it had a totally different meaning. 8 ......D...... this, the waiter wrote down my order and went away as normal, 9 ......A...... I thought I could see him smiling when he left. It didn't matter, 10 ......A....... , because he returned with the right drink. I was lucky though. I found out later that the word I'd used meant 'paint'.

1	A Despite	B Although	**C** However	D Even though
2	**A** Although	B However	C In spite of	D Yet
3	A yet	**B** even though	C however	D despite
4	A Even though	B Despite	C Although	**D** However
5	**A** Though	B Yet	C However	D Despite
6	**A** Despite	B Even though	C Although	D Though
7	A However	B Yet	C In spite of	**D** Although
8	A Although	B Yet	C However	**D** In spite of
9	**A** although	B despite	C in spite of	D however
10	**A** though	B yet	C even though	D although

E **Write a letter of complaint by forming sentences or pairs of sentences from the following, using the word or phrase in brackets.**

1 I have phoned you several times about the delivery of my order. It has still not arrived. (despite)
2 I understand that this is a busy period for you. I do not understand the length of this delay. (although)
3 Your staff have been very polite to me. I feel that this situation is unacceptable. (nevertheless)
4 You have given me many promises. Nothing has happened. (in spite)
5 I have been very patient. This will not continue. (however)
6 I don't want to take legal action. I will do so unless my order arrives within the next few days. (on the other hand)

Dear Sir / Madam,

1 Despite having phoned/phoning/the fact that I have phoned you several times about the delivery of my order, it has still not arrived.
2 Although I understand that this is a busy period for you, I do not understand the length of this delay.
3 Your staff have been very polite to me, nevertheless I feel that this situation is unacceptable.
4 In spite of giving me/of the fact that you have given me many promises, nothing has happened.
5 I have been very patient, however this will not continue/this will not continue however.
6 I do not want to take legal action. On the other hand I will do unless my order arrives within the next few days.

4.2 Causes & results

because at the beginning of a sentence, or between two clauses ***because* + subject + verb, etc.** ***because of* + noun / pronoun** ▶ note: do not use *because of* + subject + verb, etc.	 *We couldn't travel* ***because*** *the weather was bad.* ***Because of*** *the bad weather we couldn't travel.* NOT ~~*We couldn't travel because of the weather was bad.*~~
since / as • = *because*, when the cause produces an obvious, logical or expected result • often used at the beginning of a sentence	***Since / As*** *we don't have much time, we'll have to hurry.*
due to / owing to / in view of / on account of • = *because of*, in fairly formal contexts • at the beginning of a sentence, or between two clauses ***due to / owing to / in view of / on account of* + noun/pronoun** ***due to / owing to / in view of / on account of the fact that* + subject + verb, etc.** ▶ note: Do not use *due to / owing to / in view of / on account of* + subject + verb, etc.	 *The event has been cancelled* ***due to / on account of*** *lack of interest.* *The event has been cancelled* ***in view of / owing to the fact that*** *not enough tickets have been sold.* NOT ~~*The event has been cancelled due to not enough tickets have been sold.*~~

so • to introduce the result of something • used between two clauses, after a comma, or with *and*	 *I wasn't listening,* ***so*** *I don't know what he said.* *I was tired* ***and so*** *I went to bed.*
therefore • to introduce the result of something • more formal than *so* • used at the beginning of a second sentence or between two clauses with *and* • at the beginning of a sentence often followed by a comma	 *We'd lost our tickets.* ***Therefore****, we couldn't see the show.* *We'd lost our tickets* ***and therefore*** *we couldn't see the show.*
then • to respond to something with what the speaker believes to be the result of it • used at the beginning or end of the response ▶ note: Do not use *then* to link a cause and a result in a single sentence.	 *'There are no buses at this time of night.' – '****Then*** *we'll have to get a taxi.'* *'I was very rude to Jo.' – 'You'd better apologize* ***then****.* NOT ~~*I wasn't listening then I didn't know what he said.*~~ Instead, use *so* (see above).
as a result used in the following patterns: ***as a result* + subject + verb, etc.** used at the beginning of a second sentence or between two clauses with *and* ***as a result of* + *-ing*** ***as a result of* + noun / pronoun**	 *The company was doing very badly.* ***As a result****, many people lost their jobs.* ***As a result of*** *losing his job, he became depressed.* *Many people lost their jobs* ***as a result of*** *the company's difficulties.*

make* + noun / pronoun + infinitive without *to links a cause and a result ***make* + *it* + adjective + *for* + noun / pronoun + infinitive with *to*** often used with the adjectives *easy, difficult, possible, impossible* ***make* + noun / pronoun + adjective** used with many adjectives describing feelings, attitudes attitudes and characteristics	*It was a sad story and it made me cry.* *His attitude made it easy for me to relax.* *The noise made it impossible for me to concentrate.* *That failure made her even more determined to succeed.* *Her comments made me angry.*
***cause* + noun / pronoun (+ infinitive)**	*What caused the problem?* *Ill health caused him to retire from his job.*
***result in* + noun** = have as a result	*The bad weather resulted in an increase in fruit and vegetable prices.*
***lead to* + noun / pronoun** = produce as a result	*Smoking can lead to heart disease.* *What led to her financial difficulties?*
(*which*) *mean that* + subject + verb, etc. • introduces a result that is certain • with *which* links a cause with its result	*The fact that they are so rich means that they don't have to worry about paying their bills.* *They're extremely rich, which means that they don't have to worry about paying their bills.*

A **Fill in the gaps in this note with one suitable word.**

1 ......Since/As...... I seem to have lost your new mobile phone number, I thought I'd better write you a quick note. The problem is, I can't meet you at the airport on the 25th, 2 ......so...... we'll have to make another arrangement. I've got to go to a meeting that day, which will 3 ......make...... it impossible for me to get to the airport on time. 4 ......Therefore...... , I suggest that you get a taxi into the city and wait for me at that café next to my apartment building. I hope this doesn't 5 ......cause...... too much trouble, but let me know. If this arrangement doesn't suit you, 6 ......then...... I'll have to think of something else.

B **Complete the second sentence so that it means the same as the first sentence, using the word given.**

1 Because of you, I'm having difficulty concentrating on my work. (difficult)
You are making ......it difficult for me to...... concentrate on my work.

2 I wanted to visit the place because of some pictures I saw of it. (made)
Some pictures I saw of the place ......made me want...... to visit it.

3 Because of the accident, there were traffic problems that day. (resulted)
The ......accident resulted in traffic problems...... that day.

4 I lost my temper because of the assistant's unpleasant attitude. (caused)
The assistant's unpleasant attitude ......caused me to lose...... my temper.

5 Their victory in the match was caused by excellent play. (led)
Excellent play ......led to their victory...... in the match.

6 Because of your help, I was able to succeed. (possible)
Your help made ......it possible for me to...... succeed.

7 She has become much happier at work because she is earning more money now. (result)
She is earning more money now and ......as a result...... she has become much happier at work.

8 Because of some bad experiences, he became cautious about taking risks. (made)
Some bad experiences ......made him cautious...... about taking risks.

C **Read this report and decide which word or phrase (A, B, C or D) fits into each gap.**

The University Entertainments Committee

The University Entertainments Committee meeting was held 1 ......B....... recent financial losses. The Events Officer reported on the last two events. He said that students had been very busy 2 ......A........ the exams, and 3 ......D....... ticket sales had been poor. The Finances Officer blamed the losses on the high charges made by the performers at those events.

4 ......A........ these charges, he said, the events would have lost money even if every ticket had been sold. One suggestion was to increase ticket prices in future but it was felt that, 5 ......A....... many students have little money, this would not 6 ......B........ to an improvement in the financial situation. After discussion it was agreed that 7 ......C........ the seriousness of the situation and 8 ......A....... there was a real danger of the university authorities closing down the Entertainments Committee, the next two events would have to be cancelled immediately. This would 9 ......C....... that the performers in question would have to be contacted immediately, 10 ......D........ the fact that contracts had already been signed with them.

1	A owing	**B** because of	C due	D on account
2	**A** due to	B as a result	C therefore	D in view
3	A then	B since	C as	**D** so
4	**A** On account of	B Because	C Since	D As a result
5	**A** as	B therefore	C so	D then
6	A cause	**B** lead	C result	D make
7	A as a result	B because	**C** in view of	D as
8	**A** since	B then	C due to	D because of
9	A result	B cause	**C** mean	D lead
10	A therefore	B since	C on account	**D** owing to

D **Read this information about a female tennis player. Decide which was the result of each cause and link them using the word or phrase in brackets.**

	CAUSE	RESULT
0	her father was a professional player (because)	earned more than she earned from playing
1	started playing seriously at the age of five (as)	became interested in tennis as a child
2	won a lot of major tournaments (as a result)	retired from tennis completely
3	argued with an umpire (owing to)	had to find a new one
4	sacked her coach (so)	knew nothing about life outside tennis
5	did some modelling (which resulted)	got into trouble with the sport's authorities
6	became too old to stay at the top (therefore)	became the top player in the world

0 *Because her father was a professional player, she became interested in tennis as a child.*

1 As she started playing tennis seriously at the age of five, she knew nothing about life outside tennis.

2 She won a lot of major tournaments and as a result she became the top player in the world.

3 Owing to the fact that she argued with an umpire, she got into trouble with the sport's authorities.

4 She sacked her coach so she had to find a new one.

5 She did some modelling which resulted in her earning more than she earned from playing.

6 She became too old to stay at the top, therefore she retired from tennis completely.

4.3 Alternatives

instead of to introduce a possibility, choice or idea that is preferred to something also mentioned	
instead of* + *-ing when the subject of both verbs is the same	***Instead of*** *taking a bus, I walked.* *We went out for a meal* ***instead of*** *cooking at home.*
▶ note: Do not use *instead* + infinitive.	NOT ~~*Instead to take a bus …*~~
instead of **+ noun / pronoun**	*Let's sit at that table* ***instead of*** *this one.*
instead = instead of something also mentioned	*I don't feel like doing it now. I'll do it tomorrow* ***instead***.
rather than to introduce a possibility, choice or idea that is preferred to something also mentioned	
rather than **+ infinitive without *to***	***Rather than*** *waste any more time, I gave up.*
rather than* + *-ing	***Rather than*** *standing there, why don't you help?*
rather than **+ noun / pronoun**	*I bought the blue one* ***rather than*** *the red one.*
otherwise = if not, when talking about what will / would happen if another thing mentioned does not/did not happen	*If I see her today I'll tell her.* ***Otherwise****, I'll call her later.* *I was ill. I would have gone to the party* ***otherwise***.
else • = different; more • use in the following structures: *something else*, *nothing else*, etc. *what else*, *where else*, etc. • in questions and statements	*Is there* ***anything else*** *you'd like to know?* *Jack didn't know so I asked* ***somebody else***. *There's* ***nowhere else*** *to look.* ***What else*** *did he say?* *I didn't know* ***where else*** *to go.*
or (else) • to introduce an alternative • with *else* emphasizes that there will be a bad result if the first thing mentioned doesn't happen	*Are you going to phone me* ***or*** *shall I phone you?* *I'd better leave now* ***or (else)*** *I'll be late.*

whether … or (not) to talk about two possibilities	*You'll have to pay,* ***whether*** *you like it* ***or not***.
whether **+ subject + verb + *or* (+ subject) + verb**	***Whether*** *I go away this weekend* ***or*** *I stay here depends on how much money I've got.*
either … or to link two possibilities	
either **+ possibility A + *or* + possibility B**	*You* ***either*** *love her or you don't.*
negative verb (+ and + negative verb) + *either*	*George can't go and I can't (go)* ***either***. *'I can't go on Friday.' – 'I can't* ***either***.*'*

A Read this extract from a travel brochure and choose the word or phrase (A, B, C or D) that fills each gap.

Escape the Crowds!

Don't go to the crowded tourist spots, come to our region 1 ......B........ ! Nowhere 2 ......C........ in the country can offer you such comforts in such tranquil surroundings. 3 ......A........ stand in endless queues with other holidaymakers, you can take it easy all the time and do everything you could possibly want to. We have sun, sea, sand, entertainment and everything 4 ......B........ you could want. So, 5 ......D........ following the crowds, come to us. But hurry up. 6 ......B........ , you might be too late. People are already beginning to discover us, so book now 7 ......A........ else you might find that our small selection of exclusive hotels and apartments are full up. For current prices, contact us by phone 8 ......C........ e-mail us.

1	A otherwise	**B** instead	C rather	D else
2	A instead	B rather	**C** else	D otherwise
3	**A** Rather than	B Otherwise	C Instead of	D Or else
4	A whether	**B** else	C otherwise	D either
5	A or else	B instead	C rather	**D** instead of
6	A Else	**B** Otherwise	C Instead	D Rather than
7	**A** or	B instead	C either	D otherwise
8	A either	B else	**C** or	D instead

B Read this article about a football team and fill each gap with one word.

A Club of Losers

The situation at Plankton United looks hopeless. The team can't score goals and they can't stop other teams scoring against them 1 ....either.......... . 2 ....Instead.......... of cheering, the supporters boo their team off at half-time. They're not going to win the Cup and they are not going to win the League 3 ....either.......... . Something needs to be done soon, 4 ....otherwise.......... the club's finances and its ability to attract the better players will be affected. Some people say they should sack the coach, but others think the players are not good enough, 5 ....whether.......... they get a new coach or not. But one thing is sure, 6 ....either.......... serious action is taken or the situation will get even worse.

C Complete the second sentence so that it means the same as the first sentence. It is possible to rewrite some of them correctly in more than one way.

1 I didn't wait for them to phone me, I phoned them. (instead of)
Instead of waiting for them to phone me, I phoned them.

2 I'm not interested in politics and neither are my friends. (either)
I'm not interested in politics and my friends aren't either.

3 We didn't want to spend a lot of money so we stayed at a cheap hotel. (rather)
Rather than spend a lot of money, we stayed at a cheap hotel.

4 Don't criticize all the time, say something positive. (instead of)
Instead of criticizing all the time, say something positive.

5 I'd like a cold drink, not a hot one. (rather)
I'd like a cold drink rather than a hot one.

6 You can pay by cash and you can pay by credit card. (either)
Either you can pay by cash or you can pay by credit card./You can pay (either) by (either) cash or credit card.

4.4 Exceptions & additions

apart from to talk about the only way a statement is not true ***apart from* + *-ing*** only when both verbs have the same subject ***apart from* + noun / pronoun** ***apart from the fact that* + subject + verb, etc.** must be used if the verbs in the sentence have different subjects	 ***Apart from*** *going to the shop, I've done nothing today.* *We didn't do much in London,* ***apart from*** *seeing the sights.* ***Apart from*** *Helen and Eric, I didn't know anyone at the party.* ***Apart from the fact that*** *the plane was a bit late, we had a good journey.*
except / but to talk about the only way in which a statement is not completely true ***except for* + *-ing*** = apart from + *-ing* ***except / but* + noun / pronoun** = apart from + noun/pronoun ***except / but* + infinitive without *to*** to talk about the only action that is possible or the only thing that someone does	 ***Except*** *for going to the shop, I've done nothing today.* *We didn't do much in London,* ***except for*** *seeing the sights.* *He doesn't care about anything* ***except*** *money.* *She told everyone* ***but*** *me.* *There is nothing I can do* ***except / but*** *apologize for my mistake.* *You've done nothing* ***but*** *complain all day!*
no choice / alternative / option but* + infinitive with *to to talk about the only possible action	*I've got* ***no choice / alternative / option but to*** *start again.*

apart from / as well as to link two statements which are true in order to emphasize that both things are true ***apart from / as well as* + *-ing*** only when both verbs have the same subject ***apart from / as well as* + noun / pronoun** ***apart from the fact that* + subject + verb** must be used when the verbs have different subjects	 *She works in the evening* ***as well as*** *working all day.* ***Apart from*** *working all day, she works in the evening.* *I have several other bills to pay* ***apart from*** *this one.* *I'm not going to buy it.* ***Apart from the fact that*** *it's expensive, I don't really like it.* NOT ~~*As well as the fact that …*~~
in addition to = apart from / as well as, but more formal ***in addition to* + *-ing*** only used when both verbs have the same subject ***in addition to* + noun / pronoun** ***in addition to the fact that* + subject + verb, etc.** when the verbs have different subjects ***in addition*** = in addition to this / that	 ***In addition to*** *running the department, she has responsibility for staff training.* *You will require a work permit* ***in addition to*** *the appropriate qualifications.* ***In addition to the fact*** *that her work is good, she gets on very well with everyone else.* *You will require the appropriate qualifications and,* ***in addition****, a work permit.*
besides = apart from / as well as / in addition to (this/that) ***besides* + *-ing*** when both verbs have the same subject ***besides* + noun / pronoun** ***on top of* + noun / pronoun / *-ing*** to link two statements that are true in order to emphasize that they are both true	*She spends a lot of time working but she does a lot of other things* ***besides****.* ***Besides*** *eating too much, he also gets far too little exercise.* *He has lots of other interests* ***besides*** *football.* ***On top of*** *having to do a lot of school work, she also does a lot of sport.* *I'm very busy at work and* ***on top of*** *that I've got problems at home.*

also • after *and* in a single sentence • at the beginning of a second sentence	*I cooked the meal and* ***also*** *I washed up afterwards.* *I cooked the meal.* ***Also****, I washed up afterwards.*
subject (+ auxiliary / modal) + ***also*** **+ verb** ▶ note: Do not put *also* at the end of a sentence.	*She has computer skills and (****also****) she can /* ***also*** */ speak / she (****also****) speaks several languages.* NOT ~~*and she speaks / can speak several languages also.*~~
not only ... (but) also to emphasize that two things are both true	*I* ***not only*** *cooked the meal (****but****) I* ***also*** *washed up afterwards.*
too / as well • at the end of a sentence in which two clauses are linked by *and*	*I cooked the meal and I washed up afterwards,* ***too / as well****.* NOT ~~*and I too / as well washed up afterwards*~~*.*
• at the end of a second sentence	*I cooked the meal. I washed up afterwards,* ***too / as well****.*
▶ note: Do not use *too / as well* at the beginning of a sentence.	NOT ~~*Too I washed up afterwards.*~~
furthermore / moreover • to introduce another comment or point in addition to something previously said • quite formal • can be followed by a comma	*The room I was given at your hotel was unsatisfactory.* ***Furthermore / Moreover****, the service was very poor.*

A **Read this extract from a brochure and fill each gap with one suitable word.**

~ *The Diamond Home Entertainment System* ~

As 1 ....well.......... as the finest in picture quality, this system gives you the finest sound quality. In 2 ....addition.......... , it couldn't be easier to operate. Follow the simple instructions and you'll have a wonderful sound system and a home cinema 3 ....as.......... well. 4 ....Besides.......... being able to watch satellite TV channels from all over the world, you'll be able to watch sports events on TV in a variety of exciting ways. For example, at the press of a button you can follow a particular player and you can 5 ....also.......... replay the action whenever you want. You can edit your own videos 6 ....too.......... . So you can 7 ....not.......... only be a film-watcher, you can 8 ....also.......... be a film-maker!

B **Rewrite the sentence so that it means the same as the first sentence, using the word given.**

1 A sandwich is the only thing I've eaten all day.

apart

Apart from a sandwich, I haven't eaten all day. OR I haven't eaten all day, apart from ...

2 The only thing I could do was wait.

choice

I had no choice but to wait.

3 I've never taken much interest in this subject, but I have read a couple of articles about it.

except

Except for reading a couple of articles about it I've never taken much interest in this subject. OR I've never taken much interest in this subject, except for ...

4 Everything's going well at the moment, although I haven't got much money.

apart

Everything's going well at the moment, apart from not having much money. OR Apart from the fact that I haven't got much money, everything's ...

5 Work is the only thing he's interested in.

but

He's interested in nothing but work.

6 The only thing I did all weekend was watch TV.

apart

I did nothing all weekend apart from watch TV. OR Apart from watch TV I did ...

7 The only thing I can do in this situation is laugh about it.

but

I can do nothing but laugh in this situation. OR In this situation I can ...

8 The only thing you can do is admit that you were wrong.

option

You've got/You have no option but to admit you were wrong.

9 She works very hard and she runs the family home.

in addition

In addition to running the family home she works very hard.

10 He was late and he was rude to me, too.

as well

As well as being late, he was rude to me.

11 The place doesn't appeal to me and I can't afford to go there.

apart

Apart from not appealing to me, I can't afford to go there.

12 He earns a lot of money and he doesn't have to work very hard.

besides

Besides earning a lot of money, he doesn't have to work very hard.

C **Read this description and decide which word or phrase (A, B, C or D) fits into each gap.**

The US by **Greyhound Bus**

We travelled around America on Greyhound buses. It was a relatively cheap way to travel and 1 ....C......., it meant that we could see more of the country. 2 ....B....... to the fact that we saw a lot of places, we met a lot of interesting people during the journeys. From them, we heard a lot of interesting stories and 3 ....C....... we learnt a lot about the different states.

4 ....A....... , we saw a lot of places we would never have seen if we'd travelled by plane. The buses were comfortable and punctual. 5 ....A....... , they stopped regularly so that everyone could have a cup of coffee and a break. 6 ....A....... that, we saved money on hotels by taking night buses and sleeping on the bus. So, 7 ....C....... of saving money, we had a great time. I'd certainly do it again and, 8 ....B....... , I'd recommend it to anyone.

1	A apart	B on top of	**C** besides	D in addition to
2	A As well	**B** In addition	C Apart	D On top
3	A too	B as well	**C** also	D apart
4	**A** Furthermore	B Apart	C Too	D As well
5	**A** Also	B Too	C As well	D Apart
6	**A** In addition to	B Moreover	C Apart	D Furthermore
7	A moreover	B as well	**C** on top	D besides
8	A too	**B** moreover	C apart	D not only

4.5 Intentions

infinitive with *to* to talk about the purpose of an action, especially everyday actions that are usually easy to do ▶ note: Do not use a negative infinitive to express a purpose. Use *so as not to* or *so that* (see below). ▶ note: Do not use *for* to talk about the purpose of an action.	*I'm going to the shop to buy a newspaper.* *She phoned to tell me something.* NOT ~~*I ran all the way there not to arrive late.*~~ NOT ~~*I went out for buy / for to buy / for buying some chocolate.*~~
so as (not) to to talk about the purpose of an action in more formal contexts or when the purpose is more difficult	*We had a meeting so as to solve the problem.* *I ran all the way there so as not to arrive late.*
in order to to explain the purpose of an action, usually only in formal contexts	*I would like to make an appointment in order to discuss this matter with you.*
so that to express any purpose; must be used if there is a second subject ***so (that)* + second subject + present simple / *will / can*** for actions intended to have a result in the present or future ***so (that)* + second subject + *would / could*** for actions intended to have had a result in the past ▶ note: This pattern can also be used if both subjects are the same.	 *I'll explain again so that you (will / can) understand the situation clearly.* *I left quickly so that they wouldn't see me.* *He shouted so that she would / could hear him properly.* *I wrote the date in my diary so that I wouldn't forget it.*

A Join these sentences using the words in brackets.

1 I hurried home. I didn't want to miss my favourite TV programme. (so that)
I hurried home so that I didn't/wouldn't miss my favourite TV programme.

2 He went to the counter. He wanted to buy a cup of coffee. (to)
He went to the counter to buy a cup of coffee.

3 She left the country. She wanted to start a new life. (so as)
She left the country so as to start a new life.

4 I am writing to you. I want to make a complaint. (in order)
I am writing to you in order to make a complaint.

5 He was polite in the interview. He wanted to make a good impression. (so as)
He was polite in his interview so as to make a good impression.

6 I fetched a knife. I wanted to cut the vegetables. (to)
I fetched a knife to cut the vegetables.

7 I spoke slowly. I wanted him to understand me. (so that)
I spoke slowly so that he understood me.

8 She was very careful. She didn't want to make a mistake. (so as)
She was very careful so as not to make a mistake.

9 I didn't say anything. I didn't want us to have an argument. (so that)
I didn't say anything so that we didn't have an argument.

10 I'm going to bed early. I don't want to be tired tomorrow. (so that)
I'm going to bed early so that I won't be tired tomorrow.

→ Glossary p212

4.6 Intention & purpose

A **Read this extract from a magazine article and use the word given in capitals at the end of each line to form a word that fits in the space in the same line.**

I'm misunderstood, says Bubbles

Hollywood star Bubbles Pratt claims that it was never her 1 ......intention...... to become so famous. It all happened 2 ......accidentally......, she says in an interview in *Why?* magazine. According to Bubbles, she wasn't 3 ......ambitious...... and in fact when she was younger she led a rather 4 ......aimless...... life. She just wanted to enjoy herself and before she found fame she didn't have the 5 ......determination...... to reach the top. And fame just came to her, Bubbles reckons. She says that she never looked for publicity 6 ......intentionally...... . As far as she is concerned, it is purely 7 ......accidental...... that she has attracted so much of it. And she says that her well-known image as a rather wild person is 8 ......unintentional...... and was the result of a few jokes she made in an interview.

INTEND
ACCIDENT
AMBITION
AIM
DETERMINED
INTEND
ACCIDENT
INTEND

B **Read this article and decide which word (A, B, C or D) best fits each space.**

The Magazine Editor

All her life, Sheila Wall had had an 1 ......B...... – to start her own magazine. In 1993 she did just that. She called it *Why?* and it was 2 ......C...... at teenagers. At first she only 3 ......A...... on selling it locally. However, there were no other magazines 4 ......B...... for teenagers at that time quite like this one and it quickly became popular. Her first sales 5 ......D...... was 5000 copies a month but the magazine was soon selling more than that. Some people said that the magazine was rather silly but this was 6 ......A...... – Sheila didn't want the magazine to be serious, it was 7 ......A...... for entertainment only. Eventually she reached her 8 ......C...... – her magazine was a national success.

1	A goal	**B** ambition	C intention	D plan
2	A intended	B planned	**C** aimed	D meant
3	A planned	B aimed	C meant	D intended
4	A aimed	**B** intended	C determined	D deliberate
5	A ambition	B intention	C goal	**D** target
6	**A** deliberate	B aimed	C ambitious	D determined
7	**A** meant	B aimed	C deliberate	D intentional
8	A intention	B ambition	**C** goal	D aim

→ Glossary p212

C **Complete the second sentence so that it means the same as the first sentence, using the word given.**

1 I don't intend to stay here for long.

intention

I ......have no/don't have any intention of staying...... here for long.

2 He said that he was aiming to arrive at about 6.

aim

He said ......it was his aim to/his aim was to...... arrive at about 6.

3 I upset her unintentionally.

mean

I ......didn't mean to upset...... her.

4 He deliberately ignored me because he doesn't like me.

purpose

He ......ignored me on purpose...... because he doesn't like me.

5 I phoned him, intending to apologize.

intention

I phoned him ......with the intention of...... apologizing.

6 What are you planning to do this weekend?

plans

What ..plans do you have for/plans have you got for/are your plans for.. this weekend?

7 Jackie intends to travel and nobody can change her mind.

determined

Jackie ......is determined to travel...... and nobody can change her mind.

8 His insults to me were intentional – he knew what he was saying.

deliberately

He ......deliberately insulted me...... – he knew what he was saying.

9 I'm not planning to stay here for long.

plan

It isn't ......my plan to stay...... here for long.

10 I accidentally spilt his drink and he got annoyed.

accident

I ......spilt his drink by accident...... and he got annoyed.

→ Glossary p212–13

4.7 Word focus

Phrasal verbs: *break* & *fall*

A Complete these sentences with one of the particles below.

down in out up

1 Tony and Zena had a big argument and broke ....up.......... .
2 A fight broke ....out.......... during the party and several people got hurt.
3 Someone broke ....in.......... and stole my computer from my room.
4 The car kept breaking ....down.......... and the repair bills were very high.

B Look at these sentences using phrasal verbs with *fall*. Decide what happened, A or B.

1 Greg and I *fell out* because he accused me of lying.
A we stopped being friends B we are both confused
2 The table *fell apart* because it hadn't been put together properly.
A it looked strange B it broke into pieces
3 Tamara *fell over* because someone pushed her.
A she moved quickly B she landed on the ground
4 Nick's plan to travel round Europe *fell through*.
A he couldn't do what he planned B he decided to change his plan
5 I must have been stupid to *fall for* such a ridiculous idea.
A I was tricked B I misunderstood

Prepositional phrases: adjective + preposition

C Fill the gap in each sentence using one of the prepositions below.

for in of to with

1 Are you familiar ....with.......... this kind of music?
2 She's very proud ....of.......... everything she's achieved.
3 He wasn't aware ....of.......... what other people thought of him.
4 This kind of food is high ....in.......... fat.
5 I'm tired ....of.......... doing the same things all the time.
6 This area is well-known ....for.......... its restaurants and night clubs.
7 We are committed ....to.......... providing the best service possible.
8 The place was full ....of.......... people, so I didn't go in.
9 Thanks for being so kind ....to.......... me.
10 This sum of money is equal ....to.......... about 200 dollars.

→ Glossary p213

Collocations

D Complete these sentences with the correct form of one of the verbs below.

catch come give keep put

1 Something should be done to ....put............ a stop to this kind of injustice.
2 They ....kept............ me waiting for half an hour before my interview began.
3 You'll ....catch............ a cold if you don't wear some warm clothes.
4 When he ....came............ to power, the economy was in a terrible state.
5 She asked me to ....keep............ an eye on the children while she was out of the room.
6 Could you ....give............ me some help with this job I'm doing?
7 I managed to ....come............ third in the race, which was pretty good.
8 Nobody knows how the building ....caught............ fire, but it soon burnt down.
9 His parents are ....putting............ pressure on him to go to university.
10 I sat with him to ....keep............ him company while he was waiting.

Word formation: verb prefixes & suffixes

E Complete this advertisement for a course by forming verbs from the words in capitals at the end of each line using the prefixes or suffixes below. You may need to make more than one change to the word given.

Prefixes: a- dis- en- mis-

Suffixes: -en -ify -ize

Practical Computer Skills

As the name makes clear, this course 1 ....emphasizes...... the practical side of things. If you want to 2 ....broaden.......... your knowledge and skills, the course will 3 ....enable.......... you to do just that. Experienced teachers will 4 ....clarify.......... areas that confuse you. There may be some terminology which you have always 5 ....misunderstood.... .This course will 6 ....ensure.......... that this is no longer a problem. The teachers will 7 ....simplify.......... the technical language and explain certain error messages, so that you know what to do if the same problem 8 ....arises............ in the future. Many people are 9 ....disadvantaged.... when applying for jobs as their computer skills let them down. So don't be 10 ......discouraged...... if you're struggling with your computer – enrol on our course.

EMPHASIS
BROAD
ABLE
CLEAR
UNDERSTAND
SURE
SIMPLE
RISE
ADVANTAGE
COURAGE

ECCE Practice 4

Grammar

1 Jill seems very tough at work. She's a different person at home, __d__ .
  a although
  b yet
  c even though
  d though

2 __c__ I love swimming, my partner won't go near the water.
  a On the other hand
  b Nevertheless
  c Whereas
  d Even so

3 They bought a new house, __a__ the old one wasn't big enough.
  a because
  b then
  c due to
  d so

4 'Did you go to school today?' 'Yes, despite __b__ ill, I still went.'
  a of being
  b being
  c I'm feeling
  d of feeling

5 'Mary got the job __b__ she wasn't qualified.' 'Really! That's good news.'
  a actually
  b even though
  c in fact
  d despite

6 'I won't go camping next year.' 'I won't __c__ .'
  a too
  b neither
  c either
  d also

7 She's got exams at the moment and __a__ that she's working very long hours.
  a on top of
  b what is more
  c besides
  d more than

8 'Will they ever get married?' 'Yes, definitely __d__ their differences.'
  a however
  b owing to
  c although
  d despite

Vocabulary

9 The greatest __d__ in my life is to become a successful actor.
  a plan
  b intention
  c goal
  d ambition

10 'Look at that player! He kicked Ronald.' 'Yes, that was a __a__ foul.'
  a deliberate
  b determined
  c calculated
  d planned

11 Did you read about the diet that's __b__ in fat?
  a big
  b high
  c rich
  d full

12 Could you please __c__ an eye on the kids for a minute?
  a put
  b have
  c keep
  d take

13 I broke __c__ with my boyfriend because he didn't like any of my friends.
  a down
  b in
  c up
  d out

14 I can't believe she fell __b__ that old trick. Didn't she realize we were just playing a joke on her?
  a off
  b for
  c through
  d over

15 Will you __d__ me company while I wait for the train?
  a give
  b take
  c have
  d keep

16 Jo __c__ second in the competition for the best short story.
  a got
  b took
  c came
  d did

Exam techniques
→ p223

FCE Practice 4

Part 4

For Questions **1–15**, read the text below and look carefully at each line. Some of the lines are correct and some have a word which should not be there. If a line is correct, put a tick (✓) in the space next to the number of the line. If a line has a word which should not be there, put that word in the space next to the number of the line.

IS THERE TOO MUCH MONEY IN SPORT?

1 ....so.... It is certainly true that in recent times money has become ~~so~~ more and

2 ....✔.... more important in sport. I think that in some ways this is not a good

3 themselves thing. People seem to be involved ~~themselves~~ in some sports just to

4 ....of.... make money and not because ~~of~~ they really care about the sport. For

5 ..being.. example, some footballers get ~~being~~ paid an enormous amount of money

6 ....✔.... but sometimes they don't seem to care about the team they are playing

7 ....this.... for, which ~~this~~ makes the fans very angry. And sometimes it looks as if

8 ....✔.... some sports are run so that television companies, the people who own

9 ....✔.... clubs and the companies that provide sponsorship can make a big profit;

10 ....like.... the public who watch these sports don't seem ~~like~~ to matter at all. On

11 ....in.... the other hand, you could say that ~~in~~ these days sport has become a

12 ....✔.... global business, and so it is not surprising that money plays such an

13 ....right.... important part in it. Also, it could ~~right~~ be argued that the top players

14 ....be.... are so famous and ~~be~~ under so much pressure both from fans and the

15 ....for.... media that they deserve ~~for~~ the enormous amounts of money they earn.

Unit 5 Reported speech

Grammar
5.1 Reported speech
5.2 Reported questions
5.3 Verb patterns

Vocabulary
5.4 Speech
5.5 Word focus

5.1 Reported speech

Stop & check

Look at these sentences from newspaper reports. Tick (✓) the speaker's actual words, A or B.

1 The star of the film said that she was surprised at its success.
A 'I am surprised' ...✓... B 'I would be surprised' ......
2 The manager said that the team's results would improve.
A 'They have improved' ...... B 'They will improve' ...✓...
3 The judge said that he had made a decision.
A 'I've made a decision' ...✓... B 'I've been making a decision' ......
4 The losing player said that she had been unlucky.
A 'I'm unlucky' ...... B 'I was unlucky' ...✓...

Actual words	Reported speech
present simple *'I **like** France,' he said.*	past simple *He said (that) he **liked** France.*
present continuous *'I'**m not feeling** well,' she said.*	past continuous *She said (that) she **was not feeling** well.*
past simple *'I **passed** my test last year,' he said.*	past perfect *He said (that) he **had passed** his test the previous year.*
past continuous *'I **wasn't listening**,' she said.*	past perfect continuous *She said (that) she **hadn't been listening**.*
present perfect *'I'**ve been** very busy,' he said.*	past perfect *He said (that) he **had been** very busy.*
present perfect continuous *'I'**ve been waiting** for you,' she said.*	past perfect continuous *She said (that) she'**d been waiting** for me.*
will *'I'**ll help** you,' he said.*	*would* *He said (that) he **would help** me.*
can *'I **can't hear** you,' she said.*	*could* *She said (that) she **couldn't hear** me.*
am / is / are going to *'I'**m going to leave**,' he said.*	*was / were going to* *He said (that) he **was going to leave**.*

▶ note: It is not necessary to use *that* when reporting speech.
▶ note: There are other changes apart from the tense changes:

this ➔ that
here ➔ there
today ➔ that day
tomorrow ➔ the following day
yesterday ➔ the previous day
last week ➔ the previous week
next week ➔ the following week

A **Complete the second sentence using the correct form of reported speech.**

1 'I'm working in a factory,' said Luke.
Luke said (that) he was working in a factory.

2 'I've been working very hard today,' said Alison.
Alison said (that) she had been working very hard that day.

3 'I'm in love with Tom,' said Ruth.
Ruth said (that) she was in love with Tom.

4 'I don't want to watch that programme,' said Lucy.
Lucy said (that) she didn't want to watch that programme.

5 'I can't go to the party,' said Fred.
Fred said (that) he couldn't go to the party.

6 'I'll phone you later,' Keith said to me.
Keith said to me (that) he would phone me later.

7 'I wasn't thinking clearly,' said Wendy.
Wendy said (that) she hadn't been thinking clearly.

8 'I'm not going to do anything this weekend,' said Christine.
Christine said (that) she wasn't going to do anything that weekend.

9 'I didn't do anything wrong,' said David.
David said (that) he hadn't done anything wrong.

10 'I haven't seen Ralph recently,' said Harry.
Harry said (that) he hadn't seen Ralph recently.

11 'I don't know what you're talking about,' George said to me.
George said to me (that) he didn't know what I was talking about.

12 'I can't do what I've agreed to do,' I said.
I said (that) I couldn't do what I had agreed to do.

13 'You've made a mistake,' Alan said to her.
Alan said to her (that) she had made a mistake.

14 'This problem is my fault,' the manager said to me.
The manager said to me (that) that problem was his fault.

B **These sentences are all incorrect. Rewrite them all correctly.**

1 They said that they will contact me last week.
They said that they would contact me the previous week.

2 I said her that I was getting confused.
I told her/I said to her that I was getting confused.

3 She said she didn't liked musicals very much.
She said she didn't like musicals very much.

4 I said to her that I can lend you some money.
I said to her that I could lend you some money.

5 He said that he were going to learn how to play the guitar.
He said that he was going to learn how to play the guitar.

5.2 Reported questions

Actual words	Reported question
asked (someone) + *what* / *where*, etc. + subject + reported speech (see p65) • for questions asking for information *'How much is it?' he asked* *'What time did they arrive?' she asked.* *'When will you arrive?' I asked them.* ▶ note: Do not use a question pattern after *what* / *when*, etc. in reported questions.	 *He asked how much it was.* *She asked what time they had arrived.* *I asked them when they would arrive.* NOT ~~*He asked me what did I want.*~~
asked someone + *whether* / *if* + subject + reported speech (see p65) • for questions asking for the answer *yes* / *no* *'Do you need any help?' I asked her.* *'Have you heard the news?' he asked me.* *'Will you have enough money?' she asked him.*	 *I asked her whether* / *if she needed any help.* *He asked me whether* / *if I had heard the news.* *She asked him whether* / *if he would have enough money.*
asked someone + infinitive with *to* • for requests *'Could you give me some advice?' she asked me.* *'Would you come back later?' he asked her.* *'Please don't tell anyone about it.' she said to me.*	 *She asked me to give her some advice.* *He asked her to come back later.* *She asked him not to tell anyone about it.*
asked (someone) + *for* + noun • for requests *'Could I have another coffee, please?' he asked me.*	 *He asked (me) for another coffee.*

A Complete the second sentence to report the questions.

1 'Have you seen my brother recently?' he asked me.
He asked me if/whether I had seen his brother recently.

2 'Could you wait in reception, please?' she asked me.
She asked me if I could (please) wait in reception.

3 'Why didn't you mention the problem before?' I asked them.
I asked them why they hadn't mentioned the problem before.

4 'Could I have two tickets, please?' I asked her.
I asked (her) for two tickets./(her) if I could have two tickets.

5 'What are you thinking about?' she asked me.
She asked me what I was thinking about.

6 'Will you be staying long?' I asked him.
I asked him if he would be staying long.

7 'What do you want me to do?' I asked her.
I asked her what she wanted me to do.

8 'How long have you been waiting?' she asked me.
She asked me how long I had been waiting.

9 'Please don't smoke in the house,' she said to us.
She asked us not to smoke in the house.

10 'Are you going to celebrate your birthday?' I asked her.

I asked her ....if she was going to celebrate her birthday.............

11 'Would you lend me some money, please?' she asked me.

She asked me ....if I would lend her some money......................

12 'What were you doing that afternoon?' the police asked him.

The police asked him ....what he had been doing that afternoon...............

13 'Could I have the bill, please?' I asked the waiter.

I asked (the waiter) for the bill./(the waiter) if I could (please) have the bill..

14 'Please don't be late,' she said to him.

She asked him ....not to be late...................................

15 'Can you hear me properly?' she asked me.

She asked me ....if I could hear her properly...........................

B These sentences are all incorrect. Rewrite them correctly.

1 I asked him what he did mean.

I asked him what he meant.

2 She asked me whether did I need anything.

She asked me whether I needed anything.

3 I asked the assistant how much did it cost.

I asked the assistant how much it cost.

4 We asked an official when did the next train leave.

We asked the official when the next train left.

5 I asked her why was she upset.

I asked her why she was upset.

5.3 Verb patterns

say (that) **+ reported speech** ***say to*** **someone *(that)* + reported speech** ▶ note: Do not use *say someone* without *to*.	*He said (that) he was feeling tired.* *She said to the interviewer (that) she wouldn't answer the question.* NOT ~~*He said me that he was happy.*~~
tell **someone *(that)* + reported speech** ***tell*** **someone + infinitive with *to*** ▶ note: The verb *tell* must be followed by an object.	*They told us (that) the hotel was full.* *The boss told me not to be late again.* NOT ~~*They told (that) the hotel was full*~~. Or ~~*The boss told not to arrive late again.*~~
explain (that) **+ reported speech** ***explain to*** **someone *(that)* + reported speech** ▶ note: Do not use *explain* followed by a person.	*I explained (that) I was going to be late because I was delayed.* *She explained to me (that) she couldn't finish the work on time.* NOT ~~*I explained him that I wanted my money back.*~~
promise **+ infinitive with *to*** ***promise (that)*** **+ reported speech** ***promise*** **someone *(that)* + reported speech** ▶ note: Do not use *promised somebody to do something*.	*You promised to cook the meal tonight.* *You promised (that) you would cook the meal.* *You promised me (that) you would cook the meal.* NOT ~~*I promised him to arrive on time.*~~
suggest **(to someone) *(that)* + reported speech** = say something as an idea; propose	*He suggested to me that we went to the cinema.*

→ ExA p71

complain **(*to* someone) *(that)* + reported speech** = say you are not satisfied with or happy about something ***complain*** **(*to* someone) *about* + noun**	*We complained (to the neighbours) (that) the music was too loud.* *We complained (to the neighbours) about the noise.*
argue **(*with* someone) (*about* + noun)** = say that you don't agree, especially angrily	*He often argues with her about money.*
criticize **someone *for* + *-ing*** = say you don't like something that somebody does	*She's always criticizing him for being lazy.*
protest **(*to* someone) (*about* + noun)** = say very strongly that you do not like or agree with something or that something is unfair ***apologize*** **(*to* someone) (*for* + *-ing*)** = say 'I'm sorry' ▶ note: Do not use *apologize someone* without *to*.	*They protested to the government.* *We protested about the low pay rise.* *I apologized for embarrassing her.* *He apologized to us for keeping us waiting.* NOT ~~*I apologized him.*~~
thank **someone (*for* + noun / *-ing*)** = say 'thank you' ***blame*** **someone (*for* + noun / *-ing*)** = tell somebody that you think they are responsible for something bad that has happened	*They thanked me for my help / for helping them.* *You can't blame me for the terrible weather.* *She blamed me for making us late.*
discuss **+ noun (*with* someone)** = talk about a subject, especially an important one ▶ note: Do not use *discuss about* + noun.	*He discussed his future with his teachers.* NOT ~~*He discussed about his future.*~~

→ ExB p72

agree* + infinitive with *to = say 'yes' when asked to do something ***agree (that)* + reported speech** = say 'yes, it's true'	*She agreed to lend me some money.* *She agreed (that) she had made a mistake.*
admit (to)* + *-ing agree that something is true, especially when it is unpleasant or something that you are not happy about ***admit (that)* + reported speech** = admit to + *-ing*	*He admitted to lying to her before.* *He admitted (that) he had lied to her before.*
deny* + *-ing = say that something is not true ***deny (that)* + reported speech** = deny + *-ing*	*They denied breaking the law.* *They denied (that) they had broken the law.*
refuse* + infinitive with *to say 'no' when asked or told to do something, or offered something	*I tried to explain but he refused to listen to me.*

➔ ExC p72

insist on* + *-ing = say that you will do something because you really want to do it, even though somebody else says it is unnecessary or unwanted ***insist (that)* + reported speech** • = say firmly that something is the case, especially when someone else doesn't believe you or agree with you • = say firmly that somebody must do something, especially when they are refusing to do it	*We told him we would pay for ourselves but he insisted on paying all the costs himself.* *She insisted (that) she had not taken my pen.* *I insisted (that) the assistant served me next.*
demand* + infinitive with *to = ask to do something very firmly, in a way that suggests you will not accept the answer 'no' ***demand (that)* + reported speech** = ask somebody to do something very firmly, in a way that suggests you will not accept the answer 'no'	*She demanded to speak to the person in charge.* *I demanded that she gave me an answer immediately.*
accuse someone of* + *-ing = tell somebody that you believe they have done something wrong or bad	*Are you accusing me of stealing?*
***threaten* + infinitive with *to* (+ *unless / if*)** = tell somebody that you will hurt or punish them if they don't do what you want them to do ▶ note: Do not use *threaten* + object + infinitive.	*She threatened to sack him unless his work improved / if his work didn't improve.* NOT ~~*She threatened him to sack.*~~

➔ ExD p72

encourage **someone + infinitive with *to*** = tell somebody that they are able to do something and that it is a good idea for them to do it; support and give confidence to somebody	*She encouraged me to keep trying.*
urge **someone + infinitive with *to*** = tell somebody that it is very important for them to do something; try hard to persuade somebody to do something; recommend something strongly	*I urged her not to give up trying.* *She urged me to act quickly.*
persuade **someone + infinitive with *to*** = succeed in making somebody agree to do something by giving them good reasons for doing it ***persuade (that)*** **+ reported speech** = succeed in making somebody believe that something is true	*I persuaded him to lend me his car.* *He persuaded me (that) it was a good idea to buy it.*
convince **someone + infinitive with *to*** = persuade somebody to do something ***convince*** **someone *(that)* + reported speech** = make somebody believe something	*I convinced him to reduce the price.* *She convinced me (that) I was making a mistake.*

→ ExE–G p73

A **Complete the sentences using the correct verb patterns.**

The Team Meeting

At half-time the manager called the team together. 'You're playing very badly,' he said. 'I'm not feeling very well,' said Rick, the star player. 'I feel ill too,' said another player. 'Stop making excuses,' said the manager. 'We aren't making excuses,' they said, 'we're telling the truth.' The manager looked at them angrily and said, 'Why don't you take an aspirin?' 'We'll try harder in the second half,' they said, 'we won't give up. We'll win the match.'

1. The manager told ....the team they were playing.... very badly.
2. Rick explained ....(that) he wasn't feeling........ very well.
3. Another player said ....that he felt.................. ill too.
4. The manager told ....them to stop................ making excuses.
5. They said ....they weren't making.......... excuses.
6. They explained ....(that) they were telling........ the truth.
7. The manager suggested ....(that) they took.............. an aspirin.
8. They promised ....(that) they would try/to try..... harder in the second half.
9. They promised ..(that) they wouldn't give/not to give... up.
10. They promised ....(that) they would win/to win..... the match.

B **Complete the sentences using the correct verb patterns.**

The Staff Meeting

The manager started the meeting by saying, 'I'm sorry I've arrived late. Thank you for attending this meeting. Now, does anyone have any problems?' Janice said, 'I have a complaint. The coffee machine isn't working properly.' Frank said, 'And there isn't enough fresh air in the office.' Anne said, 'Keith causes that problem. He keeps closing the windows.' 'That's not true,' said Keith. 'Yes, it is,' said Anne. The manager interrupted them. 'Don't act like children,' he said. 'That's an unfair comment,' they said, 'we're not acting like children.' Eventually, they talked calmly about the problems.

1 The manager apologized ....for arriving.......... late.
2 He thanked ....them for attending.......... the meeting.
3 Janice complained ....that the coffee machine wasn't working.......... properly.
4 Frank complained ....about.......... the lack of fresh air in the office.
5 Anne blamed ....Keith for.......... that problem.
6 Keith argued ....that he wasn't to blame for.......... the problem of fresh air.
7 The manager criticized ....them for acting.......... like children.
8 They protested ....about.......... his comment.
9 Eventually they discussed ....the problems.......... calmly.

C **Complete the sentences using the correct verb patterns.**

The Court Case

When questioned by the prosecution lawyer in court today, he said, 'I was at the scene of the crime but I was not involved in anything illegal. I know the accused but we were not acting together. I will answer all questions about this case but nothing else. It is true that I have committed crimes in the past but I will not discuss them here.'

1 He agreed ....that he had been.......... at the scene of the crime.
2 He denied ....being involved/that he had been involved.......... in anything illegal.
3 He admitted ....knowing/that he knew.......... the accused.
4 He denied ....acting/that they had been acting.......... together.
5 He agreed ....to answer.......... all questions about the case.
6 He admitted ....to having committed/that he had committed.......... crimes in the past.
7 He refused ....to discuss.......... them.

D **Complete the sentences using the correct verb patterns.**

THE COMPLAINT

'We want to see the manager!' we said. In his office, we said, 'Give us our money back!' He wasn't very pleasant. He said, 'You've invented these problems. I want to see some proof of them.' 'We have every right to complain,' we said, 'and we'll complain to your Head Office. We'll take the company to court if we have to.'

1 We insisted ....on seeing/that we saw.......... the manager.
2 We demanded ....(that) he gave.......... us our money back.
3 He accused ....us of inventing.......... the problems.
4 He demanded ....to see.......... some proof of them.
5 We insisted ....(that) we had.......... every right to complain.
6 We threatened ....to complain to.......... his Head Office.
7 We threatened ....to take the company.......... to court.

E Complete the sentences using the correct verb patterns.

The Job Offer

I wasn't sure whether to accept the job or not, so I asked a few friends. 'I think you should definitely take it,' said Tom. 'I think you should think very carefully before you decide,' said Alison. 'Ask them for more money,' said Eric. Finally, Ruth said, 'I think it's a good idea to take the job,' and because of what she said I took it.

1 Tom encouraged ....me to take.......... the job.
2 Alison urged ....me to think about it.......... very carefully.
3 Eric tried to persuade ....me to ask.......... them for more money.
4 Ruth convinced ....me to take.......... the job.

F In the text below some lines are correct but some have a word that should not be there. Indicate the correct lines with a tick (✓). For the incorrect lines, write the word that should not be there.

Planning the Party

1 ....about.......... Yesterday we discussed ~~about~~ our plans for the party next week.
2 ....us.......... Donna said ~~us~~ that she would organize all the food and drink and
3 ....✓.......... Jeff promised us that he would arrange the music. After that, I
4 ....everybody.......... explained ~~everybody~~ that there was a problem with the room. The
5 ....✓.......... manager had told me that the party would have to end at 11 pm.
6 ....me.......... He had even threatened ~~me~~ to cancel the party if I didn't agree.
7 ....✓.......... I explained to them that I had tried hard to make him change his mind
8 ....them.......... and I promised ~~them~~ to speak to him again about the matter. They said
9 ....✓.......... to me that they hoped I would succeed or the party would be ruined. I
10 ....them.......... apologized ~~them~~ for the problem and said that I would do my best.

G Fill the gaps in this article with one of the words below.

complained admitted threatened insisted accused denied encouraged refused criticized demanded blamed convinced

The Press Conference

Best-selling author Brian Slime yesterday 1 ....accused.......... the press of treating him unfavourably and 2 ....threatened.......... not to give any more interviews if this continued. He 3 ....admitted.......... to having signed 'a very good contract' for three new books but he 4 ....denied.......... being a multi-millionaire. He 5 ....complained.......... to the journalists present that they seemed to be more interested in his income than his books and he 6 ....criticized.......... them for ignoring the quality of his writing. However, some journalists 7 ....insisted.......... on discussing the financial aspect of his new contract and 8 ....demanded.......... to know how much he would be receiving. He 9 ....refused.......... to discuss the matter further and left the room. His agent 10 ....encouraged.......... him to return and after a while he 11 ....convinced.......... him to do so. Later, he 12 ....blamed.......... the press for ruining the interview.

→ Glossary p213–14

5.4 Speech

A Use the word given in capitals at the end of each line to form a word that fits in the space in the same line.

The Minister's statement

The Transport Minister today issued a 1 ....denial.......... of the rumour that he	DENY
was being forced to resign. He said that 2 ....demands.......... for his resignation	DEMAND
were only from certain people and he was 3 ....insistent.......... that he would not	INSIST
be influenced by 4 ....criticisms.......... of that kind. He accepted politicians have	CRITICIZE
to expect 5 ....complaints.......... from people sometimes, but this incident had been	COMPLAIN
very unpleasant. He thanked his family for their 6 ...encouragement... at this	ENCOURAGE
difficult time. He said that after a long 7 ....discussion.......... with them, he had	DISCUSS
decided not to give up because they had been very 8 ....persuasive.......... .	PERSUADE
Because of their 9 ....persuasions.........., and as a result of a number of very long	PERSUADE
10 ....conversations.......... with colleagues, he had decided to stay. He said that he	CONVERSE
had also found the public's attitude to the matter very 11 ....encouraging.......... . He	ENCOURAGE
finished his statement by saying that his 12 ....refusal.......... to resign and his	REFUSE
13 ....insistence.......... on remaining in office indicated how determined he was.	INSIST
'I won't be resigning in the near future, either,' he 14 ....promised..........'.	PROMISE
Experts described his performance as 15 ....convincing.......... .	CONVINCE

B Complete the second sentence so that it means the same as the first sentence, using the word given.

1 John and I discussed the subject last night.

discussion

I ....had a discussion with.......... John about the subject last night.

2 She promised not to tell anyone my secret.

promise

She ....made a promise.......... not to tell anyone my secret.

3 Her parents encouraged her when she was at school.

encouragement

Her parents ....gave her encouragement.......... when she was at school.

4 I'm not criticizing your work.

criticism

I'm not ....making a criticism of.......... your work.

5 We have talked about this problem before.

conversation

We have ....had a conversation about.......... this problem before.

6 We told the waiter that we thought the food was unsatisfactory.

complaint

We ....made a complaint to.......... the waiter about the food.

→ Glossary p213–14

C **Use the word given in capitals at the end of each line to form a word that fits in the space in the same line.**

Incident at work

The manager came up to me and asked me for an 1 ......explanation...... . He said	EXPLAIN
documents must not be removed from his office without his 2 ......agreement...... .	AGREE
I said I didn't know what he meant but he ignored my 3 ......protests...... . He	PROTEST
said, 'I'm not going to have an 4 ......argument...... about this. You took a	ARGUE
document. Give it back or you'll be in serious trouble.' This 5 ......accusation......	ACCUSE
upset me and I was very worried about him 6 ......threatening...... me. He had never	THREATEN
been 7 ......critical...... of me before. I could hardly speak but I told him that	CRITICIZE
he shouldn't have 8 ......blamed...... me and he stormed away angrily.	BLAME
Ten minutes later he returned and he was very 9 ......apologetic...... . 'I'm sorry,'	APOLOGIZE
he said. 'It was my mistake. I owe you an 10 ......apology...... .'	APOLOGIZE

D **Complete the second sentence so that it means the same as the first sentence, using the word given.**

1 Kate and Philippa were arguing when I arrived.

argument

Kate ......was having an argument with...... Philippa when I arrived.

2 Eventually, we agreed to pay half of the bill each.

agreement

Eventually, we ......came to/made/reached an agreement...... to pay half of the bill each.

3 Did she explain her strange behaviour last week?

explanation

Did she ......give an explanation for...... her strange behaviour last week?

4 He protested about the referee's decision.

protest

He ......made a protest...... about the referee's decision.

5 The police accused him of several things when they interviewed him.

accusations

The police ......made several accusations...... when they interviewed him.

6 He threatened me and I got frightened.

threat

He ......made a threat against me...... and I got frightened.

7 Did you apologize for letting them down?

apology

Did you ......give/offer/make (them) an apology for letting...... them down?

8 They said the mistake was my fault, but it wasn't.

blame

I ......got the blame for...... the mistake, but it wasn't my fault.

→ Glossary p214

5.5 Word focus

Phrasal verbs: *run* & *catch*

A Complete these sentences with the correct form of one of the phrasal verbs below. The meanings for each phrasal verb are given in brackets at the end of each sentence.

run after run into run out of run over catch on catch up with

1 I've ....run out of.......... coffee so I can't offer you any. (= *used all of and have none left*)

2 I ....ran after.......... him and stopped him before he could leave. (= *ran and tried to catch*)

3 You'll never guess who I ....ran into.......... yesterday! (= *met by chance*)

4 His invention ....caught on.......... and he became a very wealthy man. (= *became popular*)

5 Be careful crossing the road or you might get ....run over.......... . (= *hit by a car while walking*)

6 Having been off school for some time, I had to ....catch up with.......... the rest of the class when I got back. (= *try hard to reach the same level as*)

Collocations

B Complete the second sentence so that it means the same as the first, using one of the verbs below and the word given.

do have make pay take

1 You would feel better if you did more exercise. (good)
It would ....do you good.......... to do more exercise.

2 Let's use this opportunity to sit down and rest. (advantage)
Let's ....take advantage of this opportunity.......... to sit down and rest.

3 His decision was not affected by his personal opinions. (effect)
His personal opinions ....had no effect on.......... his decision.

4 'Don't forget to bring your passport with you,' I told her. (sure)
I told her to ....make sure (that) she remembered.......... to bring her passport with her.

5 She was finding it difficult to stay awake during the meeting. (difficulty)
She ....was having difficulty (in) staying.......... awake during the meeting.

6 He told me to focus on the small details in the contract. (attention)
He told me to ....pay attention to.......... the small details in the contract.

7 Will this matter affect your chances of promotion? (effect)
Will this matter ....have an/any effect on.......... your chances of promotion?

8 She used the opportunity to earn some money. (use)
She ....made use of the opportunity.......... to earn some money.

9 I was finding it difficult to hear what she was saying. (trouble)
I ....was having trouble hearing.......... what she was saying.

10 I contacted someone who had been recommended by a friend. (contact)
I ....made contact with someone.......... who had been recommended by a friend.

→ Glossary p214

Word formation: nouns (people & jobs)

C Complete this text by forming nouns using the words in capitals at the end of each line and the suffixes below. You may need to make more than one change to the word given to form the correct noun.

-ian -er -ist -ant -or

What former pupils are doing now

As the 1 ....editor.......... of this magazine, I am always pleased to be able to give information on former pupils in this section. 2 ....Readers.......... will be interested to see that they include a rising 3 ....politician.......... , three highly successful 4 ....lawyers.......... and one person who has become a well-known 5 ....journalist.......... on a national newspaper. In the arts, we have someone who has become the 6 ....creator.......... of a popular cartoon series and a number of professional 7 ....musicians.......... . In sport, one former pupil is now the 8 ....assistant.......... coach at a major football club and another has become a fitness 9 ....instructor.......... . And we must not forget that one of our former pupils was recently a 10 ....participant.......... in the TV show *Sing Like The Stars!*

EDIT
READ
POLITICS
LAW
JOURNAL
CREATE
MUSIC
ASSIST
INSTRUCT
PARTICIPATE

Word sets

D Complete each sentence with one of the words below.

cause reason grounds influence

1 We were discussing the ....influence.......... of climate on people's personalities.
2 Nobody knows what the ....cause.......... of the accident was.
3 He was sacked from his job on the ....grounds.......... that he was totally incompetent.
4 I can see no ....reason.......... why this plan shouldn't work.

required called demanded insisted

1 They ....insisted.......... on payment of the full amount in advance.
2 In this situation, a big effort from everyone is ....called.......... for.
3 What exactly will I be ....required.......... to do on the course?
4 The job ....demanded.......... both skills and personal qualities.

maintain stand support cope

1 I just can't ....stand.......... listening to this kind of music – it's horrible.
2 I said in the meeting that I didn't ....support.......... the plan.
3 She has a lot of problems to ....cope.......... with at the moment.
4 He's finding it difficult to ....maintain.......... a high standard of work.

ECCE Practice 5

Grammar

1 'Why is Lily angry?' 'Philippe promised her he __a__ be on time for dinner.'
- **a** would
- b will
- c may
- d could

2 'Hello, darling – sorry I'm late.' 'I thought you said that you __c__ leave work early today.'
- a will
- b are going to
- **c** were going to
- d going to

3 'What did Jenny tell you yesterday?' 'Well, she __d__ me to look after her children.'
- a talked
- b made
- c spoke
- **d** asked

4 I asked him __c__ he wanted a lift home.
- a what
- b where
- **c** whether
- d which

5 'Why are you angry with Kelly?' 'Because she insisted on me __a__ Paul again.'
- **a** seeing
- b to seeing
- c see
- d to see

6 'Did he plead guilty?' 'Yes, he admitted __c__ the crime.'
- a to being
- b committed
- **c** to having committed
- d to have committed

7 They threatened to sack him if he __c__ change his attitude.
- a don't
- b doesn't
- **c** didn't
- d won't

8 He __d__ stealing the watch.
- a threatened
- b demanded
- c refused
- **d** denied

Vocabulary

9 I had a long __c__ with my neighbor yesterday. We talked for hours.
- a explanation
- b protest
- **c** conversation
- d accusation

10 'Were you involved in the accident?' 'Yes, but I wasn't to __c__ for it.'
- a charge
- b accuse
- **c** blame
- d apologize

11 I __b__ an old friend yesterday. It was really nice to see her after all this time.
- a ran after
- **b** ran into
- c ran over
- d ran up

12 'They are expanding the business because the __b__ for their product is so high.
- a need
- **b** demand
- c claim
- d request

13 I don't mind walking long distances, because I know it does me __d__ .
- a advantage
- b sure
- c more
- **d** good

14 In order to __b__ our high standards we have to be very strict on quality control.
- a hold
- **b** maintain
- c preserve
- d carry on

15 Safety experts are trying to establish the __a__ of yesterday's train crash.
- **a** cause
- b reason
- c grounds
- d creation

16 They are investigating the __b__ global warming will have on us over the next 50 years.
- a change
- **b** effect
- c result
- d outcome

Exam techniques
→ p223

FCE Practice 5

Part 2

For Questions **1–15**, read the text below and think of the word which best fits each space. Use only **one** word in each space.

THE VIOLIN MAKER

A physicist-turned-violin-maker believes that he has found a way to make new violins sound **(1)** .....like...... old ones. Alan Beavitt puts his violins through a repeated cycle of damp and dry conditions, re-creating in **(2)** ....a....... few months the natural changes that he believes are responsible **(3)** .....for...... making older violins sound better. Why older violins sound better **(4)** .....has...... long been a mystery. The best ones of all, made **(5)** ......by....... Antonio Stradivari in Cremona, Italy, 300 years ago, have a tone that other makers have tried but failed to match.

Mr Beavitt argues that the changes in the sound of a violin over time **(6)** .....are...... the result of slow changes in the wood. The process leads **(7)** ......to...... a gradual stiffening of the wood, which improves the playing quality and depends on regular changes in humidity. He reproduces the effect in two ways. He **(8)** ...either.... puts his violins in a sealed container and controls the humidity with saturated salt solutions or he pumps air of controlled humidity through rubber pipes into the interior of the violin. The weight of the instrument increases in high humidity as **(9)** ......it....... takes up water and falls again in low humidity as it loses it. Each complete cycle takes ten days and Mr Beavitt says that no further improvement takes place after six cycles. **'(10)** ....There.... is nothing unnatural about the process. The effect could **(11)** .....be...... obtained by travelling repeatedly between Arizona and Zaire, staying a few weeks at each location with the violin case open.'

He now uses the method with all the violins he makes and **(12)** ...would.... like other makers to try it. He finds all the previous explanations of **(13)** .....the...... beauty of the Stradivari violins unconvincing. 'People **(14)** ....have..... said that it is caused by the varnish but **(15)** ......in....... fact some of the best-sounding ones have no varnish,' he says.

Unit 6

Infinitives + *-ing* forms

Grammar
6.1 Start & stop
6.2 Think, decide & remember
6.3 Prefer & would rather
6.4 Mind & not mind
6.5 Want, like & dislike

Vocabulary
6.6 Like & dislike
6.7 Word focus

6.1 *Start & stop*

Stop & check

Look at these pairs of sentences. Tick (✓) the correct sentence in each pair.

1 A I'm starting to get tired. ...... ✓
  B I'm starting getting tired. ......
2 A He kept on to arguing with me. ......
  B He kept on arguing with me. ...... ✓
3 A She stopped to walk and talked to me. ......
  B She stopped walking and talked to me. ...... ✓
4 A I couldn't avoid spending all my money. ...... ✓
  B I couldn't avoid that I spent all my money. ......

start / begin* + *-ing for things that continue for a period *begin* is much less common than *start* in this pattern	 *When did you start smoking?*
start / begin* + infinitive with *to for things that start but are not completed ▶ note: If the verb *start* is in a continuous form, use an infinitive after it	 *She started / began to speak but couldn't continue.* *Are you starting to feel better now?* NOT ~~*Are you starting feeling better?*~~
continue* + *-ing* / *continue* + infinitive with *to both patterns used with the same meaning ***continue (with)* + noun**	*He continued talking / to talk, although nobody was listening.* *Are you going to continue with your studies?*
keep* (*on*) + *-ing = continue doing / to do; not stop doing	*If you keep trying, I'm sure you'll succeed.* *I said 'no' but he kept on asking me.*
carry on = continue ***carry on* + *-ing*** ***carry on with* + noun** ***can't help* + *-ing*** = be unable to stop doing something; find it impossible not to do something	 *Despite the noise, she carried on working.* *Despite the noise, she carried on with her work.* *I can't help thinking I'm doing the wrong thing.*
go on* + *-ing = continue doing / to do; keep doing ***go on with* + noun** ***go on* + infinitive with *to*** = do later, often as a result of progress or after a series of events ***go on to* + noun** = do next; do after something else ***Go on!*** = continue speaking	 *Despite the noise, she went on working.* *Despite the noise, she went on with her work.* *He was a good player at school and he went on to become one of the best in the country.* *Let's go on to the next topic on the list.* *Go on! Tell me what happened next.*

stop* + *-ing = not continue; stop something that has been continuing for a period of time ▶ note: It is not correct to use the pattern *stop* + infinitive with *to* to express this idea. ***stop* + infinitive with *to*** = interrupt/stop an action in order to do something else ***stop for* + noun** = interrupt/stop an action in order to have or get something	*Stop worrying, everything's going to be fine.* NOT ~~*Stop to worry, everything's going to be fine.*~~ *On my way there, I stopped to buy a paper.* *We'll have to stop for petrol during the journey.*
finish* + *-ing* / noun** = complete something; reach the end of something ***finish / end use *finish* and *end* without another verb form or object to talk about the end of something	*Have you finished (writing) that letter yet?* *The game finished at 6 o'clock.* *What time does the film end?*
end up / finish up* + *-ing to talk about what happens finally after a series of actions, events or developments ▶ note: Do not use only *finish* or *end* to talk about what happens finally after a series of actions, events or developments. ***end up / finish up* + place / situation** same meaning	*I was only going to stay for a week but I ended / finished up staying for a month.* NOT ~~*I ended staying for a month.*~~ *They ended up / finished up with no money and nowhere to live.*
give up* + noun / *-ing = stop a habit; not continue something	*Helen gave up smoking years ago.* *He gave up his job and went travelling.*

stop* someone / something *(from)* + *-ing = cause something not to happen or continue happening; cause someone not to do something or continue something	*Doctors couldn't stop the illness (from) getting worse.*
prevent* someone / something *(from)* + *-ing = make it impossible for something to happen or for someone to do something	*She couldn't prevent the car from going off the road.* *His illness prevented him from going to university.*
avoid* + *-ing = succeed in not doing something you don't want to do; find a way not to do something you don't want to do ▶ note: Do not use *avoid* + someone / something + *-ing*. With an object, use *stop* or *prevent*. ▶ note: Do not use *avoid* + *that*.	*I left early to avoid getting stuck in the traffic.* *It's impossible to avoid paying this bill.* NOT ~~*Doctors couldn't avoid the illness getting worse.*~~ NOT ~~*I left early to avoid that I got stuck in the traffic.*~~
save = make it unnecessary for something unpleasant or requiring effort to happen ***save* + *-ing*** ***save* someone / something *(from)* + *-ing*** ***save* + noun *(time, energy, space, money, etc.)*** = use less of; not use too much of	*I bought a ticket in advance to save queuing.* *Computers are supposed to save you (from) doing a lot of extra work.* *To save time, I bought a ready meal.* *These light bulbs save energy.*

A **Fill in the correct forms of the verbs in brackets.**

1 In the middle of his speech, he stopped ....to drink.......... (drink) some water.
2 I went to bed because I was starting ....to fall............ (fall) asleep.
3 I wish you'd stop ....making.......... (make) that noise, it's driving me mad.
4 She began ....to leave.......... (leave) the room but he asked her to stay.
5 Have we finished ....discussing....... (discuss) this matter now?
6 Start ....eating........... (eat), you don't have to wait for me.
7 I started ....to explain......... (explain) but he interrupted me.

B **Read these sentences and decide whether they are correct or not. Correct those which are not.**

1 Students who are continuing with their studies should complete this form. correct
2 I couldn't avoid her finding out the truth. I couldn't stop/prevent her from finding out the truth.
3 Let's stop for to have lunch now. Let's stop for lunch now./Let's stop to have lunch now.
4 If you continue to arrive late, you will be sacked. correct
5 They kept on complaining all day long. correct
6 She's quite lazy and likes to avoid that she has to work hard. She's quite lazy and likes to avoid working hard.
7 Let's continue discussing this later. correct
8 He paused for a moment and then went on with his story. correct
9 If you carry on to practise, you're sure to improve. If you carry on practising, you're sure to improve.
10 Suddenly, he stopped to talk and ran out of the room. Suddenly he stopped talking and ran out of the room.

C **Complete the second sentence so that it means the same as the first, using the word given.**

1 I used to watch soap operas but I haven't watched one for months.

gave

I ....gave up watching.............................. soap operas months ago.

2 I took the lift so that I wouldn't have to climb up all the stairs.

save

To ....save (me from) climbing (up).............................. all the stairs, I took the lift.

3 In the end, I spent all my money in that nightclub.

ended

I ....ended up spending.............................. all my money in that nightclub.

4 I gave him something to read in case he got bored.

stop

I gave him something to read ....to stop him from getting.............................. bored.

5 To my surprise, he became an important politician years later.

went

To my surprise, ...he went on to become.............................. an important politician.

6 Eventually, I agreed to do everything they asked me to do.

finished

I ....finished up agreeing.............................. to do everything they asked me to do.

7 I shut the door so that nobody would hear what I was saying.

prevent

I shut the door to ....prevent anybody from hearing.......... what I was saying.

8 He's trying to find a way not to pay the tax he owes.

avoid

He's trying to find a way ....to avoid paying.......... the tax he owes.

9 I laughed, even though the situation was serious.

help

I ....couldn't help laughing.......... even though the situation was serious.

10 I told her that I was going to be late so that she wouldn't cook dinner for me.

save

I told her that I was going to be late ....to save her (from) cooking.......... dinner for me.

11 I'll tell you about the course in general and then I'll give you some details.

go

After I've told you about the course in general, ...I'll go on to give..........
you some details.

12 She continued to hope that something good would happen.

kept

She ....kept (on) hoping.......... that something good would happen.

13 I continued with my plans for the holiday, despite her objections.

carried

I ....carried on with my plans/planning.......... for the holiday, despite her objections.

14 We continued to lose money.

went

We ....went on losing.......... money.

D **Complete this story by choosing the correct word A, B, C or D.**

The Secret Performance

I had a fantastic night out at the weekend. First I went to a restaurant with some friends. We were just 1 ....C.... our food when someone came up to us and offered us some free concert tickets. We couldn't believe our luck when we realized it was one of our favourite bands doing a secret concert before going on tour. The concert 2 ....C.... on for ages and it was fantastic. At first they played some new songs and then they 3 ....D.... on to some songs from their last CD. The concert 4 ....A.... very late, and after it 5 ....D.... , we were all too excited to go straight home. We 6 ....A.... in a park, talking about it until the sun came up.

1	A stopping	B ending	**C** finishing	D giving up
2	A continued	B kept	**C** went	D stopped
3	A carried	B started	C continued	**D** went
4	**A** finished	B gave up	C ended up	D stopped
5	A stopped	B finished up	C gave up	**D** ended
6	**A** ended up	B finished	C ended	D stopped for

6.2 *Think, remember & decide*

think of* + *-ing* / *consider* + *-ing to think about something in order to make a decision	*I'm thinking of going to the USA for my summer holiday.*
imagine* + *-ing to think of something as possible	*She never imagined becoming so famous.*
dream of* + *-ing to think about something that is desired but unlikely to happen	*I've always dreamt of living by the sea.*
wouldn't dream of* + *-ing = wouldn't consider doing; would never do	*I wouldn't dream of behaving as badly as him.*

wonder = ask yourself; not be sure	
***wonder* + *what* / *where*, etc. + second subject + verb, etc.**	*I wonder why he's late.*
***wonder* + *whether* / *if* + second subject + verb, etc. (+ or *not*)**	*I wonder whether / if it will happen (or not).*
wonder* + *what* / *where*, etc. / *whether* + infinitive with *to	
• use when the infinitive has the same subject as *wonder*	*I'm wondering what to do next.*
• use when the infinitive refers to an action done after wondering	*I'm wondering whether to buy it (or not).*
▸ note: Do not use the pattern *wonder if* + infinitive.	NOT ~~*I'm wondering if to buy it.*~~
***I was wondering whether* / *if* ...** to make polite requests in the present	*I was wondering whether / if you could give me some information.*

remember* / *forget* + infinitive with *to = remember something and then do it; forget something and then not do it	*I must remember to send her a birthday card next week.* (= I must remember and then do it.) *I forgot to buy milk when I was at the shop.* (= I forgot and then I didn't do it.)
remember* / *not forget* (+ object) + *-ing = remember / not forget something that happened in the past	*I'll never forget living in that flat.*
***remember* / *forget* (+ *that ...*)** = remember or forget facts and situations	*I remembered that she didn't eat meat.*
***remember* / *forget* + *what* / *whcrc*, ctc. + second subject + verb, etc.**	*I'vc forgotten what I'm supposed to do next.*
***remember* / *forget* + *what* / *where*, etc. + infinitive with to** • when the infinitive and remember / forget have the same subjects • when the infinitive refers to an action after remembering or forgetting	*I can't remember how to cook this dish.*

remind* someone + infinitive with *to = tell someone not to forget to do something; make someone remember to do something	*Remind me to phone my parents this evening.*
***remind* someone (+ *that*)** = make someone remember a fact or situation	*Remind me that I've arranged to meet Kathy tomorrow.*
***remind* someone *of* someone / something** = cause someone to remember something = seem to someone to be similar to someone / something	*Your story reminds me of something that once happened to me.* *She reminds me of someone I used to know.*

***decide / choose* + infinitive** use when *decide / choose* and the infinitive have the same subject	*I've decided not to stay.* *She has chosen to make her career in tourism.*
***decide* (+ *that*) + subject + verb, etc.** use when the subject of the second verb is different from the subject of *decide*; can also be used when both subjects are the same	*I've decided that the whole thing is a waste of time.* *I've decided that I'm not going to stay.*
***decide* + *what / where*, etc. + subject + verb, etc.**	*I couldn't decide what the best offer was.*
***decide* + *whether* + subject + verb, etc. (+ *or not*)**	*I couldn't decide whether it was a good offer or not.*
decide* + *what / where*, etc. / *whether* + infinitive with *to • use when the infinitive has the same subject as *decide* • use when the infinitive refers to an action done after deciding	*I couldn't decide whether to accept the offer or not.*
***decide on* + noun / pronoun**	*We saw ten flats before we decided on this one.*

▶ note: Do not use question patterns after ***whether***, ***what***, ***where***, etc. with any of the verbs in this section.
Instead, use *whether / what / where*, etc. + subject + verb, etc.
It is not correct to say ~~*I wonder what did she mean.*~~ Instead say *I wonder what she meant.*

A Complete the second sentence so that it means the same as the first, using the word given.

1 Joe thinks that he might do a course in computing.

considering

Joe ......is considering doing...... a course in computing.

2 As a child, it was always her wish to be a famous actress.

dreamt

As a child, ...she always dreamt of being...... a famous actress.

3 Please make sure that I remember to phone Sally later.

remind

Please ......remind me to phone...... Sally later.

4 We might decide to have a big party at the end of the year.

thinking

We ......are thinking of having...... a big party at the end of the year.

5 This film is similar to another film I've seen.

reminds

This film ......reminds me of another film...... I've seen.

6 Stealing from a friend is something he would never do.

dream

He ......would never dream of stealing...... from a friend.

7 Please don't let me forget that the train leaves at 8.30.

remind

Please ......remind me that the train...... leaves at 8.30.

8 I'm sure I'll never be as confident as Paul.

imagine

I ..never/can't ever imagine being/don't imagine I'll ever be/imagine I'll never be.. as confident as Paul.

9 She has decided that she isn't going to accept the offer.

chosen

She ....has chosen not to accept........ the offer.

10 He said that he had changed his mind and wouldn't come with me.

decided

He said that he ....had decided not to come/that he wouldn't come........ with me.

B **Complete the second question so that it means the same as the first. Sometimes there may be more than one correct answer.**

1 'What are you going to do about the problem?'

Have you decided ....what you are going to do about the problem........?

2 'Could you give me a lift, please?'

I was wondering ....if/whether you could give me a lift........ .

3 'Should I believe him or not?'

I can't decide ....whether (or not) to believe him (or not)........ .

4 'Why did she get so angry?'

I wonder ....why she got so angry........ .

5 'Was he joking or being serious?'

I can't decide ....if/whether he was joking or being serious........ .

6 'Did I do the right thing?'

I wonder ....if/whether I did the right thing........ .

7 'Should I look for another job?'

I'm wondering ....if/whether I should look for another job........ .

8 'Which way should I go from here?'

I'm wondering ....which way I should go from here........ .

9 'Which one should I buy?'

I can't decide ....which one to buy/I should buy/on which one to buy........ .

C **Complete these sentences using the correct form of the words in brackets.**

1 On the bus, I realized that I had forgotten ....to lock........ (lock) the door before going out.

2 I was surprised when they arrived because I had forgotten ....(that) they were coming........ (they come).

3 ....Did you remember/Have you remembered........ (you remember) ....to get........ (get) the information I asked you for?

4 ....Do you remember me telling........ (you remember) (me) (tell) you about a friend of mine who lives in China?

5 He'll never forget ....falling........ (fall) in love for the first time.

6 I can't remember how ....to spell........ (spell) his name.

7 I'm sorry, I forgot ....it was........ (it) (be) your birthday yesterday.

8 Can you remember what ....their address is........ (their address) (be)?

6.3 *Prefer & would rather*

Compare

prefer

Use *prefer* for general preferences (see second note at the bottom of the page for structures)

I don't save money, I prefer to spend / spending it.
I'm not keen on football, I prefer tennis.

would prefer

Use *would prefer* for particular preferences that are true at a particular time

I don't want to stay here, I'd prefer to leave.
'Tea or coffee?' 'I'd prefer coffee.'

***would prefer*: present & future**	***would rather*: present & future**
would prefer + infinitive with ***to*** *I'd prefer to leave now.* ***would prefer*** + object + infinitive with ***to*** OR ***would prefer it if*** + second subject + past simple *I'd prefer them to do it now.* *I'd prefer it if they did it now.*	***would rather*** + infinitive without ***to*** *I'd rather leave now.* ***would rather*** (+ ***that***) + second subject + past simple *I'd rather (that) they did it now.*
***would prefer*: past**	***would rather*: past**
would prefer to have + past participle OR ***would have preferred*** + infinitive with ***to*** *I'd prefer to have gone somewhere else.* *I'd have preferred to go somewhere else.* ***would prefer*** + object + ***to have*** + past participle OR ***would have preferred*** + object + infinitive with ***to*** *I'd prefer them to have come on another day.* *I'd have preferred them to come on another day.* ***would have preferred it if*** + second subject + past perfect *I'd have preferred it if they had come on another day.*	***would rather have*** + past participle OR ***would have rather*** + past participle *I'd rather have gone somewhere else.* *I'd have rather gone somewhere else.* ***would rather*** (+ ***that***) + second subject + past perfect *I'd rather (that) they had come on another day.*

▶ note: if the pattern includes an infinitive, the negative infinitive forms are as follows:

infinitive with *to (to do)* ➜ ***not* + infinitive with *to (not to do)***
I'd prefer not to continue.

perfect infinitive with *to (to have done)* ➜ ***not* + perfect infinitive with *to (not to have done)***
I'd prefer not to have gone there.

infinitive without *to (do)* ➜ ***not* + infinitive without *to (not do)***
I'd rather not continue.

perfect infinitive without *to (have done)* ➜ ***not* + perfect infinitive without *to (not have done)***
I'd rather not have gone to that place.

▶ note: the verb *prefer* is used in the following structures:

prefer + infinitive with *to* — *They prefer to go abroad on holiday.*
prefer + *-ing* — *They prefer going abroad on holiday.*
prefer + object + infinitive with *to* — *I prefer people to be honest with me.*

A **Complete the second sentence so that it means the same as the first.**

1 I'd prefer to eat later because I'm not very hungry now.
I'd rather ....eat later because I'm not very hungry now.........

2 I don't want you to tell anyone else what I've told you.
I'd rather ....you didn't tell anyone else what I've told you.........

3 I don't want to spend any more money than I have to.
I'd prefer ....not to spend any more money than I have to.........

4 I don't want to say anything about this matter at the moment.
I'd rather .....not say anything about this matter at the moment......

5 I don't like them playing their music so loud.
I'd prefer ....them not to play their music so loud..............

6 I wanted to stay at home last night but I had to go out.
I'd prefer ...to have stayed at home last night but I had to go out....

7 I don't want you to come with me.
I'd rather ....you didn't come with me.........................

B **Complete the second sentence so that it means the same as the first, using the word given.**

1 I don't want you to keep criticizing me.
rather
I ....would/'d rather you didn't keep.................... criticizing me.

2 I wish they hadn't stayed so long.
preferred
I ....would/'d have preferred them not to stay........... so long.

3 I don't want to think about that problem now.
rather
I ....would/'d rather not think........................ about that problem now.

4 I'm not happy that they phoned me so late at night.
rather
I ....would/'d rather they hadn't phoned............... me so late at night.

5 It would be better for me if you gave me the money now.
prefer
I ....would/'d prefer you to give....................... me the money now.

6 I wish I'd stayed at home.
rather
I ....would/'d rather have stayed....................... at home.

7 I didn't want to tell him the horrible truth but I had to.
rather
I ....would/'d rather not have to tell................... him the horrible truth but I had to.

8 I don't want to do something as dangerous as that.
prefer
I ....would/'d prefer not to do......................... something as dangerous as that.

6.4 *Mind* & *not mind*

(not) mind **(someone) + *-ing*** • be willing to do something • most often used in the negative to mean (not) be angry or upset about something that could annoy or upset someone	*I don't mind helping them.* *Do you mind having to work such long hours?* *Louise doesn't mind people criticizing her.*
wouldn't mind **+ *-ing*** = would quite like to do, when talking about things that seem like an attractive idea or situation	*I wouldn't mind living in a place like that.* *I wouldn't mind being as rich as them.*
***(not) mind what / where,* etc. / *whether* + second subject + verb, etc.** • = it makes no difference; it doesn't matter; it isn't important • use the present simple to talk about the future	*I don't mind what other people think of me.* *I didn't mind whether I got the job or not.* *I don't mind where we go tonight.* *Do you mind whether you get the job or not?*
Would / do you mind (someone) **+ *-ing*?** • to ask someone to do something • *Would you mind …?* is more polite than *Do you mind…?*	*Would you mind waiting here for a moment?* *Do you mind me talking so much?*
Do you mind if **+ second subject + present simple?**	*Do you mind if I sit here?*
Would you mind if **+ second subject + past simple?** • to ask someone for permission to do something • in informal, spoken English, the pattern *Is it OK / all right if* + subject + present simple? is often used to ask for permission	*Would you mind if I sat here?* *Is it OK / all right if I sit here?*
not matter = not be important to someone; make no difference to someone	*Don't worry about this, it doesn't matter.*
not matter to **someone**	*Money doesn't matter to him.*
not matter **(to someone) *what / where,* etc. / *whether* + second subject + verb, etc.** *it doesn't matter to me* = I don't mind use the present simple to refer to the future ▶ note: Do not use *it* + *mind*. Use a subject with *mind* and *it* with *matter*.	*It doesn't matter to me what other people say about me.* *It doesn't matter to me where we go tonight.* *It didn't matter to me whether I got the job or not.* NOT ~~*It doesn't mind (to me).*~~
not care = not be at all interested in something; consider something totally unimportant	
not care about **+ *-ing* / noun / pronoun**	*He doesn't care about doing his job properly.* *He doesn't care about his work.*
***not care what / where,* etc. / *whether* + second subject + verb, etc.** use the present simple for the future	*I don't care what other people think of me.* *I don't care where we go tonight.* *I didn't care whether I got the job or not.*

A Complete the second sentence so that it means the same as the first, using *mind*.

1 I think it would be nice to live in a house like that.
I ......wouldn't mind living...... in a house like that.

2 I'm sure Louise will be willing to lend you some money.
I'm sure ......Louise wouldn't mind lending...... you some money.

3 They can stay with us for as long as they like, as far as I'm concerned.
I ......don't mind how long...... they stay with us.

4 Seeing that film isn't important to me.
I ......don't mind whether I see...... that film or not.

5 I'm willing to do the washing-up.
I ......don't mind doing...... the washing-up.

B Rewrite these questions using the word *mind*.

1 Can I ask you a personal question? Would/Do you mind if I ask/me asking you a personal question?

2 Could you say that again, please? Would/Do you mind saying that again, please?

3 Is it embarrassing for you to talk about this subject? Do you mind talking about this subject?

4 Can I come with you? Would you mind if I came with you?/Do you mind if I come with you?

C Read these reports and complete the sentences with the correct form of *mind*, *matter* or *care*.

Annual Report on Staff Members

John is a very easy-going person who never 1 ......minds...... helping other people. At work, it doesn't 2 ......matter...... to him how long it takes to do a job, he always wants to do it properly.

Leslie doesn't 3 ......care...... enough about the customers. She seems to think that their feelings don't 4 ......matter...... and she doesn't 5 ......care...... about looking after them properly. The only thing that 6 ......matters...... to Leslie is doing as little work as possible.

D Complete the second sentence so that it means the same as the first, using the word given.

1 Apparently, it isn't important to Gerald how much the car costs. (care)
Apparently, ...Gerald doesn't care how much...... the car costs.

2 Maybe I'll win, maybe I won't – it isn't important to me. (mind)
I ......don't mind if I win...... or lose.

3 Excuse me, may I use your pen? (mind)
Excuse me, ...would you mind if I used/would you mind lending me... your pen?

4 Being popular isn't important to Charles. (care)
Charles ......doesn't care whether he's popular or...... not.

5 Excuse me, can I smoke here? (all right)
Excuse me, ...is it all right if I smoke...... here?

6 For John, what has happened in the past is of no interest. (matter)
What ......has happened in the past doesn't matter to...... John.

7 It's clear that earning a lot of money isn't important to Helen. (matter)
It's clear that ......it doesn't matter to Helen whether she earns...... a lot of money or not.

6.5 *Want, like & dislike*

Use	Example
want **+ infinitive with *to*** ***want*** **+ object + infinitive with *to*** ▶ note: Do not use *want + that.* ▶ note: Do not use *want + for.*	*I want to go home now.* *I didn't want her to hear me.* NOT ~~*I didn't want that she heard me.*~~ NOT ~~*I didn't want for to start an argument.*~~
like / love / hate **someone + *-ing*** • = like or dislike something which is happening now or which happened over a period of time ***like / love / hate*** **someone + infinitive with *to*** • = generally prefer or choose something if it is possible, but it is not always possible ▶ note: Do not use *hate* + someone + infinitive with *to* ***like / love / hate it that*** **+ subject + verb**, etc. • = like or dislike a situation ***like / love / hate it when*** **+ subject + verb**, etc. • = like or dislike something that happens sometimes ***like / love / hate the way*** **+ subject + verb**, etc. • = like or dislike how something is done	*I like living here.* *I don't like you staring at me.* *I like to eat at the same times every day. (= if I can.)* *I like people to be honest with me.(= but this does not always happen.)* NOT ~~*I hate him to come late.*~~ *I don't like it that things keep changing.* *I like it when we go out together.* *I like the way she dances.*
would like / love **(someone) + infinitive with *to*** • = want to do; want someone to do ***wouldn't like / would hate*** **(someone) + infinitive with *to*** • = don't want to do, when talking about trying to prevent something from happening or when saying that a hypothetical situation is not attractive ***would like / love / hate*** **(someone) + perfect infinitive with *to*** (to have done) OR ***would have liked / loved / hated*** **(someone) + infinitive with *to*** (to do) • = wanted or didn't want in the past something that didn't happen	*I'd like to speak to the manager.* *Would you like me to come with you?* *I wouldn't like to give you the wrong idea, so I'll explain again.* *I wouldn't like you to get the wrong idea, so I'll explain again.* *I would like to have stayed longer but I had to leave.* *What would you like me to have said instead?* *I would have loved to see more of the country but there wasn't time.* *I would have hated my friends to know what I'd done.*

Compare

like
for a general feeling
I like listening to music.

would like
for a particular wish or desire at a particular time
I would like to listen to some music now.

Compare

want
for direct or informal statements or questions
I want to speak to you now.

would like
for more polite or formal statements or questions
I'd like to speak to you now, if that's possible.

Use	Example
enjoy **+ *-ing*** ***enjoy*** **+ reflexive pronoun (*myself*, *yourself*, etc.)** ***enjoy*** **+ noun / pronoun** ▶ note: The verb *enjoy* must be followed by *-ing*, a reflexive or a noun / pronoun. ▶ note: Do not use *enjoy* + infinitive.	*I've always enjoyed travelling to other countries.* *Did you enjoy yourself last night?* *I enjoyed that meal.* NOT ~~*I enjoyed on my holiday*~~. Instead, say *I enjoyed myself on my holiday, I enjoyed my holiday* or *I enjoyed it.* NOT ~~*I enjoyed to visit the place.*~~

A **Complete the second sentence so that it means the same as the first sentence, using the word given.**

1 I wanted to see that film but I didn't have time.

liked

I ....would/'d have liked to see.......................... that film but I didn't have time.

2 Did you have a good time at the party last night?

enjoy

Did you ....enjoy yourself.................................. at the party last night?

3 Could you give me some advice?

like

I ....would/'d like you to give.......................... me some advice.

4 I don't want you to get angry with me.

like

I ....wouldn't like you to.............................. get angry with me.

5 I'm glad I don't have such a horrible job!

hate

I ....would/'d hate to have............................ such a horrible job!

6 He's great at singing that song.

way

I love ....the way he sings................................ that song.

7 I really wanted to go to that concert but I couldn't get a ticket.

love

I ....would/'d love to have gone........................ to that concert but I couldn't get a ticket.

8 Having nothing to do bores me.

when

I don't like ....it when I have.................................. nothing to do.

9 Tell me, when you worked for that company, did you have a good time?

like

Tell me, ...did you like it when you worked/did you like working.... for that company?

10 I feel good when I spend time on my own.

enjoy

I ....enjoy spending/enjoy myself when I spend.......... time on my own.

11 I was sad that I couldn't afford such wonderful clothes.

love

I ....would/'d love to be.......................... able to afford such wonderful clothes.

12 Her family wanted her to become a lawyer.

liked

Her family ....would have liked her to....................... become a lawyer.

B In the text below some lines are correct but some lines have a word that should not be there. Indicate the correct lines with a tick (✓). For the incorrect lines, write the word that should not be there.

The Price of Fame

1 ...for...	Sometimes I just want ~~for~~ to be left alone. Don't get me wrong. I love all my
2 ...✔...	fans and I love it that they say such nice things to me and send me such
3 ...with...	lovely letters. It's just that when I'm enjoying ~~with~~ a meal in a restaurant, for
4 ...that...	example, I don't always want ~~that~~ to be bothered by people asking me for
5 ...✔...	autographs. To be honest, I hate it when that happens. But I can't be rude, can
6 ...it...	I? I mean, I'd hate ~~it~~ to get a reputation for being the sort of person who's
7 ...wouldn't...	horrible to the public. And I really don't ~~wouldn't~~ like the way some other movie
8 ...it...	stars behave. So I sign the autograph even if I don't like ~~it~~ doing that.

C Rewrite these sentences using the word in brackets.

1 Please don't carry on making that terrible noise. (**want**)
I want you to stop making that terrible noise.

2 I'm happy when my team wins but of course they lose sometimes. (**like**) (2 answers)
I like it when my team wins but of course sometimes they lose.
I like my team winning but of course sometimes they lose.

3 I had fun with my friends over the weekend. (**enjoyed**)
I enjoyed myself with my friends over the weekend.

4 I'm always pleased when my aunts, uncles and cousins visit us. (**like**) (2 answers)
I always like it when my aunts, uncles and cousins visit us.
I always like my aunts, uncles and cousins visiting us.

5 Could you make a decision now, please? (**like**)
Would you like to/I'd like you to make a decision now, please.

6 His parents wanted him to get married but he didn't. (**liked**) (2 answers)
His parents would have liked him to get married but he didn't.
His parents would like him to have got married but he didn't.

7 I really like the idea of having a career like hers. (**love**)
I love the idea of having a career like hers.

8 Having to get up early every morning is awful for me! (**hate**) (2 answers)
I hate having to get up early every morning.
I hate it that I have to get up early every morning.

→ Glossary p214–15

6.6 *Like & dislike*

A **Complete the second sentence so that it has a similar meaning to the first sentence, using the word given.**

1 I don't want to do anything too energetic today.

feel

I ....don't feel like doing.......... anything too energetic today.

2 Did you enjoy yourself when you were travelling around Europe?

time

Did ....you have good time.......... when you were travelling around Europe?

3 I don't want to listen to jokes at the moment.

mood

I am not ....in the mood for listening.......... to jokes at the moment.

4 Alan, would you like to go to the game with me?

fancy

Alan, ...do you fancy going.......... to the game with me?

5 Jane really enjoys helping other people.

pleasure

Jane ....gets pleasure from.......... helping other people.

6 Ian quite likes telling other people what to do.

fond

Ian ....is fond of telling.......... other people what to do.

7 She doesn't think that people should break the law.

approve

She doesn't ....approve of people breaking.......... the law.

8 His parents didn't think he should give up his studies but he did.

disapproved

His parents ....disapproved of him giving up.......... his studies but he did.

9 I hope you enjoy yourself on your trip.

fun

I hope ....you have fun.......... on your trip.

10 I don't like the idea of doing adventure sports.

appeal

The idea of doing adventure sports ....doesn't appeal to.......... me.

11 I don't mind doing her a favour.

objection

I ....have no objection to doing.......... her a favour.

12 Rachel enjoys listening to music.

enjoyment

Rachel ....gets enjoyment from listening.......... to music.

→ Glossary p214–15

B **Read this extract from a novel and underline the correct word 1–6.**

Trisha's 1 disapproval/dislike for Laura had started years before but now that feeling had become intense 2 hatred/detest. She 3 objected/detested hearing her voice, she intensely 4 disliked/opposed seeing her face and she 5 objected/disapproved to having to spend any time with her at all. She had 6 opposed/objected Laura's appointment as manager of the department and she simply hated seeing her in charge. No, she couldn't go on working there any longer.

C **Complete this article by forming a word from the word given in capitals at the end of each line.**

The Proposed New Entertainment Centre

Plans to create a giant new leisure complex on the outskirts of the city have been
greeted with 1 ......disapproval...... by many local people, who do not want it at all. Their — APPROVE
main 2 ......objection...... is that it will greatly increase traffic congestion in the area. — OBJECT
As a result of their 3 ......opposition...... , which has been expressed at local — OPPOSE
meetings, official 4 ......approval...... of the plan has been delayed. However, — APPROVE
there are many people in the area who think the creation of the centre is highly
5 ......desireable...... . They believe it would have economic benefits, particularly — DESIRE
since it would be an 6 ......attraction...... for visitors to the area. They also point to the — ATTRACT
amount of 7 ......enjoyment...... local people themselves would have in such a place. They — ENJOY
believe that it would be 8 ......appealing...... to families because it would provide them — APPEAL
with opportunities for many 9 ......enjoyable...... days out. They cannot understand why — ENJOY
anyone would be 10 ......opposed...... to such a thing. — OPPOSE

D **Read this article and choose the correct answer A, B, C or D to fill each gap.**

I want to be in the media

These days it seems that almost every young person in Britain is 1 ......B...... to work in the media in one way or another. The kind of people they admire are TV presenters and other 'celebrities' who are constantly on TV and in newspapers and magazines. The 2 ......A...... of these people's jobs is that they look glamorous and they're in the public eye, and a lot of young people these days have a strong 3 ......C...... to be famous. Many of them are 4 ......A...... for fame but the vast majority are only going to face disappointment. These jobs that appear so 5 ......B...... on the outside are in fact very hard to get. So if you're 6 ......D...... on the idea of such a career, think again. Don't be too 7 ......A...... to enrol on a media studies course. You may never get a job from it. The idea of fame and glamour may 8 ......C...... you to such a course but you may regret it.

1	A desirable	**B** keen	C appealing	D fond
2	**A** appeal	B desire	C approval	D fancy
3	A attraction	B appeal	**C** desire	D mood
4	**A** desperate	B fond	C keen	D eager
5	A fond	**B** attractive	C eager	D fun
6	A eager	B desperate	C fond	**D** keen
7	**A** eager	B fond	C appealing	D desirable
8	A appeal	B fancy	**C** attract	D desire

→ Glossary p215

6.7 Word focus

Phrasal verbs: *keep* & *put*

A Fill each gap with the particles below.

out of to up up with

1 She walked so fast that it was hard for me to keep ....up with.......... her.

2 I kept ....out of.......... the conversation because it didn't concern me.

3 They played well for 20 minutes but they couldn't keep it ....up.......... .

4 I've decided to keep ....to.......... my original plan rather than change it.

B Look at these sentences using phrasal verbs with *put*. Decide which situation is described, A or B.

1 I couldn't *put up with* the situation any longer.

A I had had enough B I was confused

2 Some friends are going to *put me up* while I'm there.

A they're going to accompany me B they're going to let me stay with them

3 I came home with the shopping and *put it away*.

A I left it on the floor B I put it in the right place

4 I asked to be *put through to* the head of the department.

A I was on the phone B I was writing a letter

5 His constant interruptions *put me off* while I was trying to speak.

A he made me laugh B he prevented me from concentrating

6 I *put on* some smart clothes and went out for the evening.

A I got changed B I got undressed

7 You can't *put off* the decision any longer.

A you must decide now B you musn't make the wrong decision

8 Your description has *put me off* going to that place.

A I'm keen to go there B I no longer want to go there

Collocations

C Complete this extract from a college prospectus with the correct forms of the verbs below. You will need to use some of the verbs more than once.

change keep make pay put reach take

The friendly college

At this college, we have always 1 ....put.......... the emphasis on learning in a friendly environment. We want our students to 2 ....reach.......... the level they are capable of but to feel that they can relax too. People 3 ....make.......... friends at our college and many of them 4 ....keep.......... in touch with each other long after they've left. So why not 5 ....pay.......... a visit to the college and discuss with us what you'd like to do? We'll 6 ....take.......... into consideration both your educational background and your aims in life when suggesting the right course for you. And if you 7 ....change.......... your mind after starting a course, we're flexible about you transferring to another. So 8 ....make.......... an appointment to see one of our advisors now!

→ Glossary p216

Word formation: adjective prefixes

D Complete this text by forming nouns using the words in capitals at the end of each line and the prefixes below. You may need to make more than one change to the word given to form the correct noun.

dis- il- im- in- un-

The rights of customers

MANY PEOPLE are 1 ....unaware.......... of exactly what their rights are as customers. But many people experience 2 ....inefficient.......... service, receive bills that are totally 3 ....incorrect.......... or are victims of traders who are either simply 4 ....dishonest.......... or engaged in activities that are completely 5 ....illegal.......... . What can you do in this position? Many people feel that they are 6 ....incapable.......... of doing anything about it, while others don't wish to be 7 ....impolite.......... when dealing with a shop or other trader and are 8 ....unwilling.......... to make a fuss. But this attitude is surely 9 ....unwise.......... . If you've been the victim of what you believe to be 10 ....unfair.......... treatment, you should do something about it and in this leaflet we'll explain exactly what.

AWARE
EFFICIENT
CORRECT
HONEST
LEGAL
CAPABLE
POLITE
WILLING
WISE
FAIR

Prepositional phrases: verb + preposition

E Fill each gap with one of the prepositions below.

for into on to with

1 I'm trying to concentrate ....on.......... my work at the moment.
2 It can be difficult to adapt ....to.......... life in a new country.
3 The news was received ....with.......... shock throughout the country.
4 Could I exchange this shirt ....for.......... a different one, please?
5 We were divided ....into.......... three groups.
6 I'd like to congratulate you ....on.......... your success.
7 Does this rule apply ....to.......... everyone?
8 How much he earns depends ....on.......... how many hours he works.
9 The number of people we invite will have to be limited ....to.......... 20.
10 I'm going to treat myself ....to.......... an ice-cream when I've finished work.

ECCE Practice 6

Grammar

1 George had to __c__ playing tennis when he injured his knee.
- a end up
- b stop for
- **c** give up
- d go on

2 I'll never __b__ that fantastic holiday in the Caribbean.
- a remember
- **b** forget
- c remind
- d imagine

3 Phil was wondering __d__ to do with all his old books.
- a whether
- b why
- c where
- **d** what

4 'Why are you angry with Kelly?' 'Because she insisted on me __a__ Paul again.'
- **a** seeing
- b to seeing
- c see
- d to see

5 'I told Monica the truth about him.' 'I'd rather you __b__ !'
- a don't
- **b** hadn't
- c did
- d do

6 He told us to stop __a__ .
- **a** talking
- b to talk
- c talked
- d having talked

7 I wouldn't __b__ going to the beach on the weekend.
- a matter
- **b** mind
- c care
- d want

8 'Don't you like this place?' 'I'd rather we __a__ somewhere romantic.'
- **a** had gone
- b went
- c did go
- d have gone

Vocabulary

9 I don't __a__ of smoking in public places. It's not fair to non-smokers.
- **a** approve
- b disapprove
- c appeal
- d fond

10 'I didn't know you liked sports.' 'Well, I'm __c__ on soccer especially.'
- a interested
- b eager
- **c** keen
- d anxious

11 As it was raining, Paul didn't __d__ like walking home.
- a fancy
- b wish
- c want
- **d** feel

12 Jane really __c__ to looking after her younger brother.
- a detested
- b opposed
- **c** objected
- d disliked

13 I wish you would keep __d__ the argument. You're just making things worse.
- a up with
- b up
- c to
- **d** out of

14 Jeff seemed to be __c__ of remembering anything I told him.
- a unable
- b unwilling
- **c** incapable
- d inefficient

15 I decided that I couldn't put __a__ their thoughtless behavior any longer.
- **a** up with
- b off
- c up
- d through to

16 Don't forget to __b__ in touch while you're away.
- a put
- **b** keep
- c make
- d hold

Exam techniques
→ p223

FCE Practice 6

Part 1

For Questions **1–15**, read the text below and decide which answer **A**, **B**, **C** or **D** best fits each space.

THE GRAND TOUR

Travel is so much the norm these days that it's hard to **(1)** .C. a time when the world's great historical sites, beaches and beauty spots weren't **(2)** .A. with camera-carrying tourists. But two centuries ago, **(3)** .C. before cheap rail tickets greatly reduced the cost of crossing Europe, tourism was **(4)** .D. for those with time and money. In Britain, The Grand Tour was seen as an essential **(5)** .B. of any wealthy young man's education. It was a trip of up to five years, taking in a **(6)** .A. range of Europe's artistic and architectural highlights.

Italy was the focus of The Grand Tour, **(7)** .A. it was highly regarded for both its antique and modern culture. **(8)** .D. it was to Venice, Florence, Rome and Naples that the young aristocrats flocked. The hardships of the long and sometimes hazardous journey across the Alps were all part of the **(9)** .D. and they were amply rewarded by the celebrated countryside, the antique ruins and the works of the great Italian painters, not to **(10)** .C. the parties, pageants and carnivals. Tourists were **(11)** .B. to Italy from many countries, as they still are, but it was from Britain that the majority of visitors came.

Although mass tourism was still in its infancy, all the **(12)** .B. of the modern tourist were already there, as the young aristocrats went round Italy in **(13)** .A. of paintings, drawings and a **(14)** .D. of other souvenirs to carry back home. English houses were soon filled with them. The tourists brought the craze for all things Italian and antique back to Britain, and buildings, furniture, even clothes were all **(15)** .C. by this revolution in taste.

1	**A**	think	**B**	suppose	**C**	imagine	**D**	guess
2	**A**	crowded	**B**	full	**C**	extensive	**D**	entire
3	**A**	far	**B**	plenty	**C**	long	**D**	away
4	**A**	severely	**B**	extremely	**C**	strongly	**D**	strictly
5	**A**	section	**B**	part	**C**	share	**D**	division
6	**A**	wide	**B**	grand	**C**	various	**D**	thorough
7	**A**	since	**B**	owing to	**C**	from	**D**	as for
8	**A**	As	**B**	For	**C**	That	**D**	So
9	**A**	involvement	**B**	participation	**C**	incident	**D**	experience
10	**A**	state	**B**	refer	**C**	mention	**D**	tell
11	**A**	appealed	**B**	drawn	**C**	fetched	**D**	fascinated
12	**A**	clues	**B**	signs	**C**	figures	**D**	notices
13	**A**	search	**B**	hunt	**C**	chase	**D**	track
14	**A**	pack	**B**	gang	**C**	flock	**D**	host
15	**A**	impress	**B**	reacted	**C**	influenced	**D**	concerned

Unit 7

Articles, determiners & pronouns

7.1 Articles 1

Stop & check

A Decide whether these sentences are correct or not. Correct them by taking out *a* or *the* where necessary.

1 I've got lots of ~~the~~ good friends. ..✗..
2 I feel ill, I think I've got ~~a~~ 'flu. ..✗..
3 Alan left a message for you. ..✓..
4 He enjoys the work he does. ..✓..

B Decide whether these sentences are correct or not. Correct them by adding *a* or *the* where necessary.

1 My father is [a] businessman. ..✗..
2 Life is very difficult for some people. ..✓..
3 Heavy metal is a type of rock music. ..✓..
4 He ignored [the] advice I gave him that day. ..✗..

Use *a / an*	Use *the*
• when mentioning something or someone for the first time and the person you are speaking to does not know about this thing or person *Someone left a message for you.* (the person being spoken to did not know that this message existed or what it contains before now)	• when mentioning the same thing or person again and the person you are speaking to knows about this thing or person *The message shocked me.* (the person being spoken to now knows that the message exists)
• when you are talking about one of a number of things or people but not specifying which one *She took a CD off the shelf.*	• when you are specifying which one of a number of things or people you are talking about, often with a relative clause *The CD that she played was by my favourite band.*
• to say what a person's job is in general *She's a dentist.* (NOT ~~*She's dentist.*~~)	• with someone's job title or if there is only one person doing that job *the Managing Director; the school caretaker*
• to talk about some common illnesses *I've got a headache.* *She's got a cold.*	
• to give a definition of something *The London Eye is a tourist attraction in London.* *The Beatles were a pop group.*	

▶ note: Do not use *a / an* with the names of some medical conditions; they are uncountable and have no article.
He is suffering from cancer.
She has 'flu.

Countable and uncountable nouns

Use	Example
• some nouns can be used in the plural and some cannot	
• countable nouns, which can be used in the plural, can be used with *a / an* in the singular and *the* in the singular and plural	*I read a book.* *The book you bought me was very enjoyable.* *She put the books in her bag.*
• uncountable nouns, which cannot be used in the plural, cannot be used with *a / an*. Instead, use a word like *some*, *any*, etc, or a phrase like *a piece of*	*I bought some food. Have you got any money?* *It was a nice piece of meat.*
• many physical nouns describing food, drink, substances and materials are uncountable, for example: *meat / fish / rice / pasta / wine / gold / wood / leather / wool*, etc.	*I've got an interesting piece of news for you.* *I bought some meat.* *Would you like some pasta?* *It's made of wood.*
• many abstract nouns describing ideas are uncountable, for example: *information / news / advice / fun / health / knowledge / education / research / progress / weather / work*, etc.	*I'd like some information.* *I've had some good news.* *Do some work.*
▸ note: Do not say *a new*.	NOT ~~*I heard a new yesterday.*~~
• some physical nouns describing objects are uncountable, for example: *furniture / rubbish / traffic / luggage / hair*	*We got some new furniture.* *I got stuck in traffic.*
▸ note: The noun *travel* is uncountable and means 'the general activity of travelling'.	*Her job involves a lot of travel.*
It cannot be used as a singular noun.	NOT ~~*I had a good travel.*~~ Instead, use *journey* or *trip*.
▸ note: The noun *work* is uncountable and cannot be used as a singular noun.	NOT ~~*She has a good work.*~~ Instead, use *job*.

Using and not using *the*: generalizing and specifying

Use	Example
• do not use *the* with a plural noun if you are talking about things or people in general	*It's nice to have friends.* *I like visiting other countries.*
• use *the* with a plural noun if you are talking about particular things or people and you specify which ones you mean, often with a relative clause	*I don't want to leave because of the friends I've made here.* *He talked about the countries he had visited.*
• do not use *the* with an uncountable noun if you are talking about something in general	*He's an expert on food and drink.* *Money isn't the only important thing to him.*
• use *the* with an uncountable noun if you are talking about a specific example or quantity of it	*I didn't like the food in that country.* *I regret the money that I wasted.*
• many uncountable nouns describe abstract ideas or concepts, for example philosophical ideas or feelings. Do not use *the* with such nouns if you are talking about the idea in general but use *the* if you are giving a specific example of the idea, often with a relative clause.	*Education is important.* *The education I had was excellent.* *You should try to enjoy life.* *I like the life I live here.* *What's your idea of happiness?* *I'll never forget the happiness I felt at that moment.*

Exclamations

A strong feeling about something can be expressed with these patterns:

***What a / an* + singular noun + !**

What a terrible idea!
What an unusual present!

▸ note: Do not use *what a / an* + uncountable noun.
NOT ~~*What a terrible weather!*~~

***What* + uncountable / plural noun + !**

What delicious coffee you make!
What beautiful children they are!

A Complete this text using the articles *a* or *the*.

Frank Leonard – Private Eye

When private investigator Frank Leonard got back to his office, there was 1 ....a.......... woman waiting for him, 2 ....a.......... woman he had never seen before. Or at least, he thought he had never seen her before, but when 3 ....the.......... woman began to speak, he felt that there was something familiar about her. 'My name is Toyah Hart,' she said, offering him 4 ....a.......... business card. 'I'm 5 ....a.......... dancer,' she said, smiling in 6 ....a.......... way that made Frank highly suspicious. She clearly wasn't 7 ....the.......... person she said she was, he decided instantly. He looked at 8 ....the.......... card closely and then took 9 ....a.......... file out of his desk. He opened 10 ....the.......... file. It was full of papers and photographs. He took 11 ....a.......... photograph out of it and placed it on 12 ....the.......... desk so that 13 ....the.......... woman could see it. She looked briefly at 14 ....the.......... photograph and 15 ....the.......... smile that had been on her face disappeared. 'OK,' she said, her voice hardening, 'let's talk business.'

B Complete this text by filling the gaps with *a* or *the*.

Newspapers in Britain

An enormous number of people in Britain read 1 ....a.......... national newspaper every day. Some have 2 ....a.......... newspaper delivered to their home, while others buy one from 3 ....a.......... shop, usually a newsagent. 4 ....The.......... paper that people choose to read is 5 ....the.......... paper which they feel corresponds with their own interests, often with regard to their political opinions.

There are basically two kinds of national newspaper in Britain: the 'broadsheets' and the 'tabloids'. Broadsheets focus on 6 ....the.......... news and serious social matters; tabloids focus more on 7 ....the.......... latest gossip and scandal concerning famous people. *The Sun*, which is 8 ....a.......... tabloid, is 9 ....the.......... daily newspaper with 10 ....the.......... highest sales figures. Some people are critical of 11 ....the.......... approach taken by the tabloids, saying that they have 12 ....a.......... bad effect on society. Nevertheless, 13 ....the.......... fact that so many people buy them shows that there is 14 ....a.......... big demand for 15 ....the.......... kind of story they print.

C In this text, *a*, *an* and *the* are sometimes used when they should not be. Cross out those words when they are used incorrectly. Some lines contain more than one error.

The Trip

After months of doing ~~a~~ hard work, I decided that I needed a break. I wanted to go on a trip and I asked a friend for ~~an~~ advice about where I could go. I really enjoy ~~the~~ travel and I love meeting people from ~~the~~ other countries – it's always ~~a~~ great fun. My friend said that I should go to Italy, which was a place I had never been to before. I got ~~an~~ information about ~~the~~ train tickets and ~~the~~ accommodation from the Tourist Board office and off I went.

I travelled all over Italy and what a fantastic time I had! I really like ~~the~~ pasta so I loved the food there and I like ~~the~~ extrovert people so I made ~~the~~ friends there everywhere I went. We talked about all kinds of ~~the~~ things, like ~~the~~ life, ~~the~~ love and a lot of less serious subjects, too! I found the countryside in Italy beautiful and the cities I went to were amazing.

In particular, I will always remember the atmosphere and the buildings in Venice – it's a place that makes a big impression on everyone who goes there. I'd love to go there every year – going on a trip like that is my idea of ~~the~~ happiness. I'm planning the next one now.

D For the following sentences, fill the gaps with *a*, *an* or *the*, or put a dash (–) into the gaps if it is correct to leave them blank.

1 Don't lose ..–.. hope! I'm sure that ..–.. things will get better.

2 Ken feels that ..–.. job satisfaction is more important than ..–.. money.

3 Many people feel that ..–.. violence is a big problem in ..–.. society.

4 You need both ..–.. determination and ..–.. luck to succeed in that profession.

5 I read ..an.. interesting article about ..the/–.. changes that have been happening in ..the.. climate in this country recently.

6 Many people don't trust ..–.. politicians because all they want is ..–.. power.

7 This used to be ..a.. job that only ..–.. men did, but now ..–.. women do it, too.

8 They're protesting because they want ..–.. democracy, ..–.. freedom and ..–.. human rights.

9 What ..a.. surprise! I didn't expect you to buy me ..a.. present.

10 She finds ..the.. work she has to do quite easy; ..–.. boredom is her biggest problem.

11 I think ..–.. life must be ..a.. terrible struggle if you haven't got enough money to buy ..the.. things that you need.

12 You take ..–.. life too seriously – there's a place for ..–.. fun, too!

13 To achieve ..–.. success in some careers often depends on ..the.. support of ..–.. friends and ..–.. family.

14 Passing exams is not simply ..a.. matter of ..–.. knowledge or ..–.. intelligence; ..the.. techniques you use are also important.

15 ..–.. TV documentaries don't interest him; ..the.. programmes he likes are purely for ..–.. entertainment.

16 I told ..the.. Head of Department that I had ..a.. bad cold and couldn't go to ..the.. meeting that day.

17 She has never liked ..–.. authority; she won't take ..–.. orders and she hates ..–.. discipline.

18 Be careful what you say – ..–.. strangers find it difficult to understand ..the.. sense of humour in this region.

19 What ..–.. wonderful music this is and what ..–.. amazing songs they write! I think they are ..the.. group I like best of all.

20 I never discuss ..–.. religion or ..–.. politics; it always leads to ..–.. arguments.

E These sentences are all incorrect. Rewrite them correctly.

1	I heard a terrible news last week.	I heard some terrible news last week.
2	Could I have a wine, please?	Could I have some wine, please?
3	She gave me an interesting information.	She gave me some interesting information.
4	I got delayed in a traffic on my way there.	I got delayed in the traffic on my way there.
5	Someone has done a research into this subject.	Someone has done some research into this subject.
6	He told me a very surprising new in his letter.	He told me some very surprising news in his letter.
7	He has a very well-paid work.	He has a very well-paid job.
8	There was a good weather throughout the holiday.	There was good weather throughout the holiday.
9	Did you have a pleasant travel?	Did you have a pleasant trip.
10	She's been in a bad health for some time.	She's been in bad health for some time.
11	What a lovely food this is!	What lovely food this is!
12	We'll need to get a new furniture for our new house.	We'll need to get (some) new furniture for our new house.

7.2 Articles 2

Using and not using *the*: individual cases

Use	Example
school / university / hospital / church / prison	
• use *the* if you are talking about these places as a physical building and not referring to taking part in what happens inside them	*The school was built in 1853.*
• use *the* if you are specifying a particular one, often with a relative clause	*She goes to the local school.*
• do not use *the* if you are talking about being someone who receives what is provided in the building; in other words, if you or the person you are talking about is a pupil, a student, a patient, someone attending a religious service or a prisoner.	*Do you like school?*
• notice the prepositions that are used without *the* in these contexts: ***at** school / university / church* ***in** hospital / prison* ***go to** school / university / hospital / church / prison*	 *I was at church yesterday morning.* *John is in hospital at the moment.* *He'll be going to university next year.*
• use *leave* and no preposition to talk about no longer being a pupil, student, patient, etc.	*He left school at the age of 16.*
• use *the Church* to refer to the organization (priests, etc.)	*The Church is very powerful in that country.*
work / bed / home	
• do not use *the* with *work* if you are talking about the place where you work or the activity of working	*I went to work early today.* *I was at work yesterday.* *Let's start work now.*
• use *the* with *work* if you are talking about a specific type of work or a particular piece of work	*She really enjoys the work she does.* *I found the work difficult and left the company.*
• do not use *the* with *bed* if you are talking about being in it	*I went to bed late last night.* *I was still in bed when they arrived.*
• use *the* with *bed* if you are talking about one as a piece of furniture	*I moved the bed to the other side of the room.* *They sat on the bed talking.*
• do not use *the* with *home* in these phrases: ▶ note: Do not use *to* + *home*.	*After that, we went home.* *I stayed at home all day.* *When are you coming home?* NOT ~~*We went to home.*~~
• Use *the* with *house*	*I left the house early this morning.*

➔ ExA p105

transport	
• do not use *the* after *by* to talk about the kind of transport used for a journey	*I went by car / bike / bus / train / plane / coach / boat / ship / ferry / taxi / air / sea / tube.*
• you can also talk about the kind of transport you use with these patterns:	*I went in the / my car.* *I went on my bike.*
• the phrase *on foot* means 'walking' *I went on foot.* (NOT ~~*by foot*~~)	*I went on the bus / train / boat / ship / ferry / plane / tube.*

music • *the* is sometimes used with musical instruments but it is not essential • do not use *the* with types of music	*She plays (the) piano very well.* *He likes rock / classical music.*
sports and games • do not use *the* before sports and games	*She's very good at chess / football.*
radio / television / theatre / cinema • use *the* with radio, theatre and cinema but not usually with television	*I heard it on the radio.* *Have you been to the theatre lately?* *Let's go to the cinema tonight.* *I watched television last night.*
academic subjects • do not use *the* with academic subjects, for example: *chemistry / maths / economics*	*She's doing a course in economics.* (NOT ~~*the economics*~~)
parts of society • use *the* with nouns referring to parts of society, for example: *the public / the government / the rich / the poor*, etc.	*The public approved of the idea.*
meals • do not use *the* before meals if you are talking about the act of eating one • use *a* or *the* before meals if you are describing the content of one or giving an opinion of one	*What did you have for breakfast?* *Let's go for lunch.* *What time will dinner be?* *I had a very small breakfast.* *The lunch she cooked was lovely.*
times • do not use *the* with years or months • *the* is sometimes used with seasons and sometimes it isn't • do not use *the* with days of the week unless you are specifying a particular one • use *the* in the phrases *in the morning / afternoon / evening* and *at the weekend* • do not use *the* in the phrase *at night*	*I last came here in 1998 / September.* *Let's go there in (the) summer.* *Let's meet on Friday.* *It happened on the Friday after I arrived there.*

→ ExB–D p106

A **In this text, *the* is sometimes used when it should not be. Cross it out whenever it is used incorrectly.**

MY FAMILY

My father is a lecturer at the university in the city where I live and my mother is a nurse at the local hospital. They both go to ~~the~~ work at different times on different days and they both tell me that they like the work they do. My younger brother is still at ~~the~~ school. He says that he hates the school he goes to. He can't wait to leave ~~the~~ school and go to ~~the~~ work. My parents would like him to go to ~~the~~ university to get a degree but he's not interested in studying. He prefers to go out with his friends, come back ~~the~~ home late and then stay in ~~the~~ bed for as long as he can. If he does get a job after ~~the~~ school, he'll never leave the house on time and he'll always turn up late for ~~the~~ work!

B **In this text, *the* is sometimes used when it should not be. Cross it out whenever it is used incorrectly.**

A Typical Week

I lead a busy life. I get up early in the morning and I always make sure I have enough time for ~~the~~ breakfast. Before ~~the~~ work I go to a gym and play ~~the~~ squash with a colleague of mine. I go there by ~~the~~ bike, although if the weather's really bad I sometimes go on the bus. Then I work all day – sometimes I don't even stop for ~~the~~ lunch – and I usually get home late in the afternoon. I don't waste time in the evening watching TV; sometimes I listen to the radio, sometimes I practise the trumpet (I really like ~~the~~ jazz), occasionally I go to the theatre if there's a play I want to see and from time to time I go out for ~~the~~ dinner with friends. I'm usually pretty busy at the weekend, too. For example, on ~~the~~ Saturday mornings, I do a part-time course in ~~the~~ computing – it's useful for work. And one thing's for sure: I do so many things that I never have trouble sleeping at ~~the~~ night! I'm far too tired!

C **Complete these sentences using *the* if it is required and a preposition if one is required. It may be correct to put nothing (–) in the gap.**

1 She's very ill and she's been ....in.......... hospital for a couple of weeks.
2 Which subjects did you study when you were ....at.......... university?
3 The police caught him and he is ....in.......... prison now.
4 I go ....to.......... church every Sunday.
5 Whereabouts in the city is ....the.......... university?
6 ....The.......... prison here was built centuries ago.
7 The ambulance took the injured people ....to the.......... nearest hospital.
8 ....The.......... Church has a big influence on the community in that place.
9 I met him when we were in the same class ....at.......... school.
10 I found ....the.......... bed in my hotel room rather uncomfortable.
11 I came ....–.......... home and went straight ....to.......... bed.
12 I went ....to.......... hospital to visit a friend.

D **Complete these sentences using *the* if it is required. It may be correct to put nothing (–) in the gap.**

1 I haven't been to ....the.......... cinema for ages.
2 The tourists arrive by ....–.......... ferry.
3 It's too far to walk, so we'll go in ....the.......... car.
4 It says that ....the.......... public do not agree with what ....the.......... government is saying on that subject.
5 I travelled around the country on ....the.......... train.
6 He's not very good at ....–.......... physics but he's very good at ....–.......... Spanish.
7 I don't know anything at all about ....–.......... cricket – what are the rules?
8 He plays ....the/–.......... saxophone in a local group.
9 Sometimes it's true that ....the.......... rich get richer and ....the.......... poor get poorer.
10 Did you know that ....–.......... poker is my favourite card game?
11 They usually play ....–.......... dance music in that club.
12 We were sitting next to each other on ....the.......... plane.

7.3 Pronouns, possessives & reflexives

personal pronouns as subjects *I / you / he / she / it / we / you / they* **personal pronouns as objects** *me / you / him / her / it / us / you / them* the object form of a personal pronoun is usually used after the verb *be* ▶ note: Do not use a personal pronoun immediately after a subject.	*I don't know. / You told me. / He / She came back. / The car made a noise and then it broke down.* *Can you help me? / I've already told you. / When did you meet her? / I quite like him.* *'Who's there?' 'It's only me'.* NOT ~~*The man he spoke to me.*~~
possessive adjectives + noun *my / your / her / his / its / our / your / their* **possessive adjective + *own* + noun** to emphasize that something belongs to or relates to the person mentioned and not someone else ▶ note: Remember that *its* is a possessive adjective and *it's* is a short form of *it is* or *it has*.	*Where's my pen?* *How are your parents?* *He hurt his leg.* (NOT ~~*the leg.*~~) *She took off her coat.* *She used her own money – the company didn't pay for her.* *Is this your own idea?*
possessive *'s* • with singular nouns and names the possessive is formed by adding *'s* • if a plural noun ends with *s*, the possessive is formed by adding an apostrophe (') • if a plural noun doesn't end with *s*, the possessive is formed by adding *'s* **possessive pronouns** *mine / yours / hers / his / ours / yours / theirs* ***a / some*, etc. + noun + *of* + possessive pronoun** to talk about one or a few of many things belonging to or relating to someone	*Is that Jill's brother?* *The company's profits have risen.* *my parents' house* *the children's toys* *That car is mine. / Is that pen yours? / George says that the mistake wasn't his.* *I rang a friend of mine.* *We listened to some CDs of theirs.*
***whose* + noun?** to ask who something belongs to or relates to ***whose* as pronoun**	*Whose car is that?* *Whose idea was this?* *Whose is this umbrella? (= who does this umbrella belong to?)*

→ ExA p109

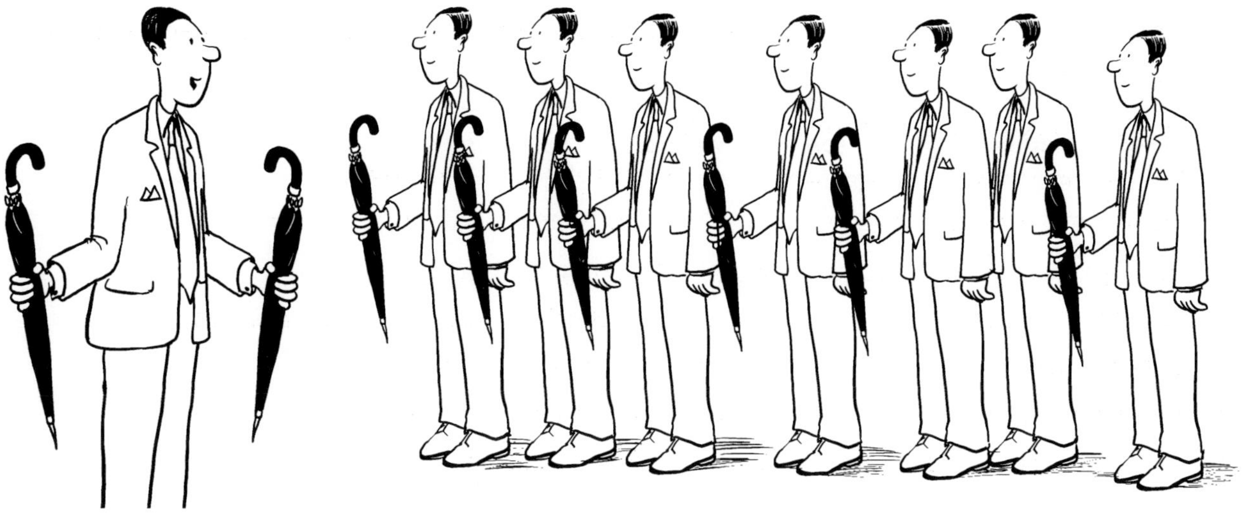

somebody / someone / somewhere / something	
• in positive sentences, = a particular but unspecified person / place / thing	*I'm sure you'll find it somewhere.* *There's something I want to tell you.*
• in questions, = a particular person / place / thing	*Could somebody / someone help me, please?* *Is there somewhere you'd like to go tonight?*
everybody / everyone / everywhere / everything = all people / in all places / all things	*Everybody / Everyone at the party had a good time.* *Everything is fine in her life at the moment.*
nobody / no one / nowhere / nothing = no people / no places / no things	*Nobody / No one heard what I said.* *Nowhere in the country is as beautiful as this.* *She said nothing all evening.*
▶ note: Do not use *nobody*, etc. with a negative verb.	NOT ~~*I haven't done nothing*~~.
anybody / anyone / anywhere / anything	
• = not a person / place / thing • with negative verbs	*I didn't see anybody / anyone.* *I can't find it anywhere.*
• = it doesn't matter which person / place / thing	*Anybody / anyone would tell you the same thing that I'm telling you.*
• = a very large number of people / places / things	*You can find this sort of thing anywhere these days.*
• in questions, = a person / a place / a thing	*Is there anything I can do for you?*
▶ note: adjectives can be used after all of the above words.	*Something strange happened today.* *Have you done anything interesting lately?*

➔ ExB p109

reflexive & emphatic pronouns *myself / yourself / herself / himself / itself / ourselves / yourselves / themselves*	
subject + verb + reflexive pronoun to say that the subject does an action to or for the subject and that another person doesn't do the action to or for the subject, or that another person doesn't help	*It will be quicker if I do this job myself.* *Be careful or you'll hurt yourself.* *She taught herself how to do it.* *He cooked a meal himself.* *The company considered itself successful.* *We repaired it ourselves.* *Did you think of this idea yourselves?* *They built the house themselves.*
▶ note: Use a reflexive pronoun after the verb *enjoy* (see p91).	*They really enjoyed themselves last night.*
▶ note: There are some verbs with meanings that suggest that they require a reflexive pronoun but which in fact are not used with reflexive pronouns, for example: *relax / afford / fall / wonder / concentrate*, etc.	NOT ~~*I relaxed myself*~~ or *She* ~~*concentrated herself*~~.
subject + emphatic pronoun + verb	
• to emphasize that the subject and not someone else does the action	*The President himself replied to my letter.*
• to emphasize that you are distinguishing one thing from another	*The room itself was quite nice but the hotel in general wasn't.*
***by* + reflexive pronoun (*by myself*, etc.)**	*He went to the cinema by himself.*
***on* + possessive adjective + *own* (*on my own*, etc.)** = alone; without another person; without help from anyone	*She painted the whole house on her own.*
each another / one another	
• to talk about the relationship between two people	*Philip and Carl don't like each other. (= Philip doesn't like Carl and Carl doesn't like Philip)*
• Person A does something to or for person B and person B does the same thing to or for person A	*They exchanged addresses with one another.*

➔ ExC–E p109–110

A **Complete this text by putting a suitable word into each gap.**

Blues Music

Blues musicians developed their 1 ....own.......... kind of music in the early 20th century in the Southern states of the US. 2 ....They.......... were originally people who lived in rural areas and 3 ....their.......... songs were about their 4 ....own.......... lives and experiences. They developed a kind of music that was completely 5 ....theirs.......... and totally unlike anything else. The early blues singers took songs from each other. It didn't matter 6 ....whose.......... song it was, they would perform 7 ....it/them.......... in 8 ....their.......... own individual way. A legendary figure in the history of blues is Robert Johnson. Many songs of 9 ....his.......... were later played by lots of other musicians and singers, and are still played now. Blues singers played an important part in the history of popular music and people haven't always given 10 ....them.......... the recognition 11 ....they.......... deserve. Blues music was the basis of rock 'n' roll and so 12 ....it.......... was the starting-point for today's most popular music.

B **Complete these sentences with *something*, *everyone*, *nobody*, *anywhere*, etc.**

1 I've got ....something........ important to tell you.
2 It was totally unexpected and .everybody/everyone. was amazed when it happened.
3 ...Nobody/No one... said anything so I assumed that they all agreed.
4 She's so famous that she can't go ....anywhere........ without being recognized.
5 I'm sure there's ....something........ I've forgotten to do today.
6 A lot of letters arrived but there was ....nothing.......... for me.
7 ......Everywhere...... I went in that country, people were friendly towards me.
8 'Where have you been today?' '........Nowhere........ . I stayed here all day.'
9 ....Something........ very strange happened yesterday.
10 ..Anybody/Anyone.. would have done the same thing that I did – there was no other choice.
11 I'm not going to apologize because I've done ....nothing.......... wrong.
12 Andrew, there's .somebody/someone. I'd like you to meet. Andrew, this is Fiona.
13 I don't trust ...anybody/anyone... apart from you.
14 He didn't have ....anything........ new to tell me.
15 Have you been ....anywhere........ exciting recently?

C **Complete this extract from a novel by putting a suitable word into each gap.**

PARTY INVITATIONS

Steve and Tim were chatting on the college steps. The conversation began innocently enough.
'Any plans for the weekend?' Steve asked.
'Yeah, I'm going to a party,' Tim replied cheerfully.
'Oh yeah? 1 ....Whose.......... party is it?' asked Steve.
'Elena's. I don't know why she invited 2 ....me.......... , we don't really know 3 ....each.......... other very well. Apparently, it's to celebrate 4 ....her.......... birthday. Anyway, I've told 5 ....her.......... that I'll go. Haven't you been invited?'
'Yeah,' said Steve. 'She sent 6 ....me.......... an invitation. I got 7 ....it.......... yesterday.'
'Really?' said Tim, 'I got 8 ....mine.......... over two weeks ago. I wonder why 9 ....yours.......... came so late.'
'I suppose,' said Steve, 'she only decided to ask 10 ....me.......... at the last moment. We don't really like 11 ....one.......... another, you know.'
'Why's that?' asked Tim. Steve shook 12 ....his.......... head. 'I don't want to talk about that,' he said.

D **Decide whether these sentences are correct or not. Correct those which are not.**

1	She likes to go home and relax ~~herself~~ after a hard day's work.	... and relax after ...
2	I fell down and hurt myself when I was coming down the stairs.	correct
3	The boss herself told me about the pay rise so it must be true.	correct
4	His parents ~~they~~ live somewhere just outside the city.	... parents live ...
5	I can't do ~~nothing~~ about this problem.	anything
6	We wondered ~~ourselves~~ why such a strange thing had happened.	... wondered why ...
7	The accused himself admitted that he had been at the scene of the crime.	correct
8	The car turned over and ended up on ~~it's~~ side.	its
9	Did someone leave this bag here by accident?	correct
10	I often feel ~~myself~~ nervous with strangers.	... feel nervous ...
11	You look worried. Has something bad happened?	correct
12	I know that the details are correct because I checked them myself.	correct
13	Some relatives of hers live in Italy.	correct
14	They can't afford ~~themselves~~ a holiday this year.	... afford a holiday ...
15	Anyone would feel the same as me in this situation.	correct
16	Did you cook this yourself or did you buy it ready-made?	correct
17	The work itself is OK but the people I have to work with are a problem.	correct
18	'What would you like to eat?' 'Anything would be fine with me. It's up to you.'	correct
19	I sat down and tried to concentrate ~~myself~~ on my work.	... concentrate on ...
20	I couldn't find Martin's phone number anywhere so I couldn't ring him.	correct
21	Dave considers himself an expert on this subject.	correct
22	She doesn't like ~~nobody~~ except her small circle of friends.	anybody/anyone
23	She created the whole thing ~~by her own~~.	by herself/on her own
24	She got some advice from a colleague of hers.	correct
25	The present was still in its box weeks after she received it.	correct

E **Complete this extract by putting one suitable word into each gap.**

The First Time

MIRANDA did her first public performance last week. She's a very good guitarist – she taught 1 ....herself.........., you know. It's 2 ....somewhere........ in the centre of town where she played – I'm not sure its exact location. She went on her 3 ....own............ – she said that she didn't want 4 ...anyone/anybody... to go with her. Personally, I can't imagine 5 ....anything........ more frightening than being 6 ....by.............. yourself in front of an audience for the first time. Anyway, Miranda tried to tell 7 ....herself.......... that it was no different from playing to a group of friends at home, but she was so nervous that she didn't say 8 ....anything.......... between the songs. She played some songs she had written 9 ....herself.......... and some by other people. She says that the people in the audience seemed to enjoy 10 ....themselves........ so the evening was quite successful. The club 11 ....itself............ isn't a particularly popular one, but playing there has made 12 ....her.............. more confident about appearing in public.

7.4 Determiners & pronouns

Use	Example
one • instead of repeating a singular noun	*'Would you like a drink?' 'No thanks, I've just had one.'* (= a drink)
ones • instead of repeating a plural noun	*I like all his records but his earliest ones* (= records) *are the best.*
the one • to refer to a particular singular thing	*I found a lot of books on the subject but I couldn't find the one* (= the particular book) *I wanted.*
the ones • to refer to particular plural things	*Don't get her those chocolates, these are the ones* (= the particular chocolates) *she likes best.*
one of **+ the possessive /** ***these*** **/** ***those*** **+ plural noun** • to talk about one among a few or many	*One of my friends is playing tonight.*
adjective + ***one*** **/** ***ones***	*I've just got a new one.* *I threw away the old ones.*
▶ note: Do not use *a* + *one* without an adjective.	NOT ~~*I bought a one last week.*~~ Instead, say *I bought one last week.*

Compare

one **and** ***a / an***

- use ***one*** to emphasize that you mean 'only one' or 'not more than one' and the number is important
  There was only one ticket left.

- use ***a / an*** if you are saying that a person or thing exists but you are not saying that there is only one of them
  I bought a ticket at the box office.

each • to refer to all of the individual people or things in a group or series separately, one after the other • with singular verbs	*She spoke to each member of staff individually.*
each **+ singular noun**	*I checked each word carefully.* *Each piece of work is equally important.*
each of **+** ***the*** **/ possessive + plural noun**	*Each of the children was given a present.* *She treats each of her children equally.*
each of **+** ***them*** **/** ***these*** **/** ***those*** **(+ plural noun)**	*Each of them / these / those costs the same.* *Each of these/those cars is on sale.*
each of **+** ***us*** **/** ***them*** **/** ***you***	*Each of us was contacted.*
every • to talk about a group or series in general, with the meaning 'all of them'	*Every member of staff must attend this meeting.*
every **+ singular noun (+ singular verb)**	*Have you read every page of the report?* *Every player has a bad game sometimes.*

Compare

each and every

- *each* refers to two or more people and things, but *every* can only refer to more than two. For example, in a game between two players you can talk about *each player* but not ~~*every player*~~, but in a team game you can say *each player* or *every player*.

both • to talk about two things or people	
***both* + plural noun (+ plural verb)**	*Both hotels were full.* *They suggested two dates and both were suitable for me.*
***both (of)* + *the* / possessive / *these* / *those* + plural noun**	*Both (of) the hotels I rang were full.* *Both (of) my brothers are doctors.*
both of* + *them* / *us* / *you* / OR *them* / *us* / *you* + *both	*I want to buy both (of) these / those coats.* *I told both of them / them both the same thing.*
subject (+ auxiliary / modal) + *both* + verb	*They both thought the same thing.* *The parcels should both arrive tomorrow.*
either • with negative verbs with the meaning 'not one or the other' or in questions meaning 'one or the other'	
***either* + singular noun (+ singular verb)**	*I haven't read either book.* *Either of them is OK.*
either (one)	*There were two programmes about this subject recently but I didn't see either (one).*
***either (one) of* + *the* / possessive / *these* / *those* + plural noun**	*I didn't like either (one) of the jackets.* *Do you like either of those?*
either of* + *them* / *us* / *you	*I didn't tell either of them.*
neither • with positive singular verbs • = not one or the other	
***neither* + singular noun (+ singular verb)**	*Neither idea is very good.*
***neither of* + *the* / possessive / *these* / those + plural noun (+ singular verb)**	*Neither of the / your ideas is going to work.* *Neither of these / those pictures is exactly what I want.*
neither of* + *them* / *us* / *you	*Neither of them / us / you arrived on time.*

***another* + singular noun** • = one more • = a different one	 *Could I have another piece of cake, please?* *Let's talk about another subject.*
***another* + number + plural noun** • = more ▶ note: Do not use *another* + plural noun. ▶ note: Do not use *another* + *one* + singular noun.	*It will take me another ten minutes to finish this.* (= It will take me ten more minutes …) NOT *~~another things~~*. NOT *~~another one piece~~*.
***other* + plural noun** • = different ones • = ones not already mentioned	*Have you got any other ideas?* *Fiona sent me a birthday card but my other friends didn't.*
***other* + singular noun** • = the one not already mentioned • has to be preceded by a determiner	*One of my brothers is a teacher and my other brother works in a factory.*
the other (one) / the others / the other ones • = the person/people or thing/things not already mentioned	*I can find one shoe but I can't find the other (one).* *Some people are already here and the others / the other ones will arrive soon.*
others • = other people or things	*Some people like this kind of music but others hate it.*

A Complete the following article by putting a suitable determiner or pronoun into each gap.

The Best and The Worst

The Best Game I Ever Saw
by Paul Graham

I think the Cup Final two years ago was certainly 1 ....one.......... of the most exciting games I've ever seen. 2 ....Both.......... teams were at the top of their form and right up until the end the result was in doubt. Sometimes 3 ....one.......... team looked like winning but then the 4 ....other.......... came right back into the game. 5 ....Every.......... person in the crowd was on the edge of their seat.

The Best Film I've Ever Seen
by Charlotte Hughes

I think that the best film I've ever seen was Citizen Kane, directed by and starring Orson Welles. It's the first 6 ....one.......... he made and it's the 7 ....one.......... that lots of people put on their list of 'Best Films Ever Made'. 8 ....Every.......... critic seems to agree that it was 9 ....one.......... of the most influential films ever made. Welles made a number of 10 ....other.......... films but he never had 11 ....another.......... success as great as that 12 ....one.......... .

The Worst Job I Ever Had
by Tom Brooks

The worst job I ever had was in a factory. 13 ....Every.......... day was exactly the same. I was bored and I'm sure all the 14 ....others.......... in my section were, too. I was given a pile of metal boxes and I had to clean 15 ....each.......... box with a special tool. When I'd done 16 ....one.......... pile, 17 ....another.......... pile would arrive immediately. After a few days I asked for 18 ....another.......... job, but I was told that I had to keep doing the 19 ....one.......... I was doing.

The Best Place I've Ever Visited
by Ellen Buchanan

In different ways I've enjoyed 20 ....every/each.......... place I've been to on my travels. As a travel writer, I've been on lots of trips and the 21 ....ones.......... I prefer are the 22 ....ones.......... where I've met a lot of the local people. Of all these trips, the 23 ....one.......... that really sticks in my memory is the 24 ....one.......... I took to Africa two years ago. But 25 ....each.......... of my trips has special memories.

B Complete these sentences with *both*, *either* or *neither* and *of* where appropriate.

1. I haven't met ....either of.......... his parents so I don't know what they're like.
2. ....Neither of.......... my neighbours is very friendly and they seldom speak to me.
3. They've made two CDs and I've got ....both of.......... them – they're great.
4. I went to two concerts last week and ....both.......... were fantastic – I really enjoyed them.
5. She broke ....both (of).......... her legs in the accident, so she couldn't walk for months.
6. She had two job offers but she decided that she didn't want to work for ....either.......... company.
7. ....Neither.......... date is suitable for me because I'm busy then.
8. ....Both (of).......... these problems are serious and I don't know which one to deal with first.
9. I didn't want to see ....either of.......... the two films that were on at the local cinema.
10. He's had two jobs and ....both (of).......... the jobs he's had have been in computing.
11. He gave me two explanations but ....neither of.......... them made sense.
12. I haven't met ....either of.......... those people you're talking about so I can't comment on them.
13. ....Neither of.......... the hotels I rang had any rooms left so I couldn't book anywhere.
14. ....Neither of.......... these ideas will work so we'd better think of something else.
15. Are ....either of.......... you two interested in coming with me?

C **Decide whether these sentences are correct or not. Correct those which are incorrect.**

1 I didn't agree with ~~either the suggestions~~ she made. — either (of the) suggestion(s)
2 She went to the airport and caught ~~one~~ plane. — a
3 His health is poor and he's got ~~another~~ problems, too. — other
4 I don't see a lot of films and I haven't seen ~~a~~ one for ages. — ... seen one ...
5 We discussed each item on the list. — correct
6 I've got two radios but neither works very well. — correct
7 Neither his parents agreed with his decision. — of
8 He wasn't concentrating because he had other things on his mind. — correct
9 Could I have another ~~one~~ cup of coffee, please? — ... another cup ...
10 There were two old castles there but I didn't go to either. — correct

D **Complete these sentences using one of the words or phrases below.**

one ones the one the ones another other others the other the others

1 Do you have ......other...... hobbies apart from playing sports?
2 There are some people who love golf but ......others...... who hate it.
3 This is their best record – ......the others...... they've made aren't nearly as good.
4 Could you give me ......another...... five minutes to get ready?
5 I don't like his new songs, I prefer ......the ones...... he recorded years ago.
6 I was the first person to arrive – ......the others...... got delayed and they arrived late.
7 He opened one eye and then ......the other...... .
8 He's got two jobs – ......one...... is at the college and ......the other...... is in a restaurant.
9 'I've been to lots of countries.' 'Really? Which ......ones...... have you been to?'
10 This programme is ......the one...... I was telling you about earlier.

E **Complete this extract from a novel by putting one suitable word into each gap.**

Friends

Anna and Rose were chatting in the canteen.

'I was in that café the other night,' Anna said.

'Which café?' asked Rose.

'You know, the 1 ......one...... I often go to after classes, the 2 ......one...... next to the cinema.'

'Oh yeah.'

'Anyway, I was with Mike and Paul and they were 3 ......both...... really miserable.'

'Really? I haven't seen 4 ......either...... of them lately. What was the problem?'

'Well, 5 ......neither...... of them had much money and they were 6 ......both...... asking me how they could get some,' said Anna. 'But 7 ......every/each...... time I suggested something, they didn't like it.'

'What did you suggest?'

'Well, for example, I said that there were summer jobs at the campsite but 8 ......both...... of them said that they weren't interested in that. And they weren't keen on any of my 9 ......other...... ideas, so I just left them 10 ......both...... there, looking miserable and complaining.'

'I don't blame you,' said Rose.

7.5 Quantifiers

quantifier + plural noun all, most, some, a lot, lots, many, several, any, no ▶ note: Do not use *the most* + noun.	*All visitors must report to reception.* *I've got no plans for the weekend.* NOT ~~*the most people at the party*~~.
quantifier + uncountable noun *all, most, some, a lot, lots, much, any, no* ▶ note: Do not use *the most of.* ▶ note: Use *much* with uncountable nouns; use *many* with plural nouns.	*Most food is cheap here.* *She hasn't got any talent.* NOT ~~*the most of food*~~. *I don't have much interest in this.* *He doesn't have many friends.*
quantifier + *of* + determiner + plural noun *all, most, some, a lot, lots, many, several, none, any* ▶ note: It is not necessary to use *of* after *all* and before a determiner. ▶ note: do not use the structure quantifier + *of* + noun; a determiner must be used.	*I answered some of the letters.* *None of the others agreed with me.* *They showed me all (of) their photos.* NOT ~~*most of people at the party*~~ or ~~*some of food*~~.
quantifier + *of* + determiner + uncountable noun *all, most, some, a lot, lots, much, none, any*	*She saves a lot of the money she earns.* *None of the damage was serious.*
quantifier + *of* + determiner + single noun *all, most, some, a lot, lots, much, none, any*	*I ate all (of) my meal.* *Can you understand any of this letter?*
quantifier + *of* + pronoun *all, most, some, a lot, lots, many, several, much, none, any*	*There were 20 questions and he answered all of them.* *There were lots of jackets in the shop, but I didn't like any of them.*

additional structures with *all*

it/them all	*I couldn't eat them all.*
subject + *all* + verb	*We all enjoyed ourselves.*
all + *day / morning / night / week / year*, etc.	*They spent all day shopping.*

▶ note: It is not correct to say ~~*All the day, all the night*~~, etc.
▶ note: Use *none* with positive verbs; use *any* with negative verbs and in questions.
None of the damage was serious / I haven't got any money. / Have you got any money?
▶ note: Use *no* with positive verbs; use *any* with negative verbs and questions.
We've got no food. / We haven't got any food. / Have you got any food?
▶ note: Use *no* before nouns; use *none* + *of* + a determiner + noun
I have no interest. / I have none of that money left.

few / a few **(+ countable noun)** • *few* has a negative meaning; = not many • *a few* has a positive meaning; = some ***few / a few*** **+ plural noun**	*Few tourists visit this area.* *She made a few suggestions.*
few / a few **+ *of* + determiner + plural noun**	*Few of his statements were true.* *A few of her suggestions were good.*
few / a few **+ *of* + pronoun**	*She told me her opinions and I agreed with a few of them/but I agreed with few of them.*
little / a (little) bit / a little **(+ uncountable noun)** • *little* has a negative meaning; = not much • *a (little) bit* and *a little* have a positive meaning; = some ***little / a (little) bit / a little*** **+ uncountable noun**	*There is little crime there.* *Let's have a (little) bit of fun.* *I added a little sugar.*
little / a (little) bit / a little **+ *of* + determiner + uncountable noun** ***little / a (little) bit / a little*** **+ *of* + determiner + singular noun** ***little / a (little) bit / a little*** **+ *of* + pronoun** ▶ note: Do not use *a (little) bit* + noun. If there is a noun *a (little) bit* must be followed by *of*.	*Little of the crime there is serious.* *He only spent a (little) bit of his money.* *I understood little of the lesson.* *I only saw a (little) bit/a little of the programme.* *He told me a lot of things but I remember little of it.* NOT ~~*a bit information*~~ or ~~*a little bit money*~~.

A **Read the sentences and underline the correct words and phrases in 1–20.**

1 A lot / A lot of my friends will be at the party.
2 There are few / a few things I want to discuss with you.
3 She had no / any difficulty in finding the house.
4 He was ill and ate little / a little for several days.
5 Lots / Lots of programmes on TV are rubbish!
6 She spent most / most of her life at the same company.
7 We took some sandwiches and ate the most of them / most of them on the journey.
8 There has been no / not improvement in the situation.
9 The place was full of people but I didn't know them any / any of them.
10 She has few / a few friends and is rather lonely.
11 After I'd read a bit / a bit of the article I got bored.
12 I couldn't find any / none of the books I wanted to buy.
13 You haven't eaten much / much of your breakfast.
14 None of / None of the public phones were working.
15 He speaks little / a little of the language and can go shopping easily.
16 I rang a few friends but any / none of them were in.
17 I saw little / a little of the game because there was a very tall man in front of me.
18 He writes really good books and I've read lots them / lots of them.
19 She doesn't have any / any of experience of that kind of work.
20 There was no / none surprise when the news was announced.

B **Decide which sentences are correct and which are incorrect. Correct those which are incorrect.**

ALL

1	All of my education was useful to me.	correct
2	I learnt a lot at school and all ‸ it was useful to me.	of
3	All education is good for you.	correct
4	All my friends got a good education.	correct

MOST / SOME / A LOT / LOTS

1	Most of the sightseeing we did was to museums and art galleries.	correct
2	There were lots of museums and art galleries and we visited ~~the~~ most of them.	... visited most of ...
3	~~The~~ most of our visits were to museums and art galleries.	Most of our visits ...
4	Some of our holiday was good but some of it wasn't.	correct
5	We had some bad weather on our holiday.	correct
6	Some of the weather was good.	correct
7	Some ‸ our experiences on holiday were good and some were bad.	of
8	We ate a lot of the local food while we were there.	correct
9	We spent a lot of our trip going to local restaurants.	correct
10	A lot ‸ food in that area was great.	of (the)
11	We did lots of practical work on the course.	correct
12	I gained lots of knowledge on the course.	correct
13	Lots of the course was practical.	correct

MANY/SEVERAL/MUCH

1 There aren't ⁁ ~~much~~ tourists here at this time of year.	many
2 There's a lot of tourism here but there isn't much of it at this time of year.	correct
3 There isn't much tourism here at this time of year.	correct
4 I went to several ~~of~~ shops but I couldn't find what I wanted.	... several shops ...
5 Several of the shops I went to were closed.	correct
6 There were lots of bookshops but several of them were closed.	correct

FEW / A FEW / LITTLE / A (LITTLE) BIT / A LITTLE

1 A lot of people want to be famous but few succeed.	correct
2 ⁁ ~~Little~~ of the people who want to be famous succeed.	Few
3 Many people who want to be famous have little ~~of~~ success.	... little success.
4 Lots of people want to be famous and a few succeed.	correct
5 She spends little of her time studying for the course.	correct
6 She's done a little of the work she has to do for the course.	correct
7 She has a lot of work to do for the course and she's done a little of it.	correct
8 She has a lot of work to do for the course but she's done ⁁ ~~few~~ of it so far.	little
9 I'm not very good at Spanish but I can speak a little.	correct
10 I speak ⁁ ~~few~~ Spanish so I can't talk to people in Spain.	little
11 I learnt Spanish grammar and I can remember a ⁁ ~~few~~ of it.	little
12 I learnt Spanish at school but I can remember little of it.	correct
13 I watched a bit of television last night.	correct
14 I missed most of the programme but I saw a bit of it.	correct
15 I missed most of the programme but I saw a little bit.	correct
16 I watched a little bit ⁁ the programme last night.	of

NONE/ANY/NO

1 There were ⁁ ~~any~~ jackets in the shop that suited me.	no
2 None of the jackets in the shop suited me.	correct
3 He said that none of the article was true.	correct
4 He said that there wasn't any truth in the article.	correct
5 He criticized the article and said that none of the things in it ⁁ ~~weren't~~ true.	were
6 He said that no word of the article was true.	correct
7 They didn't do any of the job properly.	correct
8 Did they do any of the work properly?	correct
9 They did the job quickly but they did none of it properly.	correct
10 They didn't do ⁁ ~~none~~ of the work properly.	any

C **In the text below some lines are correct but some have a word that should not be there. Indicate the correct lines with a tick (✔). For the incorrect lines, write down the word which should not be there.**

The Motor Car

1 ✔ Many of the developments of the 20th century have changed the way
2 a we live enormously, but ~~a~~ few of them have had the impact of the
3 the motor car. In ~~the~~ most parts of today's world, it is very difficult for
4 of most ~~of~~ people to imagine life without it – getting to work, going on
5 ✔ holiday, visiting family and friends would not be possible for a lot of
6 of people. Some ~~of~~ families have more than one car. However, despite all
7 of, a ~~of~~ the advantages the car gives us, it also has ~~a~~ several disadvantages.
8 ✔ In lots of cities there is so much congestion that none of the traffic
9 ✔ can move during the busiest periods. And much of the pollution that
10 of affects many places is caused by the motor car. Many ~~of~~ people think that
11 ✔ motorists should give a little bit of thought to these problems and
12 ✔ make a little effort to resolve them, perhaps by using their cars less.
13 ✔ With a bit of co-operation, progress could be made, they say.

D **Read the text and underline the correct words and phrases in 1–8.**

Roads

Ever since the invention of the wheel there has been a need for roads. In Britain, there were 1 no / any / none proper roads at all until the Romans built some 2,000 years ago. 2 Lot / Many / Much of Britain's roads developed naturally from footpaths. 3 Most / Most of / The most travel in the middle ages was only local and 4 all / all them / them all the roads at that time were links between neighbouring towns and villages, rather than planned routes across the country. There was 5 few / little / some progress until 6 lots / many / several of 'turnpike roads' were built in the 18th century. Britain's modern road programme started in the 1950s – it didn't have 7 any / no / none motorways until then. The idea was to build a network of efficient motorways to connect the major cities. A 8 few / little / several of these motorways were built but lack of money and local opposition meant only about half a satisfactory system was developed. Today, there is disagreement about whether it is a good idea to build more roads.

E **In the text below some lines are correct but some have a word that should not be there. Indicate the correct lines with a tick (✔). For the incorrect lines, write down the word which should not be there.**

~ *Shakespeare* ~

1 of Among all ~~of~~ writers in history, Shakespeare is perhaps the most
2 ✔ well-known. Many of the plays he wrote are still performed regularly
3 of in many ~~of~~ countries in the world. Over the years there has been a
4 ✔ lot of disagreement among scholars and experts about the meanings
5 ✔ of Shakespeare's plays; some of the books about him even suggest
6 ✔ that he didn't really write all the plays that have his name. There has
7 ✔ been a lot of research into his life and work but few of the theories
8 ✔ about him can be proved. A few people have even said that Shakespeare
9 of was really a woman but there is little ~~of~~ support for this theory!
10 ✔ Many visitors go to Shakespeare's birthplace in Stratford in England
11 ✔ and a lot of them go to see a play at the Royal Shakespeare Theatre there.
12 of A few ~~of~~ tourists find it difficult to understand the play because the
13 it language is old. Because they don't understand much ~~it~~ they either
14 the leave after a short time or are asleep all ~~the~~ evening! However,
15 of with a little ~~of~~ effort it is possible to enjoy the plays even if you don't
16 of have much ~~of~~ knowledge about them. The productions are always
17 of entertaining and few ~~of~~ people have difficulty in following what is happening.

7.6 Pronouns & demonstratives

Use *it*	
• to refer to a thing, an action or a situation	*I'm looking for my book but I can't find it.* *When you haven't got much money, it's a problem.*
▶ note: Do not use *it* together with a subject or object.	NOT ~~*My book it is lost*~~ or ~~*I can't find it my book*~~.
• to refer to the weather, time and distances	*It's going to be sunny tomorrow.* *It's just after 12.* *How far is it from here to London?*
it* with adjectives in these patterns:** ***it* + *be* + adjective + infinitive with *to	*It was nice to meet you again.* *It was hard to understand what he said.*
▶ note: the *-ing* form can also be used when the adjective describes a feeling.	*It was nice meeting you.*
it* + *be* + adjective + *for* someone + infinitive with *to	*It will be good for her to have a holiday.*
***it* + *be* + adjective + (*that*) + subject + verb, etc.**	*It's strange (that) they haven't contacted me yet.*
***find* + *it* + adjective** to talk about feelings and attitudes towards something	
find* + *it* + adjective + infinitive with *to	*I find it interesting to meet new people.*
***find* + *it* + adjective + (that) + subject + verb, etc.**	*I find it incredible (that) you said that.*
▶ note: The following pattern is also used with *find*: ***find* + object + adjective**	*I found his attitude surprising.*
***it* + *be* + relative clause** for emphasis	
▶ note: In this pattern, the person, thing, etc. that comes immediately after *be* is emphasized.	*It was Eric who told me about this place.* (= Eric and not somebody else.)
Use *there* to say that something exists or happens	
***there* + *be* (singular / plural) + singular / plural noun**	*There was a knock at the door.* *There are 25 students in the class.*
***there* + modal**	*There might be a problem.*
***there* + *be* + noun + participle**	*There was a car coming towards me. (= a car was coming)*
***there* + *be* (plural) + number + *of* + pronoun**	*There were seven of us at the meeting.*
▶ note: Use this pattern, and not subject + *be* + number, to talk about how many people or things.	NOT ~~*We were seven at the meeting*~~.

Compare

it* and *there

- *there* is often used the first time something is mentioned
- *it* is then used to refer to the same thing because it has already been established which thing is being talked about

There's a letter for you. It came this morning.

what with the meaning '*the thing / things that …*' to form emphatic sentences in these patterns:	
***what* + verb**	*What annoys me is that she's been telling lies about me.* (= it annoys me that)
***what* + subject + verb**	*What I like most about him is his sense of humour.* (= the thing that I like)

***this / that* + singular / uncountable noun** ***these / those* + plural noun**	
• *this* and *these* refer to something that is close to the speaker	*Have you read this article in the paper here?* *Look – I've just bought these clothes.*
• *that* and *those* refer to something that is not close to the speaker	*Could you pass me that book that's over there?* *Those trees in the the garden are quite tall.*
• *this*, with or without a noun, refers to the situation or place you are in at the moment or to something that is happening at the moment	*This problem is going to be difficult to solve.* *This is a very nice restaurant, isn't it?* *This is the best piece of music I've ever heard.*
• *that*, with or without a noun, refers to a fact or idea that has previously been mentioned	*You've already told me that.* *Jack was ill and that's why he couldn't come.*
• *this*, *that*, *these* and *those* can be used without a noun to refer to things, with the meaning '*this / that thing*' or '*these / those things*'	*Could you give this to Alan for me, please?* *I've never seen those before.*
• *this* refers to actions or experiences in the near future, and *that* refers to past actions or experiences	*This is going to be a very interesting journey.* *That was an excellent meal.*

A **Complete this extract from a novel by filling the gaps with a suitable pronoun or demonstrative.**

'1 ....This/It.......... won't take long,' said Mr Brandon, as Robert sat down. 'Here, look at 2 ....this.......... report,' he said, handing Robert a file. 3 ....It.......... was a report on staffing levels. Robert feared that 4 ....there.......... could be some bad news in it for him. 'Are 5 ....these.......... figures correct?' he asked, pointing at a table on the last page of the report.

'Yes,' said Mr Brandon, gravely. 'And 6 ....that.......... is why we have to take immediate action. 7 ....This.......... company needs to cut costs quickly and 8 ....that/this.......... report you're looking at shows us the way forward.'

'I see,' said Robert, but he didn't really. Mr Brandon continued: '9 .....Those/These..... figures on 10 ....that/this.......... page in front of you make it absolutely clear that we must reduce the workforce by at least 20%.'

'I have a question,' said Robert suddenly. 'Oh, and what's 11 ....that.......... ?' asked Mr Brandon, mildly surprised. 'I haven't had time to study 12 ....these/those....... properly,' Robert said, pointing again at the figures, 'but do they mean that I'm going to be out of a job?'

'No,' said Mr Brandon, laughing, '13 ....These/Those..... don't affect you, they affect some of the more senior managers.' He picked up a piece of paper from his desk. '14 ....This.......... ,' he said, smiling, and handing it to Robert, 'is 15 ....what.......... I really wanted to show you.' '16 ....There.......... is going to be a job available as Head of Department and I'm offering 17 ....it.......... to you. You don't have to give me an answer now, but let me know later this week if you want the job.'

'Well,' thought Robert when he got out of the office, 'That wasn't 18 ....what.......... I was expecting at all.' He walked away, grinning.

B **Complete this extract from a novel by filling the gaps with one suitable word.**

The Message

Martin arrived home, looking forward to a relaxing evening on his own. He checked for messages on his answerphone. 1 ....There.......... was one message. 'Martin,' he heard, 'This is Zena. 2 ....There.......... is something I must tell you and 3 ....it.......... can't wait until tomorrow. 4 ....It.......... is just after 6.30 now. Please call me back. I'll be here.' Martin was not very pleased. He had spoken to Zena that afternoon and she hadn't said that 5 ....there.......... was a problem of any kind. He was annoyed by the call and he didn't really want to return 6 ....it.......... . But he didn't want her to call again, so he picked up the phone. '7 ....This.......... is going to be a complete waste of time,' he thought.

C **Rewrite these sentences using an appropriate form of *find* and the adjective in brackets.**

1 This subject interests me. (**interesting**)
I find this subject interesting.

2 I'm having difficulty making up my mind. (**difficult**)
I'm finding it difficult to make up my mind.

3 I can't understand why you didn't tell me this before. (**strange**)
I find it strange that you didn't tell me about this before.

4 She makes friends easily. (**easy**)
She finds it easy to make friends.

5 I can't explain why she hasn't been in touch with me. (**peculiar**)
I find it peculiar that she hasn't been in touch with me.

6 His explanation confused me. (**confusing**)
I found his explanation confusing.

D **In the text below some lines are correct but some have a word that should not be there. Indicate the correct lines with a tick (✓). For the incorrect lines, write the words that should not be there.**

FORTHCOMING EVENTS

1	✓	There are a number of interesting events coming up in this city. Tomorrow
2	it	evening the Central Orchestra ~~it~~ will be giving a performance at the Town
3	that	Hall – their concert last year ~~that~~ was very well received. For fans of another
4	✓	kind of music, it will be great to see Tony Andrews appearing here again.
5	these	Tickets for his show at the Apollo ~~these~~ went on sale yesterday and by
6	✓	the time the box office opened there were people queuing for miles! It will be
7	✓	interesting for Tony's fans to hear what his new material is like and there will
8	✓	be five thousand of them at the show, so it should be a memorable occasion.
9	✓	Finally, the Ramp Band will be appearing tonight at the Golden Club. It's
10	this	great ~~this~~ that they're still playing after so many years together as a band.

E **Complete the second sentence so that it means the same as the first.**

1 I need a nice, cold drink. What I need is a nice, cold drink.

2 You caused this problem. It was you who/that caused this problem.

3 The condition of the place surprised me. It was the condition of the place that/which surprised me.

4 He really regrets his lack of education. What he really regrets is his lack of education.

5 His aggressive manner made me angry. What made me angry was his aggressive manner.

6 His previous experience got him the job. It was his previous experience that/which got him the job.

7 I meant to say that I was grateful for their help. What I meant to say was that I was grateful for their help.

8 The reaction of the crowd surprised me. What surprised me was the reaction of the crowd.

9 Something you said gave me this idea. It was something you said that/which gave me this idea.

10 Money matters most to her. What matters most to her is money.

→ Glossary p216

7.7 *Worth & no point*

A Complete the second sentence so that it means the same as the first, using the word given.

1 If you worry about things you can't change, it won't do you any good. (sense)
...........There's no sense (in)........... worrying about things you can't change.

2 Is it an interesting building to visit, in your opinion? (worth?) (2 answers)
...........Is the building worth visiting..........., in your opinion?
...........Is it worth visiting the building..........., in your opinion?

3 I argued with her but she wouldn't change her mind. (pointless)
...........It was pointless arguing........... with her because she wouldn't change her mind.

4 Don't consider the idea because it's a very bad one. (not worth) (2 answers)
...........It's not worth considering the idea........... because it's a very bad one.
...........The idea isn't worth considering........... because it's a very bad one.

5 It's not a good idea to spend so much money on something you don't really need. (point)
...........There's no point (in)........... spending so much money on something you don't really need.

6 Nothing bad will happen if you ask him to do you a favour. (harm)
...........There's no harm (in)........... asking him to do you a favour.

7 Don't get angry about such an unimportant matter. (point?)
...........What's the point in........... getting angry about such an unimportant matter?

8 Don't ask me because I don't know anything about the subject. (use)
...........It's no use asking........... me because I don't know anything about the subject.

9 Don't get upset about her criticisms, they don't matter. (worth) (2 answers)
...........It's not worth getting........... upset about her criticisms.
...........Her criticisms aren't worth........... getting upset about.

10 It would be stupid to make the problem even worse. (sense?)
...........What's/Where's the sense in........... making the problem even worse?

11 You're shouting at me but it's your own fault that this has happened. (good)
...........It's no good shouting........... at me because it's your own fault this has happened.

12 I read the book but it was extremely boring. (worth) (2 answers)
...........It wasn't worth reading........... the book because it was extremely boring.
...........The book wasn't worth........... reading because it was extremely boring.

13 It's a good idea to check because you might find a mistake. (worth)
...........It's worth checking........... because you might find a mistake.

14 I tried to fix it myself but I had no idea what to do. (useless)
...........It was useless trying........... to fix it myself because I had no idea what to do.

→ Glossary p216–17

7.8 Word focus

Phrasal verbs: *get* & *set*

A Rewrite sentences 1–8, replacing the phrases in italics with one of the phrasal verbs below.

get away with   get someone down   get on (well) with   get on with

get over   get something over with   get round to   get to

1 He *has a friendly relationship* with his girlfriend's family.
He gets on (well) with his girlfriend's family.

2 The job *made him unhappy*, so he left.
The job got him down, so he left.

3 She wanted to *complete the task* as quickly as possible.
She wanted to get the task over with as quickly as possible.

4 After a few days, he *recovered from* the illness.
After a few days, he got over his illness.

5 I haven't *found time for* writing to them yet.
I haven't got round to writing to them yet.

6 We *arrived at* the airport just before the flight left.
We got to the airport just before the flight left.

7 I needed to *make progress with* my work so that it would be ready in time.
I needed to get on with my work so that it would be ready in time.

8 People shouldn't *escape punishment for* doing such terrible things.
People shouldn't get away with doing such terrible things.

B Fill each gap with one of the particles below.

about   off   out   up

1 This organization was set ......up...... 20 years ago.
2 I didn't set ......out...... to upset everyone but unfortunately that's what happened.
3 They set ......off/out...... early in the morning in order to get there by 11.
4 I'll have to set ......about...... dealing with this problem soon.

Collocations

C Fill each gap with the correct forms of *tell* or *give*.

1 These two photos are so similar that I can't ......tell...... them apart.
2 Can you ......give...... me one good reason why I should believe you?
3 This news will ......give...... her quite a shock.
4 Do you think you could ......give...... me a hand with the washing-up?
5 Just be honest and ......tell...... the truth.

→ Glossary p216–17

6 Let me ....give............ you some advice so that you don't make a mistake.

7 You'll have to ....give............ an explanation for your absence.

8 I can't ....tell............ the difference between any of his songs – they all sound the same.

9 She ....gave............ a detailed description of the events of that day.

10 He ....told............ a lie about what he had been doing that day.

Word formation: nouns

D Complete this article about a person by forming nouns using the words in capitals at the end of each line. You will need to form nouns which are the same length as or shorter than the word given.

The right style

Fashion designer Esther Robinson's path to 1 ....fame............ and fortune — FAMOUS
hasn't been an easy one. Starting with a small 2 ....loan............ from the — LEND
bank, she set up her business in the 3 ....belief............ that there was a market — BELIEVE
for the kind of clothes she designed, but the firm made a 4 ....loss............ — LOSE
in the first few years. She was faced with the 5 ....choice............ of giving — CHOOSE
up or going bankrupt, but she never lost her 6 ....nerve............ . Instead, she — NERVOUS
produced a mail-order catalogue, and the 7 ....content(s)........ of this proved — CONTAIN
so popular that she was soon accumulating enormous 8 ....wealth............ . — WEALTHY
Today she speaks of the enormous 9 ....pride............ she takes in her — PROUD
designs and says that her success is 10 ....proof............ that she was right — PROVE
all along!

Word sets

E The underlined words do not fit correctly in the sentences in which they appear. Put each one into the sentence in which it does fit correctly.

like similar same alike

1 Her attitudes to life are just alike mine. ......like......

2 This is like to something I saw in another shop. ......similar......

3 The two courses are not completely same. ......alike......

4 Isn't this exactly the similar as the last one you bought? ......same......

imagine think bear consider

1 I knew his face but I couldn't imagine of his name. ......think......

2 I'll have to bear the situation carefully before I decide. ......consider......

3 It's hard to think how people lived 100 years ago. ......imagine......

4 If you consider in mind how much it will cost, it's not worth it. ......bear......

fault blame responsible guilty

1 You can't hold me blame for this problem. ......responsible......

2 Someone will get the fault for this terrible situation. ......blame......

3 I had to admit that I was at guilty and I apologized. ......fault......

4 Someone has been found responsible of incompetence. ......guilty......

ECCE Practice 7

Grammar

1 Can we stop running now? I don't have __d__ energy left at all.
  a an
  b the
  c some
  d any

2 Somebody left a coat in the classroom. Is it __c__ ?
  a you
  b your
  c yours
  d yourself

3 Can't you speak any louder than that? Make __b__ heard.
  a oneself
  b yourself
  c himself
  d herself

4 It's been very quiet in the shop today. I haven't spoken to __d__ all morning .
  a nobody
  b somebody
  c everybody
  d anybody

5 'Have you seen Jack or his sister?' 'No, I haven't seen __a__ of them.'
  a either
  b both
  c neither
  d each

6 They want to spend more time together even though they see __c__ everyday.
  a one after another
  b the other one
  c each other
  d one another

7 She says she has __b__ her pocket money left.
  a none
  b none of
  c not any
  d few

8 __c__ were two new members at the meeting today.
  a We
  b Their
  c There
  d These

Vocabulary

9 His father is planning to __b__ up a business for him.
  a build
  b set
  c take
  d fix

10 There's no __a__ fixing that toy. He'll just break it again.
  a point
  b worth
  c harm
  d good

11 'What made him surrender to the police?' 'It's probably his __c__ conscience.'
  a blame
  b responsible
  c guilty
  d fault

12 Look at those girls ! They are very much __a__.
  a alike
  b the same
  c similar
  d look alike

13 It's me who's at __c__, so I'll have to pay for the damage.
  a error
  b guilty
  c fault
  d responsible

14 I'm sorry I didn't __d__ writing any sooner.
  a get up
  b get over
  c get through to
  d get round to

15 I've known the twins for years, but I can still hardly __b__ them apart.
  a see
  b tell
  c say
  d notice

16 I can't __c__ why you stay with Paul. He's so mean to you.
  a bear
  b consider
  c imagine
  d tell

Exam techniques
➔ p223

FCE Practice 7

Part 3

For Questions **1–10**, complete the second sentence so that it has the same meaning as the first sentence, using the word given. **Do not change the word given.** You must use between **two** and **five** words, including the word given.

1 I couldn't run any faster.

incapable

I ....was incapable of running........................ any faster.

2 I haven't been to a concert for months.

last

It is ....months since I last went.............................. to a concert.

3 'Can I change my ticket?' I asked the assistant.

change

I asked the assistant ....whether/if I could change.................... my ticket.

4 Joe organized the party and also paid for it.

well

Joe paid for the party ....as well as organizing.................... it.

5 There was no meat left in the supermarket when I got there.

run

The supermarket ....had run out of.......................... meat when I got there.

6 Anne said that I had caused the problem.

accused

Anne ....accused me of causing............................ the problem.

7 My interest in politics isn't as great as yours.

interested

I'm not ....as interested as you.............................. are in politics.

8 James works late at the office fairly often.

unusual

It is ....not unusual for James to....................... work late at the office.

9 We didn't see each other again for three years.

before

It was ....three years before we saw............................ each other again.

10 I couldn't decide which course I wanted to do.

mind

I couldn't ....make up my mind (about)............... which course I wanted to do.

Unit 8

Modals

Grammar
8.1 Obligation & permission
8.2 Necessity
8.3 Ability & possibility
8.4 Assumptions & interpretations
8.5 Suggesting & advising 1
8.6 Suggesting & advising 2
8.7 Probability & certainty

Vocabulary
8.8 Chance & possibility
8.9 Word focus

8.1 Obligation & permission

Stop & check

Some of these sentences are correct and some contain a common error. Tick (✓) the correct sentences and correct the errors.

1 You really must ~~to~~ be more careful in future. ... must be ...
2 You really must hear this record, it's great. ✔
3 Where do I have to sign my name on this form? ✔
4 You mustn't go to the party if you don't want to. ✔
5 I ~~don't have to~~ make this mistake again or he'll get angry. mustn't
6 It's OK, you don't have to help me. ✔
7 We~~'ll~~ must get there on time tomorrow. We must ...
8 I had to wait ages for a ticket. ✔

Use	Example
Use *must / mustn't* + infinitive without *to* • to talk about an obligation or order that depends on the person speaking or listening • has a present or future meaning • to say that it is very important that someone does or doesn't do something • to recommend something very strongly ▶ note: There is no future or past form of *must*. Instead, use a form of ***have to***.	*You must get to bed early.* *You mustn't tell lies.* *I mustn't forget to buy a present for my mother.* *I must go home now, it's very late.* *You must see that film, it's fantastic.*
Use *have to* + infinitive with *to* • to talk about an obligation or order from somebody else, especially in authority • for the present or future; use ***will have to*** to talk about the future and ***had to*** to talk about the past • to say that it is very important that someone does or doesn't do something • to talk about actions that are required because of the circumstances (not because a person in authority has demanded them)	*Where I work, everyone has to dress smartly.* *We'll have to work harder next week.* *I had to do the work again.* *She had to tell them what she really thought.* *I'll have to phone them later – they won't be in now.*
Use *not have to* • to say that there is no obligation to do something • to say that the subject can choose to do something or not to do it and that it is not very important whether they do it or not • to say that the circumstances do not require a particular action	*I didn't have to get a work permit to work there.* *You don't have to talk about this if you don't want to.* *We won't have to book a ticket in advance, there will be plenty left.*

Use ***have got to / haven't got to*** • with exactly the same meanings as *have to* and *not have to* • quite informal • no future or past forms	*I've got to go home now.* *I haven't got to finish this work today.* *We haven't got to leave yet.* *I haven't got to get up early tomorrow.*
Use ***have to*** and ***have got to*** • to form questions for all the above ideas. • *have to* has future and past forms but *have got to* does not ▶ note: We usually only use *must* in questions when the speaker is protesting or complaining about something that they have to do, not asking if they have to do it.	*Do I have to / Have I got to fill in this form?* *When will you have to / have you got to leave?* *When did you have to leave?* *'You've got to work overtime tomorrow.' 'Oh, must I?'*

Compare

mustn't & *not have to*

- use *mustn't* to say that something is not permitted, that there is an obligation not to do something
  You mustn't write anything in that space on the form. (= it is wrong to write anything)

- use *not have to* to say that something is not an obligation, a matter of importance or a requirement, but it is not forbidden
  You don't have to write anything in that space. (= if you don't want to, but you can write something if you choose to)

→ ExA p129

Use ***can / can't / be allowed to*** • to say that something is or is not permitted in the present ▶ note: do not use *It is not allowed to do*. To say that something is not allowed, we have to use a person as the subject.	*You can't / aren't allowed to park here.* *How much can you earn before you pay tax?* NOT ~~*It is not allowed to park here*~~. The subject of *be allowed to* must be a person.
Use ***may / may not*** • in formal contexts with the same meaning as *can / can't / be allowed to*	*Visitors may park here for short periods.* *Pupils may not be rude to teachers.*
Use ***could / couldn't / be allowed to*** • to say that something was or was not permitted in the past	*When I was quite young I could / was allowed to stay out late at night.*
Use ***will be able to / will be allowed to*** • to say that something will or will not be permitted in the future	*You'll be able / allowed to use a dictionary in that exam.*
can / may / could • use *can* and *may* to give someone permission to do something • *may* is more formal than *can* • use *can, may* and *could* to ask for permission to do something • *may* is more formal and polite than *can / could* • *could* is more polite than *can*	*You can use my phone if you want to.* *Guests may smoke in this room.* *Can I sit here?* *May I leave my suitcase here, please?* *Could I borrow your pen?*

→ ExB+C p130

Use	Example
Use *make* + object + infinitive without *to*	
• to say that somebody forces someone to do something because they order them to do it and have power over them in that situation	*Their boss makes them work hard.* *Her parents made her stay at home last night.* *You can't make me do things I don't want to do.*
▶ note: remember that *to* is not used in this pattern	NOT ~~*Their boss makes them to work hard.*~~
Use *get* + object + infinitive with *to*	
• to say that somebody asks someone to do something for them and that person does it for them. The subject of *get* does not force the other person to do it, they ask or persuade them.	*She's always getting other people to do her work for her.* *I got a friend to fix my car for me.* *He got his parents to give him some money.*
Use *order* + object + infinitive with *to*	
• = tell someone that they must do something	*His parents ordered him to do as he was told.*

let + object + infinitive without *to*	
• = give somebody permission to do something	*The boss let us go home early.* *She lets her children do whatever they want.*
• to talk about not giving permission, use *doesn't/ won't let* for the present, *won't let* for the future and *didn't/wouldn't let* for the past	*Her parents are very strict and don't/won't let her go to parties.* *I'm sure they won't let me borrow the money.* *I asked the boss but he didn't/wouldn't let me go home early.*
allow + object + infinitive with *to*	
• = give someone permission to do something	*The boss allowed us to go home early.*
• form negatives with *allow* in the same way as with *let*	*Her parents don't/won't allow her to go to parties.* *The boss didn't/wouldn't allow me to go home early.*
permit + object + infinitive with *to*	
• used in formal contexts	*The contract permits you to redecorate the flat.*

→ ExD p131

A **Complete this information sheet for new students at a college using appropriate forms of *must* and *have to* and the verbs in brackets. Sometimes there may be more than one correct answer.**

New Students – Key Information

You 1 ......must/have to pay...... (pay) all fees in advance.

You 2 ......must not/mustn't leave...... (leave) litter in classrooms or anywhere on the college premises.

You 3 ......must/have to hand in...... (hand in) all assignments on time unless you have a valid reason for not doing so.

You 4 ...do not/don't have to dress... (dress) formally for lectures but you 5 ......must not/mustn't look...... (look) too scruffy!

You 6 do not/don't have to take part (take part) in college activities outside college hours but you are encouraged to do so.

You 7 ......must not/mustn't smoke...... (smoke) on college premises – all buildings are non-smoking.

You 8 ......must/have to provide...... (provide) written explanations for any absences from classes.

You 9 ......must not/mustn't make...... (make) noise in corridors that would disturb other students who are working in the classrooms.

You 10 ......do not/don't have to...... (buy) all books yourself – the college operates a loan scheme.

B Read this extract from a novel and choose the correct form of *must*, *have to* or *be able to*.

The New Recruit

It was Russell's first day in the new job. The first thing that he 1 must/had to do was see his Head of Department for an introductory chat. She was called Irene and she seemed pleasant enough. 'There are a few things I 2 had to/'ve got to tell you,' she said, 'but of course there are a lot of things that you 3 'll have to/'ll must find out for yourself.' Russell nodded in agreement.

'First of all,' said Irene, 'there are lots of departmental meetings here but you 4 won't have to/haven't to go to all of them. You 5 'll be able to/'ll have got to miss a lot of them.'

'Good,' said Russell, 'but which meetings 6 must I to/will I have to go to?'

'The ones where every section leader 7 has to /will have to report on current progress,' she replied. 'I see,' said Russell.

'Another thing,' said Irene, 'you 8 'll have to/'ll must meet all your deadlines – you 9 don't have to/won't be able to complete projects late even if the deadlines are completely unrealistic. So you 10 'll have to/'ll have got to get used to working under terrible pressure.' She looked at her watch. 'Any questions? I 11 have to/had to go now. I 12 've got to/got to see the Managing Director in five minutes.'

'Just one thing,' said Russell. 'In my last job, we 13 may/could work at home from time to time instead of coming into the office every day. 14 Will I be able to/Can I be able to do that here?'

'I think we 15 'll have got to/'ll have to discuss that some other time,' said Irene and then she left hurriedly. Russell sat alone in her office wondering whether he had made a terrible mistake joining this company.

C Complete these sentences with one of the words or phrases below. Sometimes there may be more than one correct answer.

have to can didn't have to couldn't had to must could
don't have to may will have to mustn't

1 You ....must/have to.......... hear this story! It's extremely funny.
2 You ....will have to.......... do this again tomorrow because you've done it all wrong.
3 I ....must/have to.......... make a phone call. ....May/Can/Could.......... I use your phone?
4 When I was young, we ....couldn't.......... behave as badly as that in a public place.
5 You ....don't have to.......... remind me because I haven't forgotten.
6 I ....didn't have to.......... help her, I did it because I wanted to.
7 What's happened is a terrible thing. It ....mustn't.......... happen ever again in the future!
8 I ....must/have to/will have to.......... go to bed now, I'm exhausted.
9 You ....don't have to.......... give me a lift, I can easily walk home from here.
10 There was a problem with the trains so I ....had to.......... wait an hour to catch one.
11 I ....must/have to/will have to.......... get some new shoes – these are getting very old.
12 When I applied, I ....had to.......... fill in a lot of forms.
13 I really wanted to speak to her because I ....had to.......... find out the truth.
14 ....May/Can/Could.......... I ask you a personal question? You ....don't have to.......... answer it if you don't want to.
15 You ....didn't have to.......... be rude to the waiter, he was doing his best.

D **Complete the second sentence so that it means the same as the first, using the word given.**

1 I told him that he had to apologize to me and he did so.

made

I ....made him apologize.......... to me.

2 The teacher said that he could leave school early that day.

permitted

The teacher ....permitted him to leave.......... school early that day.

3 You can't take food into the shop.

allowed

You ....aren't allowed to take.......... food into the shop.

4 His parents said that he could leave university if he wanted to.

let

His parents ....let him leave.......... university.

5 Other people always solve his problems for him because he asks them to.

gets

He always ....gets other people to solve.......... his problems for him.

6 My parents said that I couldn't watch that programme.

allow

My parents ....didn't/wouldn't allow me to.......... watch that programme.

7 'Leave the room immediately,' the teacher told her.

ordered

The teacher ....ordered her to leave.......... the room immediately.

8 The authorities say that he can't stay in the country any longer.

let

The authorities ....won't let him stay.......... in the country any longer.

9 She always insists that I do the washing-up.

makes

She ....always makes me do.......... the washing-up.

10 He didn't give me a chance to speak, he just shouted at me.

let

He ....didn't/wouldn't let me speak.........., he just shouted at me.

11 Passengers are permitted to stand in this area only.

may

Passengers ....may stand.......... in this area only.

12 The teacher won't allow us to use a calculator in the maths test.

can't

We ....can't use.......... a calculator in the maths test.

8.2 Necessity

need* + infinitive with *to to say that an action is necessary or very important	*I need to lose some weight.* *I'll need to think about it before I decide.* *I needed to practise a lot before I could do it.*
not need / needn't to say that an action is not necessary or important ***don't need* + infinitive with *to* OR** ***needn't* + infinitive without *to*** to talk about the present ***will / won't need* + infinitive with *to*** to talk about the future ***didn't need* + infinitive with *to*** • to say that an action was not necessary in the past • with this pattern, it is not clear whether the action actually happened or not, only that it was not necessary ***needn't have* + past participle** to say that someone did something but it was not necessary to do it	*You don't need to apologize, you've done nothing wrong.* *You needn't apologize, you've done nothing wrong.* *You won't need to book a ticket in advance.* *I didn't need to ask because I already knew the answer.* (perhaps I asked, perhaps I didn't ask, but it was not necessary to ask) *I didn't need to hurry as there was plenty of time.* *I needn't have worried because in fact everything was fine.* (I worried but it was not necessary to worry) *I needn't have hurried because I got there very early.*
***need* + *-ing* / *need to be* + past participle** • to say that an action is necessary • the action is not done by the subject of *need*: the person doing the action is not mentioned in this pattern, because that person is understood or unimportant	*Your hair needs cutting / to be cut.* *My flat will need painting / to be painted soon.* *The car needed repairing / to be repaired so I took it to a garage.*
there* + *be* + *no need* (+ *for* someone) + infinitive with *to in this pattern, *need* is used as a noun to say that something is not necessary	*There's no need (for you) to get upset – I'm only joking.* *There was no need (for him) to be rude – I didn't do anything wrong.*

A Complete the second sentence so that it means the same as the first, using correct forms of the verb *need*.

1 I couldn't decide before I'd thought about it.
I ......needed to think about it...... before I could decide.

2 It's necessary to water those plants regularly.
Those plants ......need watering/need to be watered...... regularly.

3 It's important that you spend less money.
You ......need to spend...... less money.

4 The work was easy so it wasn't necessary for me to try hard.
I ......didn't need to try...... hard because the work was easy.

5 It isn't necessary for us to discuss this matter in great detail.
We ......don't need to discuss/needn't discuss...... this matter in great detail.

6 It will be necessary for me to check my diary before I can confirm a date.
I ......will need to check...... my diary before I can confirm a date.

7 I could do it on my own so it wasn't necessary for me to get any help.
I ......didn't need to get...... any help because I could do it on my own.

8 It won't be necessary for us to spend a lot of money in that place.

We ......won't need to spend...... a lot of money in that place.

9 It's not necessary for you to give me the details, I can imagine what happened.

You ......don't need to give/needn't give me...... the details, I can imagine what happened.

10 Someone will have to post these letters this afternoon.

These letters ......will need posting/will need to be posted...... this afternoon.

B Complete the second sentence so that it means the same as the first, using the word given.

1 Thanks, but it isn't necessary for you to repeat yourself, I heard you the first time.

needn't

Thanks, but ......you needn't repeat...... yourself, I heard you the first time.

2 I cooked more food than was necessary.

needn't

I ......needn't have cooked...... so much food.

3 It will be necessary to pay this bill before the end of the week.

need

This bill ......will need paying/will need to be paid...... before the end of the week.

4 You lost your temper but it wasn't necessary.

need

There ......was no need (for you) to lose...... your temper.

5 Someone had to fix the heating system because it broke down.

needed

The heating system ......needed fixing/needed to be fixed...... because it broke down.

6 Don't worry about this because it really doesn't matter.

no

This really doesn't matter so ......there is no need (for you) to...... worry about it.

7 It is necessary to consider this situation very carefully.

needs

This situation ......needs considering/needs to be considered...... very carefully.

8 She worked harder than was necessary.

needn't

She ......needn't have worked...... so hard.

8.3 Ability & possibility

ability	possibility
Use *can / can't* + infinitive without *to* • to talk about abilities in the present *She can play the guitar very well.* *Can you hear what I'm saying?*	Use *can / can't* + infinitive without *to* • to talk about things that are possible / impossible in the present / future *What can we do now? I'm bored.* *I can't see you tomorrow.*
Use *could(n't)* + infinitive without *to* • to talk about abilities in the past *I could speak French quite well when I was at school.* *When I was younger, I couldn't sing at all.*	Use *could(n't)* + infinitive without *to* • to talk about things that are possible in the present but which do not happen (positive form only) *I could blame others for my problems but I don't.* • for things you cannot imagine happening (negative only) *I couldn't do a job like that – it looks awful.* • for things you believe to be possible / impossible in the present / future (positive and negative) *With her qualifications she could get a good job.*

➔ ExA p134–35

be good at + noun / *-ing* • = be able to do something well *George is good at crosswords.* *I'm not very good at cooking.*	Use *could(n't)* + continuous infinitive without *to (be doing)* • to talk about things that you believe are possible / impossible at this moment or during this period of time *I could be making a lot of money now but I missed my chance.*
be capable of + noun / *-ing* • = have the ability or qualities required to do something *Tom is capable of achieving a lot in his career.* *She's capable of better work than this.*	Use *could(n't)* + perfect infinitive without *to (have done)* • to talk about things you believe were possible / impossible in the past *The assistant couldn't have been more helpful.* Use *could(n't)* + perfect continuous infinitive without *to (have been doing)* • to talk about things you believe were possible / impossible for a period of time in the past *I was wasting my time when I could have been doing something useful.*
Use *be able to* • to talk about abilities in the future; use future forms *The baby will be able to walk soon.* • Use past forms to talk about abilities in the past *Were you able to repair the car yourself?*	Use *will / won't be able to* • to talk about things that are possible or impossible in the future *The manager will be able to see you at 3 o'clock tomorrow.*

➔ ExB p135

A Complete the second sentence so that it means the same as the first, using *can*, *can't*, *could* or *couldn't*.

1 He was a fast runner when he was younger.
He .... could run fast .... when he was younger.

2 It wasn't possible for me to get a ticket for the concert.
I .... couldn't get .... a ticket for the concert.

3 It's impossible for me to make it to the party tomorrow.
I .... can't make it .... to the party tomorrow.

4 Some people would get angry in this situation but I'm not going to.

I ....could get angry.......... like other people in this situation.

5 I would hate to live in a dirty place like that.

I ....couldn't live.......... in a dirty place like that.

6 It wouldn't be possible for her to become a good actress, she isn't talented enough.

She ....couldn't become.......... a good actress, she isn't talented enough.

7 This letter is too complicated for me to understand.

I ....can't understand.......... this letter.

8 He's not doing a better job because he's too lazy.

He ....could be doing.......... a better job but he's too lazy.

9 For them, life is as good as it can be.

Life ....couldn't be.......... better for them.

10 I was saving as much money as I possibly could.

I ....couldn't have been saving.......... more money.

B Complete the second sentence so that it means the same as the first, using the word given.

1 Those bags will be too heavy for me to carry on my own.

able

I ....won't be able to.......... carry those bags on my own.

2 Anne wouldn't be able to do a job with a lot of responsibility.

capable

Anne wouldn't ....be capable of doing.......... a job with a lot of responsibility.

3 You weren't helping me, you were standing and watching while I struggled.

could

You were standing and watching while I struggled when ....you could have been helping.......... me.

4 He had the chance to start his own company but he decided not to.

could

He ....could have started.......... his own company but he decided not to.

5 Things at work are going as well as possible.

couldn't

Things at work ....couldn't be going.......... better than they are.

6 James can't organize his social life very well.

good

James ....isn't (very) good at organizing.......... his social life.

7 You'll have learnt how to play this tune soon.

able

You ....will be able to play.......... this tune soon.

8 I tried as hard as I could but I didn't succeed.

couldn't

I ....couldn't have tried.......... any harder but I didn't succeed.

9 We didn't succeed in finding a cheap hotel.

able

We ....weren't able to find.......... a cheap hotel.

8.4 Assumptions & interpretations

assumptions: *must & can't*

- Use *must* and *can't* to talk about things that you believe to be true because of the information or evidence that you have. You do not have absolute proof but you have good reasons to be certain that something is true.
- Use *must* to express a positive idea concerning the present or past and *can't* to express a negative idea concerning the present or past.
- Use an appropriate form of the infinitive after *must* and *can't*.

Belief	Assumption
present simple Situation: 'I rang the number but nobody answered the phone.' *They're out.* *They're **not** there.*	***must / can't*** **+ infinitive without *to*** *They **must be** out* *They **can't be** there.*
present continuous Situation: 'Jack says that he's won the lottery.' *He's **joking**.* *He's **not telling** the truth.*	***must / can't*** **+ continuous infinitive without *to*** *He **must be joking**.* *He **can't be telling** the truth.*
past simple / present perfect Situation: 'Helen didn't do what I asked her to do.' *She **misunderstood** you.* *She **didn't hear** you.* Situation: 'Fred hasn't replied to my letter.' *He **has lost** my address.* *He **hasn't received** my letter.*	***must / can't*** **+ perfect infinitive without *to*** *She **must have misunderstood** you.* *She **can't have heard** you.* *He **must have lost** my address.* *He **can't have received** my letter.*
past continuous / present perfect continuous Situation: 'She was always short of money.' *She **was spending** too much.* *She **wasn't earning** much.* Situation: 'He looks very tired.' *He**'s been working** too hard.* *He **hasn't been resting** enough.*	***must / can't*** **+ perfect continuous infinitive without *to*** Situation: 'He looks very tired.' *She **must have been spending** too much.* *She **can't have been earning** much.* *He **must have been working** too hard.* *He **can't have been resting** enough.*

→ ExA p137

possible interpretations: *may / might / could*

- Use *may*, *might* and *could* to express a possible interpretation of a situation, action or event. With this pattern, you are not sure that you are right, you are guessing or only suggesting what you think might be true.
- Use *may*, *might* and *could* to express a positive idea concerning the present or past, and *may not / might not* to express a negative idea concerning the present or past. Do not use *couldn't* to express this idea.
- Use an appropriate form of the infinitive after *may*, *might* and *could*.

Possibility	Interpretation
present simple Situation: 'I rang the number but nobody answered the phone.' *They're out.* *They're **not** there.*	***may (not) / might (not) / could*** **+ infinitive without *to*** *They **may / might / could be** out.* *They **may not / might not be** there.*
present continuous Situation: 'Jack says that he's won the lottery.' *He's **joking**.* *He's **not telling** the truth.*	***may (not) / might (not) / could*** **+ continuous infinitive without *to*** *He **may / might / could be joking**.* *He **may not / might not be telling** the truth.*

past simple / present perfect Situation: 'Helen didn't do what I asked her to do.' *She* ***misunderstood*** *you.* *She* ***didn't hear*** *you.* Situation: 'Fred hasn't replied to my letter.' *He* ***has lost*** *my address.* *He* ***hasn't received*** *my letter.*	***may (not) / might (not) / could*** **+ perfect infinitive without *to*** *She* ***may / might / could have misunderstood*** *you.* *She* ***may not / might not have heard*** *you.* *He* ***may / might / could have lost*** *my address.* *He* ***may not / might not have received*** *my letter.*
past continuous / present perfect continuous Situation: 'She was always short of money.' *She* ***was spending*** *too much.'* *She* ***wasn't earning*** *much.* Situation: 'He looks very tired.' *He's* ***been working*** *too hard.* *He* ***hasn't been resting*** *enough.*	***may (not) / might (not) / could*** **+ perfect continuous infinitive without *to*** *She* ***may / might / could have been spending*** *too much.* *She* ***may not / might not have been earning*** *much.* *He* ***may / might / could have been working*** *too hard.* *He* ***may not / might not have been resting*** *enough.*

→ ExB p138

A Complete the following using *must* or *can't* and the correct infinitive form.

Example: It's impossible that you saw me in the street at 3 o'clock. I was at work at that time.
You ***can't have seen*** *me in the street at 3 o'clock. I was at work at that time.*

1 Robert's always spending lots of money. Obviously he's rich.
Robert's always spending a lot of money. He ....must be.......... rich.

2 I haven't got my bag. The only possible explanation is that I left it on the bus.
I haven't got my bag. I ....must have left.......... it on the bus.

3 I'm sure it isn't very pleasant living in that terrible place.
It ....can't be.......... very pleasant living in that terrible place.

4 You don't know about this story? Clearly you haven't been reading the papers lately.
You don't know about this story? You ......can't have been reading...... the papers lately.

5 Erica hasn't come yet. Obviously she's working late.
Erica hasn't come yet. She ....must be working.......... late.

6 It's impossible that you've forgotten this already. I only told you five minutes ago.
You ....can't have forgotten.......... this already. I only told you five minutes ago.

7 It shouldn't be so difficult to do this. Clearly I'm not doing it right.
It shouldn't be so difficult to do this. I ....can't be doing.......... it right.

8 I'm sure it's taken you a long time to do all this work.
It ....must have taken.......... you a long time to do all this work.

9 I'm sure you weren't pleased when it happened.
You ....can't have been.......... pleased when it happened.

10 I couldn't find what I wanted anywhere. Clearly I was looking in the wrong shops.
I couldn't find what I wanted anywhere. I ......must have been looking...... in the wrong shops.

11 You're much better at this game now. Clearly you've been practising a lot.
You're much better at this game now. You ....must have been practising.... a lot.

12 Tom wasn't as cheerful as he usually is. Obviously he wasn't feeling very well.
Tom wasn't as cheerful as he usually is. He ......can't have been feeling...... very well.

B **Complete the second sentence so that it means the same as the first, using the word given.**

1 It was a ridiculous thing to say and obviously he wasn't thinking clearly.

can't

He .... can't have been thinking .... clearly because it was a ridiculous thing to say.

2 It's possible that Edward looks tired because he's working too hard.

might

Edward .... might be working .... too hard and that's why he looks tired.

3 What you're saying isn't right and clearly you've made a mistake.

must

You .... must have made a mistake .... because what you're saying isn't right.

4 Perhaps we can't find their house because they gave us the wrong address.

may

They .... may have given us .... the wrong address and that's why we can't find their house.

5 I'm sure my friends are wondering what I'm doing.

must

My friends .... must be wondering .... what I'm doing.

6 It's possible that you can't contact them because they're away.

could

They .... could be away .... and that's why you can't contact them.

7 Perhaps he didn't do what you wanted because he didn't understand your instructions.

might

He .... might not have understood .... your instructions and that's why he didn't do what you wanted.

8 I'm sure he isn't enjoying himself in such a terrible job.

can't

He .... can't be enjoying himself .... in such a terrible job.

9 Perhaps he didn't mention the subject because he isn't interested in it.

may

He .... may not be interested .... in the subject and that's why he didn't mention it.

10 It's possible that she knows about this because she heard you talking about it on the phone.

could

She .... could have heard you talking .... about this on the phone and that's why she knows about it.

11 Perhaps he's been having too many late nights.

might

He .... might have been having .... too many late nights.

12 It's possible that she doesn't care about the matter at all.

may

She .... may not care about .... the matter at all.

8.5 Suggesting & advising 1

Use	Example
should / ought to **+ infinitive without *to***	
• = present / future	
• to give / ask for fairly strong advice	*Should I take the job or not?*
• to talk / ask about things we believe to be right or wrong	*You ought to / should tell the truth at all times.* *She shouldn't be so rude to people.*
• to talk about expectations which are or were not reality or things which are or were not expected	*You should know / ought to know how to do this because I told you yesterday.*
should / ought to **+ continuous infinitive**	
• = present continuous	
• to talk / ask about things we believe to be right or wrong	*You should be thinking about your future.* *I shouldn't be earning such a low salary.*
• to talk about expectations which are or were not reality or things which are or were not expected	*I've taken the tablets and I should be feeling / ought to be feeling better, but I still feel bad.* *The car shouldn't be making that noise.*
should / ought to **+ perfect infinitive**	
• = past simple / present perfect	
• to talk/ask about things we believe to be right or wrong	*You should / ought to have been more careful.*
• to talk about expectations which are or were not reality or things which are or were not expected	*They shouldn't have lost because they were the better team.*
should / ought to **+ perfect continuous infinitive**	
• = past continuous / present perfect continuous	
• to talk / ask about things we believe to be right or wrong	*I should have been studying / ought to have been studying but I was enjoying myself.*
• to talk about expectations which are or were not reality or things which are or were not expected	*I should have been making / ought to have been making more progress than I was.*

▶ note: The negative forms of *ought* are *oughtn't* and *ought not*, e.g. *You oughtn't to / ought not to complain.* However, *shouldn't* is usually used instead of these forms. Question forms using *ought* are very rare.

A Complete the second sentence so that it means the same as the first, using the word given.

1 It's wrong that the government isn't doing anything about that problem.

ought

The government ......ought to be doing...... something about that problem.

2 You aren't careful enough about who you trust.

should

You ......should be...... more careful about who you trust.

3 Why didn't I write the number down?

ought

I ......ought to have written...... the number down.

4 It's wrong that he's earning so much money – he's useless.

shouldn't

He ......shouldn't be earning...... so much money – he's useless.

5 What's the right place for me to sign my name?

should

Where ......should I sign...... my name?

6 It was wrong of you to say that.

shouldn't

You ....shouldn't have said.. that.

7 I don't understand why he's not enjoying life – everything's fine for him.

should

He ....should be enjoying.. life – everything's fine for him.

8 I haven't been working hard enough lately.

should

I ....should have been working.......................... harder lately.

9 You don't take enough care of your health.

ought

You ....ought to take.................................... more care of your health.

10 What would have been the right thing for me to say in that situation?

should

What ....should I have said.. in that situation?

11 It's wrong that you haven't been taking the tablets that the doctor gave you.

ought

You ....ought to have been taking.......................... the tablets that the doctor gave you.

12 You work too hard.

shouldn't

You ....shouldn't work.................................... so hard.

13 I'm annoyed because you didn't ask me before you changed the plans.

should

You ....should have asked.. me before you changed the plans.

14 It's wrong that you were listening to their private conversation.

shouldn't

You ....shouldn't have been listening.......................... to their private conversation.

8.6 Suggesting & advising 2

Suggest / recommend / propose

suggest

- to talk about things you believe to be a good idea in the circumstances or the right thing to do, and things that you believe will produce a good result

recommend

- to tell somebody that something is a good idea for them or suitable for them because you have had a good experience of it

propose

- to suggest ideas and plans, usually in formal contexts

Structures	Examples
present verb (*that*) + second subject + subjunctive / (*should*) infinitive without *to*	*I **suggest (that) you accept** the offer.* *I **recommend (that) you should visit** the north of the country.* *I **propose (that) he raise** this matter in the next meeting.*
past verb (*that*) + second subject + subjunctive / (*should*) infinitive without *to*	*She **suggested (that) he should accept** the offer.* *A friend **recommended (that) we stay(ed)** at that hotel.* *She **proposed (that) they (should) start** their own company.*
verb + *-ing* • if the subject of the *-ing* verb is clearly understood or will also do the action suggested	*I don't know who **suggested coming** to this place.* (= … that we come …) *They **recommended living** there because of the pleasant way of life.* *She **proposed selling** their house.*

▶ note: Do not use *suggest / propose someone* + infinitive with *to*.
It is not correct to say *~~I suggest you to accept the offer~~*.

Additional structures with *recommend*:

recommend* someone + infinitive with *to	*They recommend you to book early.*
***recommend* someone something**	*Could you recommend me a good hotel?* (questions only)
***recommend* something *to* someone**	*I wouldn't recommend this make of car to anyone.*

advise / warn

advise

- to tell people what you think they should do, particularly if you think you know a lot about the subject
- also used in formal or professional contexts

warn

- to tell people that they should or shouldn't do something because something bad or unpleasant will happen to them if they do not do as they are told

Structures	Examples
verb + someone (+ *not*) + infinitive with *to*	*My teacher has advised me to read this book.* *I warned you not to trust him – he's dishonest.*
verb + someone (+ *that*) + second subject + *should* + infinitive without *to*	*My teacher advised me (that) I should read this book.* *I warned you that you shouldn't trust him.*
verb + someone (+ *that*) + second subject + reported speech	*I advised her that it was a bad idea.* *I warned her she would regret her actions.*
verb + someone *against* + *-ing* • = advise / warn not to do	*He advised me against signing the contract.* *I warned you against trusting him.*

→ ExA p143

Other structures used for suggesting & advising

Use	Example
Use ***had better*** • to give very strong advice or express the idea that an action is necessary or urgent and that there will be a bad result if it is not done • to refer to the present and future only ***had better*** **+ infinitive without** ***to*** ***had better not*** **+ infinitive without** ***to*** ▶ note: short forms (*you'd* / *we'd*, etc.), are usually used in these patterns, not full forms.	*You'd better leave now or you'll miss your train.* *You'd better not leave your bag there.*
Use ***would be better off*** **+ *-ing*** • to say that there is a better way to do something than the way that someone is planning or doing it Use ***would have been better off*** **+ *-ing*** • to say that there was a better way to do something in the past than the way it was done	*'I'm going into the city by car.' 'Don't do that, you won't be able to park. You'd be better off using public transport.'* *You arranged things very badly. I'd have been better off doing it myself.*
Use ***it's better / best*** **+ infinitive with** ***to*** • to suggest how to avoid a problem or how to get the best result, in general Use ***it would be better / best*** **+ infinitive with** ***to*** • to suggest how to avoid a problem or how to get the best result, in a particular case	*It's better / best to do this kind of thing slowly or you make mistakes.* *I decided it would be better / best not to disturb her when she was busy.*
why don't you ... ? • the question form *why don't you / we*, etc. can be used to suggest something	*Why don't you come with me? I'm sure you'll enjoy yourself.* *Why don't we go for a coffee now?*
If I were you ... • to give advice • usually followed by *would* or *should*	*If I were you I should study more.* *If I were you I would tell the truth.*
Use ***let's*** • to suggest something that the speaker will also do ***let's*** **+ infinitive without *to* (+ , *shall we?*)** ***let's not / don't let's*** **+ infinitive without** ***to***	*Let's go out for a meal together one evening (, shall we?).* *Let's not / Don't let's argue about such a silly thing.*
Use ***it's (about / high) time*** **+ subject + past simple** • to say that someone should do something now or something should happen now • to say that something probably should have been done or should have happened earlier and so it is now a very important or urgent matter	*It's about time you got ready to go out.* *It's high time you made a decision, I can't wait any longer.* *It's time I had a holiday, I'm exhausted.*
Use ***may / might as well*** **+ infinitive without** ***to*** • to suggest something, not because it is particularly desirable but because there isn't a better idea or choice • to suggest that somebody does something they would prefer to do or that is easy for them	*There won't be a bus for ages so we might as well walk home.* *You've done all your work so you might as well go home now.*
Use ***might (just) as well*** **+ infinitive without** ***to*** • to express a negative view that something is a waste of time and that it would be better to do something easier.	*I'll never understand this – I might (just) as well give up.*

→ ExB+C p144

A **Complete the second sentence so that it means the same as the first, using the word given.**

1 'Think carefully before making such an important decision,' he said to me.

advised

He advised me to think OR advised me (that) I should think carefully before making such an important decision.

2 You're not considering the situation calmly enough.

suggest

I suggest (that) you consider/should consider OR suggest considering the situation more calmly.

3 What do you think I should order from the menu?

recommend

What do/would you recommend (that) I order/I should order OR do/would you recommend me to order OR do/would you recommend ordering from the menu?

4 Let's get legal advice about this.

propose

I propose (that) we get/should get OR propose getting legal advice about this.

5 'I think we should have a break soon,' I said.

suggested

I suggested (that) we had/should have/ have OR suggested having a break soon.

6 'Don't believe everything in the newspapers,' she said to me.

advised

She advised me not to believe/against believing OR advised me (that) I shouldn't believe everything in the newspapers.

7 A friend told me that this was a good place a few weeks ago.

recommended

A friend recommended this place to me a few weeks ago.

8 'Get as much experience as you can,' he said to me.

suggested

He suggested (that) I got/should get/get OR suggested getting as much experience as I could.

9 'Don't give up your course,' I said to her.

advised

I advised her not to give up/against giving up OR advised her (that) she shouldn't give up her course.

10 'Go to the exhibition at the Modern Art Gallery,' the guide said to us.

recommended

The guide recommended (that) we went/should go/go OR recommended going to the exhibition at the Modern Art Gallery.

11 'Don't take unnecessary risks,' he said to her.

warned

He warned her not to take/against taking OR warned her (that) she shouldn't take unnecessary risks.

12 'Something bad is going to happen in a minute,' I said to her.

warned

I warned her (that) something bad was going to happen in a minute.

B Complete this article by filling the gaps with one suitable word or a contracted form.

➜ ➜ ➜ ➜ ➜ ➜ The Safe Way to Fitness ➜ ➜ ➜ ➜ ➜ ➜

Do you feel in bad condition physically? Do you look at yourself and think that you'd 1 ....better.......... get fit. Many people who have inactive, unhealthy lifestyles get to the point where they feel that it's 2 ....time.......... they did something to improve their physical condition. However, there are dangers in doing too much too soon. Why 3 ....don't.......... we see what our health expert advises?

- ➜ it's 4 ......best/better...... not to try to do too much at first
- ➜ if I 5 ....were.......... you, I'd start slowly, gradually building towards fitness
- ➜ you'd be better 6 ....off.......... going for brisk walks to begin with
- ➜ choose a sport you enjoy – you 7 ....might.......... as well have fun
- ➜ don't expect too much. Let's 8 ....not.......... imagine that you'll make it to the Olympics!

C Complete the second sentence so that it means the same as the first, using the word given.

1 John said, 'I think we should go somewhere different for a change.' (**why**)
John said, '..........why don't we go.......... somewhere different for a change?'

2 I decided it wasn't a good idea to say anything. (**best**)
I decided that ....it was/would be best not.......... to say anything.

3 If I don't go to the bank now, I won't have any money for the weekend. (**better**)
I ....had/'d better go.......... to the bank now or I won't have any money for the weekend.

4 He hasn't grown up yet but I think he should stop behaving like a child. (**time**)
I think ....it's (about/high) time he grew up.......... and stopped behaving like a child.

5 You bought a new one but a second-hand one would have been cheaper and just as good. (**better**)
You would ....have been better off buying.......... a second-hand one.

6 Anna said, 'I think it would be nice if we went out for a meal tonight.' (**let's**)
Anna said, '..........let's go out.......... for a meal tonight.'

7 I said to her, 'You should have started taking things seriously by now.' (**time**)
I said to her, '..........it's (about/high) time you started.......... taking things seriously.'

8 I think that it would be a very bad idea if you argued with him about this. (**better**)
I think you ....had/'d better not argue.......... with him about this.

9 In my opinion, you really should make up your mind now. (**about**)
In my opinion, ...it's about time you.......... made up your mind.

10 We've done enough for today so let's stop now. (**might**)
We've done enough for today so we ....might as well stop.......... now.

11 If I ask him again, he'll get angry. (**better**)
I ....had/'d better not ask.......... him again or he'll get angry.

12 It would be easier for me to stop trying because I'm not making any progress. (**just**)
I ....might just as well stop.......... trying because I'm not making any progress.

8.7 Probability & certainty

Use	Example
Use *may (not)* / *might (not)* + infinitive without *to* • to say that it is possible but not certain that something will happen in the future ▶ note: Do not use *can* to talk about future possibilities.	*I might be a bit late home tonight.* *I may not see you again for a while.* NOT ~~*It can be sunny next week.*~~
Use *may* / *might well* + infinitive without *to* • to say that you believe that something probably will happen in the future, but you are not completely sure	*She may well change her mind about this.* *I might well change my job soon.*
Use *should* / *shouldn't* + infinitive without *to* • to talk about things that you think probably will / won't happen or probably are / aren't true	*The meal should be ready soon.* *It shouldn't take me long to get there.*
Use *I should* / *shouldn't think* + subject + positive verb • to introduce something that you think probably will / won't happen or probably is / isn't true	*I should think the meal will be ready soon.* *I shouldn't think it will take me long to get there.*
Use *doubt whether* / *if* / *that* • to say that you think something probably won't happen or probably isn't true ▶ note: Use a positive verb form after *doubt* because the verb *doubt* has a negative meaning.	*I doubt whether / if / that the party will finish before 12.* NOT ~~*I doubt whether / if / that it won't happen.*~~
Use *it* + *be* + *possible* (+ *that*) + subject + verb, etc. • to say that something may / might happen or be true	*It's possible (that) we won't get in, but we might.*
probably / *certainly* / *definitely* • these adverbs are used in the following patterns: subject + adverb + positive verb subject + adverb + negative auxiliary / modal subject + positive auxiliary / modal + adverb	*She probably hates me.* *She probably doesn't like me.* *I'll probably see you later.*

Use *likely* / *unlikely* • to say that something probably will or won't happen • use the following structures: *It* + *be* + *likely* / *unlikely* (+ *that*) + subject + verb, etc. subject + *be* + *likely* / *unlikely* + infinitive with *to*	*It's likely (that) they'll lose the game.* *They're unlikely to win.*
Use *sure* / *certain* • to say that you think you know something will happen • use the following structures: subject + *be* + *sure* / *certain* + second subject + verb, etc. subject + *be* + *sure* / *certain* + infinitive with *to* / negative infinitive with *to (not to do)*	*I'm sure he'll be angry.* *I'm sure the plan won't work.* *He's sure to be angry.* *The plan is sure not to work.*
likely and *sure* / *certain* follow the same patterns: present simple *It's likely / I'm sure that John* ***knows*** *the answer.*	infinitive (*to do*) *John is likely / John is sure* ***to know*** *the answer.*
present continuous *It's unlikely / I'm certain that she****'s working*** *now.*	continuous infinitive (*to be doing*) *She's unlikely / She's certain* ***to be working*** *now.*
past simple / present perfect *It's likely / I'm sure that they* ***left / have left*** *early.*	perfect infinitive (*to have done*) *They're likely / They're sure* ***to have left*** *early.*
past continuous / present perfect continuous *It's unlikely / I'm certain that he* ***was / has been lying****.*	perfect continuous infinitive (*to have been doing*) *He's unlikely / he's certain* ***not to have been lying****.*

A **Complete the second sentence so that it means the same as the first, using the word given.**

1 I shouldn't think they'll enjoy themselves very much there.

doubt

I ....doubt whether/if/that they'll enjoy.... themselves very much there.

2 This mistake will not happen again, I promise you.

certainly

This mistake ....certainly won't happen again.... , I promise you.

3 I suppose that things might get better soon.

possible

I suppose ....it's possible (that) things will get.... better soon.

4 They have no intention of going back there again!

definitely

They ....definitely won't go.... back there again!

5 I should think Bob will be there as well.

probably

Bob ....will probably be there.... as well.

6 The meal probably won't be ready until 2pm.

doubt

I ....doubt whether/if/that the meal will.... be ready before 2pm.

7 The situation probably won't improve in the near future.

unlikely

The situation ....is unlikely to improve.... in the near future.

8 I don't think she'll change her mind about this.

likely

I don't think she ....is likely to change.... her mind about this.

9 In my opinion, he'll definitely be angry about this.

sure

In my opinion, he ....is sure to be.... angry about this.

10 Your luck will certainly change soon.

certain

Your luck ....is certain to change.... soon.

11 He'll probably turn up late.

likely

It's ....likely that he'll turn up.... late.

12 Harry will definitely be there tonight.

sure

I ....am sure (that) Harry will be.... there tonight.

B Complete these short newspaper previews by deciding which word or phrase (A, B, C or D) fits into each gap.

Football Preview

Denton City face a tough game on Saturday against Lonsdale United but they 1 ......C....... win comfortably. Star striker Felix Andrews will 2 ......A...... be fit to play, although team coach Robert Deans 3 ....B........ decide that he isn't quite ready yet, following his leg injury. Stan Green will 4 ....C...... play in goal, according to the coach. It will be one of the big games of the season and there 5 ....D....... be a record crowd.

1 A likely	B probably	**C** should	D sure
2 **A** probably	B well	C likely	D certain
3 A can	**B** may	C possible	D doubt
4 A sure	B certain	**C** definitely	D likely
5 A should well	B likely	C probably	**D** might well

Film Preview

I 6 ....A........ think that most people will see a better film all year than *Dreamland*, just released and showing at The Odeon from Friday. It is 7 ....C........ the best film Roland Lang has ever made. I'm 8 ....B........ it will set records at the box office and it 9 ....A........ pick up many awards over the coming year. Roland Lang fans 10 ....B........ be surprised to see him playing a romantic role but he has surely never acted better.

6 **A** shouldn't	B may not	C might not	D don't doubt
7 A sure	B well	**C** certainly	D certain
8 A likely	**B** sure	C definitely	D possible
9 **A** may well	B likely	C probably	D should well
10 A can	**B** might	C likely	D certainly

Music Preview

It's 11 ....D........ that the gig by The Temples at the Golden Bowl on Friday night will be their last appearance in this country for some time. They're off on a tour of the US next month and it's 12 ....D........ that they'll be so successful there that they won't come back for a while. It 13 ....C........ be too difficult for fans to keep in touch with them, though, as they're setting up a website that will allow fans to follow them on their adventures in America. Says singer Chas Davies: 'I'm 14 ....A........ that the gig on Friday will be an emotional one but I 15 ....B........ think that all our fans here will want to give us a big send-off.'

11 A sure	B certainly	C probably	**D** possible
12 A definitely	B probably	C certainly	**D** likely
13 A doubts	B unlikely	**C** shouldn't	D may not well
14 **A** certain	B likely	C probably	D definitely
15 A may	**B** should	C might	D can

C **Complete the second sentence so that it means the same as the first.**

1 I'm sure that they've received my letter by now.
They're sure to have received my letter by now.

2 It's likely that she was telling you the truth.
She's likely to have been telling (you) the truth.

3 I'm certain that he's planning something terrible.
He's certain to be planning something terrible.

4 It's unlikely that she was upset by what you said.
She is unlikely to have been upset by what you said.

5 It's likely that he's left his office by now.
He's likely to have left his office by now.

6 I'm sure she's wondering where I am.
She's sure to be wondering where I am.

7 I'm certain that he was earning a lot of money in that job.
He's certain to have been earning a lot of money in that job.

8 It's unlikely that he misunderstood what I told him.
He's unlikely to have misunderstood what I told him.

D **Complete this letter by filling the gaps with one suitable word or a contracted form. Sometimes there may be more than one correct answer.**

The European Tour

Tom

I thought I'd write you a quick note because I'm off on my travels around Europe next week and I 1 ......shouldn't...... think I'll have time to see you before then. I haven't completely decided where I'm going yet but I 2 ......may/might...... well go to Holland and it's 3 ......likely/possible...... that I'll go to Scandinavia as well. I 4 ......doubt...... whether I'll go to Britain though, because it's 5 ......unlikely...... that I'll have enough time. It's 6 ......likely/possible...... that I'll pay a quick visit to Switzerland but I really don't know about that. I'm 7 ......sure/certain...... I'll be able to find good places to stay – I've got a very good guidebook – but I 8 ......may/might...... not have enough money to go to all the places I want to. I 9 ......should...... think I'll be back by the end of August, and I'll 10 ......definitely/certainly...... get in touch with you as soon as I get back, I promise!

Love, Alice

→ Glossary p217

8.8 Chance & possibility

A **Complete the second sentence so that it means the same as the first, using the word given. There may be more than one possible correct answer.**

1 I'll never become a millionaire.

chance

There's no chance of me (ever) becoming/that I'll (ever) become a millionaire.

2 You probably won't find a cheaper one anywhere.

chances

The chances are that you won't find a cheaper one anywhere.

3 Do you think you'll have the information for me by tomorrow?

chances

What are the chances of you having/that you'll have the information for me by tomorrow?

4 Is it possible that you'll get your money back?

chance

Is there any chance of you getting/that you'll get your money back?

5 The meeting might be cancelled.

possibility

There is a possibility that the meeting will be cancelled.

6 We definitely won't be able to afford such a high price.

chance

There is no chance of us being /that we'll be able to afford such a high price.

7 It's possible that you'll get what you want there.

chance

There is a (good) chance that you'll get what you want there.

8 It's possible that the weather will improve later but I doubt it.

slight

There is a slight chance of the weather improving later, but I doubt it.

9 I doubt he'll be chosen for the national team.

much

There is not much chance that he'll be chosen for the national team.

10 Is it likely or unlikely that you'll persuade him?

your

What are your chances of persuading him?

11 It's possible that she will get promoted.

chance

She has a chance of being promoted.

12 They are likely to win that match.

good

They have a good chance of winning that match.

→ Glossary p217–18

8.9 Word focus

Phrasal verbs: *turn* & *make*

A Fill the gaps with the correct form of *turn* or *make* to complete a phrasal verb with the meaning in brackets.

1 About 200 people ......turned...... up at the meeting. (attended)
2 She ......made...... out that everything was fine but I knew that it wasn't. (pretended)
3 When the film ended, the audience ......made...... for the exit. (went in the direction of)
4 I had to ......turn...... down the invitation because I couldn't go. (say no to)
5 I couldn't ......make...... out what he said because he spoke so quietly. (hear clearly)
6 I ......turned...... up late because I was stuck in traffic. (arrived)
7 This area has ......turned...... into a place full of tourists. (changed and become)
8 My father was always ......making...... up stories for us when we were children. (inventing)
9 I had to work harder than usual to ......make...... up for the time I'd wasted. (balance)
10 We were ......turned...... away at the door because we weren't members. (refused entry)

Word formation: adjective suffixes

B Complete the text by forming adjectives using the word in capitals at the end of each line and the suffixes below. You may need to make more than one change to the word given to form the correct adjective.

-ly -less -al -ing -able -ful -ous

~ *The Ross Hotel* ~

For the most 1 ......comfortable...... rooms in town, all available at extremely	COMFORT
2 ......reasonable...... rates, look no further than the Ross Hotel. You will always	REASON
find a warm welcome here from our highly 3 ......professional...... staff, who are	PROFESSION
keen to be 4 ......helpful...... to guests at all times. We are in the best location	HELP
in town, and many of our rooms have 5 ......exceptional...... views of the coast.	EXCEPT
There are also 6 ......countless...... tourist attractions that are well worth visiting	COUNT
in the 7 ......surrounding...... area. Our dining room has an excellent reputation,	SURROUND
particularly for the 8 ......traditional...... dishes of the region. So take advantage of	TRADITION
one of our 9 ......numerous...... special offers. Phone the number below to find out	NUMBER
about our very low 10 ......daily...... rates and our rates per week.	DAY

Collocations

C Complete the second sentence so that it means the same as the first, using one of the verbs below and the word given.

do have lose make take

1 The players' protests did not change the referee's decision at all.

difference

The player's protests ......made no difference to...... the referee's decision at all.

2 Their offer to him was generous, I think.

offer

They ......made him a generous offer......, I think.

➔ Glossary p218

3 The idea of starting a group doesn't interest Tim any more.

interest

Tim ....has lost interest in........................ the idea of starting a group.

4 We haven't contacted each other for years.

touch

We ....lost touch with each other........................ years ago.

5 She doesn't say anything about her boyfriend in this letter.

mention

She ....makes no mention of her boyfriend........................ in this letter.

6 She did not get involved in the conversation at all.

part

She ....took no part in/didn't take part in........................ the conversation at all.

7 'Why didn't you do what I advised you?' he asked me.

advice

'Why didn't ....you take my advice........................ ?' he asked me.

8 Scientists have been researching the causes of the disease.

research

Scientists ....have been doing research into........................ the causes of the disease.

9 His decision to take the job was influenced by money.

influence

Money ....had an influence on........................ his decision to take the job.

10 'Some exercise wouldn't be bad for you,' she told him.

harm

'Some exercise wouldn't ....do you (any) harm........................ ,' she told him.

Prepositional phrases: noun + preposition

D Fill each gap with one of the prepositions below.

for from in of to

1 Unfortunately, there wasn't much demand ....for.......... the goods they produced.
2 I have no recollection ....of.......... promising to do that.
3 Lots of people have a fear ....of.......... flying.
4 He has a very strange attitude ....to.......... life.
5 She has a lot of confidence ....in.......... herself.
6 He played no part ....in.......... what happened so nobody can blame him.
7 She has announced her retirement ....from.......... the sport.
8 I began to regret my involvement ....in.......... the project.
9 She wanted revenge ....for.......... the terrible thing that had been done to her.
10 There must be a better way ....of.......... solving this problem.
11 When interviewed, one ....in.......... ten people said that they were against the idea.
12 She has a real talent ....for.......... acting.

ECCE Practice 8

Grammar

1 'Monica brought some food for the party.' 'She __a__ , we have plenty.'
 a didn't need to
 b doesn't have to
 c needn't have brought
 d needn't

2 I rang the door twice. Dora wasn't at home. She __b__ left already.
 a can't have
 b must have
 c needn't have
 d should have

3 You __c__ finish your homework now. You can always do it after dinner.
 a couldn't
 b mustn't
 c don't have to
 d shouldn't

4 Why are you still here? You __a__ been helping Dianne in the yard.
 a should have
 b must have
 c might have
 d would have

5 My parents always __a__ us stay up late on the weekend.
 a let
 b allow
 c permit
 d get

6 Ray __d__ get into his house because he'd forgotten his keys.
 a can't
 b wouldn't
 c mustn't
 d couldn't

7 Why lie to him about your condition? You __c__ tell him the truth or things might get worse.
 a should better
 b would better
 c had better
 d would rather

8 I __d__ well go to the movies after work tonight.
 a could
 b should
 c shall
 d might

Vocabulary

9 'Do you think he'll recover from the accident?' 'It's not looking good, I'd say the __c__ are slim.'
 a possibility
 b opportunity
 c chances
 d likelihood

10 We can't just __b__ up at the party without an invitation.
 a go
 b turn
 c arrive
 d reach

11 Sam liked making __d__ stories to tell to his children.
 a off
 b out
 c for
 d up

12 Our house is right in the country. There are plenty of nice places to walk in the __b__ area.
 a around
 b surrounding
 c near
 d nearby

13 He doesn't use that old car any more, so I'm going to __d__ him an offer for it.
 a give
 b take
 c do
 d make

14 __a__ my advice – don't get involved with her.
 a Take
 b Have
 c Do
 d Hold

15 Sally is so successful because she has complete confidence __c__ herself.
 a at
 b of
 c in
 d for

16 My younger brother has a real talent __b__ painting.
 a in
 b for
 c at
 d with

Exam techniques
→ p223

FCE Practice 8

Part 4

For Questions **1–15**, read the text below and look carefully at each line. Some of the lines are correct and some have a word which should not be there. If a line is correct, put a tick (✓) in the space next to the number of the line. If a line has a word which should **not** be there, put that word in the space next to the number of the line.

ELVIS PRESLEY

1 ..was.. Although Elvis Presley ~~was~~ died in 1977, he is probably just as famous

2 ....✓.... today as he ever was. He became famous in the 1950s, and he was the

3 ....✓.... first rock ‘n’ roll star in the world. He was working as a truck driver

4 ..had.. when he ~~had~~ started singing and making recordings. Soon, his records

5 ..when.. were extremely successful and ~~when~~ his first appearances on television

6 ....✓.... caused a sensation because parents disapproved of the way that he

7 ....so.... danced while he was singing. Teenagers all over the world thought ~~so~~

8 ....as.... that he was wonderful, ~~as~~ though, and rock ‘n’ roll soon became their

9 ....the.... favourite kind of ~~the~~ music. Next, Elvis spent two years in Germany in

10 ....✓.... the US Army, after which he appeared in more than 30 films. In 1969,

11 ....at.... he started giving concerts again, ~~at~~ mostly in Las Vegas. His records

12 ..quite.. and concerts now consisted of love songs ~~quite~~ more than rock ‘n’ roll.

13 ..time.. He lived for much ~~time~~ of his life in a huge house called Graceland,

14 ....✓.... and since his death fans have continued to visit the house. To them,

15 ..being. he is known as ‘The King’ – some even think he is still ~~being~~ alive!

Unit 9 Conditionals

Grammar
9.1 Conditional patterns
9.2 Conditional conjunctions
9.3 Wishing & regretting

Vocabulary
9.4 Size
9.5 Word focus

9.1 Conditional patterns

Stop & check

These sentences all contain a common error. Correct the part of each sentence that is incorrect.

1 If I'd saved my money last year, I 'd be ~~am~~ able to afford it.
2 If I could play better, I would win more matches.
3 If I 'd left my house earlier yesterday, I would have got there on time.
4 If I'd seen him there, I 'd have ~~had~~ said hello to him.
5 If I~~'ll~~ see Jack at college tomorrow, I'll ask him what his plans are.
6 If I'd been thinking more carefully, I wouldn't have made ~~didn't make~~ that mistake.

Use	Example
***if* + present simple clause + , + *will / going to* clause** • the first conditional for real possibilities • = *if* + possibility in the future + result in the future • = *if* + possibility in the present + result in the future	 *If I have enough money next year, I'll buy a house.* *If you leave now, you won't be late.*
***if* + past simple clause + , + *would* clause** • the second conditional for unreal situations • = *if* + something untrue in the present + impossible result in the present or future • = *if* + something unlikely in the future + unlikely result in the future • *were* can be used instead of *was*	 *If I knew the answer, I'd / I would tell you.* (= I don't know the answer so I can't tell you) *If I won the lottery, I'd give up work.* (= I probably won't win the lottery so I won't give up work) *If I were rich, I'd buy you a new car.*
***if* + past perfect clause + , + *would have done* clause** • the third conditional for past possibilities • = *if* + something that didn't happen in the past + result that didn't happen in the past	 *If they'd invited me, I would have gone to the party.* (= they didn't invite me so I didn't go to the party)
Use *if* + past perfect clause + , + *would* clause • a mixed conditional • = *if* + something that didn't happen in the past + result that isn't true in the present	 *If you hadn't stayed out late last night, you wouldn't be tired now.* (= you did stay out late last night so you are tired now)

▶ note: all of the above patterns can be used with continuous tenses:
If I find something better to do, I won't be working here this time next year.
If you're getting bored, I'll change the subject.
If the weather was better, I'd be feeling happier.
If I was earning more money, I'd be able to have a holiday this summer.
If I wasn't working tomorrow, I'd go out tonight.
If you'd been concentrating, you wouldn't have made that mistake.
If you'd been working as hard as me, you'd be feeling tired now.

➔ ExA+B p155–6

Use *might / may* in conditional patterns • to talk about a result or consequence that is not certain, only a possibility **Use *might / may* + infinitive without *to*** • to talk about a result or consequence in the present or future (first conditional) **Use *might / may have* + past participle** • to talk about a result or consequence in the past (third conditional)	 *If I have enough money next year, I might / may buy a house.* *If you hadn't helped me, I might / may not have succeeded.*
Use *could* in conditional patterns • to talk about a result or consequence that is an opportunity or an ability **Use *could* + infinitive without *to*** • to talk about a result or consequence in the present or future (first conditional) **Use *could have* + past participle** • to talk about a result or consequence in the past (third conditional)	 *If I won the lottery, I could give up work.* *If you hadn't helped me, I couldn't have done it.*
Use *should* in conditional patterns • when the result is something that will probably happen	 *If you leave now, you shouldn't be late.*
use *should* + infinitive without *to* • when the result or consequence is a suggestion or piece of advice; use the appropriate form of *should* • when the result or consequence is something that the speaker believes to be a logical explanation; use the appropriate form of *should*	 *If you wanted to keep this secret, you shouldn't have told George.* *If their plane took off on time, it should have arrived by now.*

➔ ExC p156

A Rewrite these sentences to form first, second, third or mixed conditionals.

1 You're unfit because you don't do enough exercise.
If you did more/enough exercise, you wouldn't be unfit/you'd be fit.

2 I got angry because he was rude to me.
If he hadn't been rude to me, I wouldn't have got angry.

3 I might go to live in Australia but I'll have to find a job first.
If I find a job (first), I'll go/I might go to live in Australia.

4 You only know about this because I told you.
If I hadn't told you, you wouldn't know about this.

5 I didn't tell her about it because she didn't ask me.
If she had asked me, I would have told her about it.

6 You don't know this programme because you don't watch television a lot.
If you watched a lot of/more television, you'd know about this programme.

7 We're not sitting outside because it's raining.
If it wasn't raining, we would be sitting outside.

8 We're friends again because he apologized to me.
If he hadn't apologized to me, we wouldn't be friends again.

9 You didn't hear what I said because you weren't listening.
If you had been listening, you would have heard what I said.

10 I'm feeling ill because I ate too much.
If I hadn't eaten so much, I wouldn't be feeling ill.

B **The following are quotations from interviews in which famous people talk about their lives. Rewrite them using first, second, third or mixed conditionals.**

1 'I might stop being famous but it won't worry me.'
If I stop being famous, it won't worry me.

2 'I'm having a wonderful time because I'm doing a lot of interesting things.'
If I wasn't doing a lot of interesting things, I wouldn't be having a wonderful time.

3 'I'm rich and famous because the public like me.'
If the public didn't like me, I wouldn't be rich and famous.

4 'I became extremely famous because I was lucky.'
If I hadn't been lucky, I wouldn't have become extremely famous.

5 'People go to see my films because they're entertaining.'
If my films weren't entertaining, people wouldn't go to see them.

6 'I only got to the top because I have a lot of talent.'
If I didn't have a lot of talent, I wouldn't have got to the top.

7 'I don't know why my music is so popular, so I can't explain it.'
If I knew why my music is/was so popular, I would be able to/could explain it.

8 'I might win an award and then I'll be very pleased.'
If I won an award, I'd be very pleased.

9 'I'm successful today because I was determined to succeed when I was younger.'
If I hadn't been determined to succeed when I was younger, I wouldn't be successful today

10 I'm not living an ordinary life because I'm working in show business.
If I wasn't working in show business, I would be living an ordinary life.

C **Rewrite these sentences using the words in brackets.**

1 If I'd known all the facts, it's possible that I wouldn't have made that decision. (**may**)
If I'd known all the facts I may not have made that decision.

2 If you gave me a hand, it would be possible for me to do this much more quickly. (**could**)
If you gave me a hand, I could do this much more quickly.

3 If you need any advice in the future, it's possible that I'll be able to give you some. (**might**)
If you need any advice in the future, I might be able to give you some.

4 If I'd applied earlier, it's possible that I would have got the job. (**might**)
If I'd applied earlier, I might have got the job.

5 Concentrate and you probably won't find this too difficult. (**shouldn't**)
If you concentrate you shouldn't find this too difficult.

6 I have so much to do that I can't relax. (**could**)
If I didn't have so much to do I could relax. .

7 He got a green card and that's why he was able to work in the US. (**couldn't**)
If he hadn't got a green card he couldn't have worked in the US.

8 They sent it last week. I expected it to be here by now. (**should**)
If they sent it last week, it should be here by now.

9.2 Conditional conjunctions

Use	Example
Use *unless* • to talk about the only thing that could stop something from happening or being true ***unless* + present tense clause + , + *will / going to* + clause** • *unless* is used in the first conditional pattern with the meaning *if ... not*. In this pattern, the verb after *unless* refers to the future but is in a present form. ***unless* + any tense** • *unless* can refer to any present or past situation, with the meaning *except if*.	*Unless you help me, I won't be able to do it.* (= if you don't help me, ...) *We're going to go for a long walk tomorrow, unless it's raining.* (= ... if it isn't raining) *Unless he's been working late, he'll get here on time.* *I don't know why she was angry, unless my comments had annoyed her.*
Use *in case* • to talk about something that might possibly happen or be true. The other part of the sentence concerns an action that is taken because that possibility exists. ***in case* + present tense** • as in the first conditional pattern, a present verb form is used to refer to the future	*I'm going to leave early in case it takes a long time to get there.* *Take my number in case you need to phone me later on.*
***in case* + any tense** • use *in case* with the appropriate verb form to refer to the present or past	*I reminded her in case she had forgotten.* *I took a sandwich in case I got hungry on the journey.* *In case you haven't heard the news, I'll tell you.*
Use *as long as / provided (that) / providing (that)* • to talk about something that must happen or be true in order for the other part of the sentence to happen or be true ***as long as / provided (that) / providing (that)* + present tense** • again, when referring to the future, use a present form ***as long as / provided (that) / providing (that)* + any tense** • use the appropriate verb form to refer to the present and past	*As long as you leave before 3, you'll catch the plane.* *I'll go back to work tomorrow provided / providing (that) I'm feeling better.* *He told me I could stay as long as I was quiet.* *Provided / Providing (that) you've followed my instructions, everything will be fine.*
Use *even if* • to talk about a possibility which does not affect or make any difference to what is stated in the other part of the sentence ***even if* in conditional patterns** • in all the patterns for conditionals used with *if* (see Conditional Patterns p154) ***even if* + any tense** • use *even if* with any appropriate verb tense to talk about the consequences of possible facts	*Even if she apologizes, I won't forgive her.* *Even if I'd tried hard, I would have failed.* *Even if I'd done what you suggested, I'd be in the same position now.* *Even if you speak the language, it isn't easy to make friends here.*

▶ note: Do not confuse *even if* and *even though*. Use *even if* to refer to possibilities but *even though* to refer to facts, things that are actually true.
Even if we ran, we'd miss the train. (= we can run but we will miss the train anyway)
Even though we ran, we missed the train. (= we ran but we missed the train)

▶ note: A present tense is always used to refer to the future after all the above words and phrases.
It is not correct to say ~~*Unless it will rain, in case you will go, as long as you'll leave, even if she will run, etc.*~~

A **Complete the second sentence so that it means the same as the first, using the word given.**

1 Write my address down because you might want to contact me. (case)
Write my address down ......in case you want...... to contact me.

2 I'll lend you the money but you must give it back to me next week. (long)
I'll lend you the money ......as long as you give...... it back to me next week.

3 You can ask me a thousand times but I'll never agree. (even)
I'll never agree ......even if you ask...... me a thousand times.

4 If you don't work hard, you won't get anywhere in life. (unless)
You won't get anywhere in life ......unless you work...... hard.

5 To catch that train we must leave now. (providing)
We'll catch that train ......providing (that) we leave...... now.

6 He hasn't got a lot of money but he'd be unhappy anyway. (even)
He'd be unhappy ......even if he had...... a lot of money.

7 I'll be polite to him but he must be polite to me. (provided)
I'll be polite to him ......provided (that) he is...... polite to me.

8 If she doesn't get promoted soon, she'll leave the company. (unless)
She'll leave the company ......unless she gets promoted...... soon.

9 Let's talk about this now because we might not have an opportunity later. (case)
Let's talk about this now ......in case we don't have...... an opportunity later.

10 I didn't run all the way there but I would have been late anyway. (even)
I would have been late ......even if I'd/I had run...... all the way there.

B **Rewrite these sentences, using one of the words or phrases below.**

unless in case as long as provided providing even if

1 The match will be cancelled if the weather doesn't improve.
The match will be cancelled unless the weather improves. OR Unless the weather improves, the match ....

2 She took a lot of warm clothes because she thought it might be cold there.
She took a lot of warm clothes in case it was cold there. OR In case it was was cold there, she took ....

3 I didn't want to see the concert but I couldn't afford a ticket anyway.
Even if had wanted to see the concert, I couldn't have afforded a ticket. OR I couldn't have afforded a ticket, even if ....

4 I'll help you this time but you mustn't expect me to do it every time.
I'll help you this time as long as/ providing (that)/provided (that) you don't expect me to do it very time. OR As long as/Providing (that)/Provided (that) you ....

5 I'll give you a key because I might not be here to let you in when you get back.
I'll give you a key in case I'm not here to let you in when you get back. OR In case I'm not here to let you in when you get back, I'll give ....

6 I might not succeed but I'm going to do my best anyway.
Even if I don't succeed, I'm going to do my best. OR I'm going to do my best even if ....

7 Perhaps something unexpected will happen – otherwise, it's going to be another boring day.
Unless something unexpected happens, it's going to be another boring day. OR It's going to be another boring day, unless ...

8 He told me that I could use his computer but that I had to be careful with it.
He told me that I could use his computer as long as/provided (that)/providing (that) I was careful with it. OR He told me that, as long as/provided (that)/providing (that) I was careful with it, ...

9.3 Wishing & regretting

wish	
wanting a situation or fact to be different	
subject + *wish* + second subject + past simple / past continuous	*He wishes he was younger.*
wanting a present fact or situation to be different	*I wish it wasn't raining.*
subject + *wish* + second subject + *would*	*I wish she would phone me.*
wanting something to happen or stop happening	*I wish you wouldn't keep arguing with me.*
subject + *wish* + second subject + *could*	*I wish I could play the piano.*
wanting to have the ability or opportunity to do something	*They wish they could have a holiday.*
subject + *wish* + second subject + past continuous	*I wish I wasn't working tomorrow.*
to say that someone is not happy about something that has been fixed for the future	*She wishes he wasn't leaving next week.*
Use subject + *wish* + second subject + past perfect	
• with a negative verb to express regret that something happened in the past and to say that someone would prefer it not to have happened	*I wish I hadn't agreed to help them.*
• with a positive verb to express regret that something did not happen in the past and to say that someone would prefer it to have happened	*I wish I'd taken your advice.*

→ ExA p160

Use *if only*	
• to express the same idea as *I wish* and use in the same patterns	
• used in emphatic sentences and expresses a very strong desire for a situation or fact to be different	
• *if only* can be used in exclamations or in conditional sentences	
***if only* + subject + past simple**	*If only I was younger!*
***if only* + subject + past continuous**	*If only it wasn't raining, we could go out.*
if only* + subject + *would	*If only she'd phone me, I'd stop worrying.*
if only* + subject + *could	*If only I could play the piano like that!*
***if only* + subject + past continuous**	*If only I wasn't working tomorrow, I could take it easy.*
***if only* + subject + past perfect**	*If only I hadn't agreed to help them!*

→ ExB p160

Use *regret*	
to talk about feeling that something someone did or didn't do in the past was a bad idea	*I regretted being rude to her.*
regret* + (not) + *-ing	*I regret not taking that opportunity.*
regret* + infinitive with *to	*We regret to inform you that your application has been unsuccessful.*
= I don't want to say this but I have to (formal)	

→ ExC p160

A **Imagine that these are facts and situations that you are not happy about. Write sentences for each one beginning with *I wish*.**

1 You're leaving tomorrow. I wish you weren't leaving tomorrow.
2 I took the job. I wish I hadn't taken the job.
3 I can't afford it. I wish I could afford it.
4 I don't know what to do. I wish I knew what to do.
5 You didn't tell me about this earlier. I wish you'd/you had told me about this earlier.
6 I'm living in this horrible place. I wish I wasn't living in this horrible place.
7 The letter hasn't arrived yet. I wish the letter would arrive.
8 You're acting liking a child. I wish you wouldn't act like a child/you'd stop acting like a child.
9 You're not listening to me. I wish you'd/you would listen to me.
10 I bought this jacket. I wish I hadn't bought this jacket.

B **Complete the second sentence so that it means the same as the first.**

1 You don't listen and that's why you make so many mistakes.
If only you listened, you wouldn't make so many mistakes.
2 I made that mistake and that's why I'm in this position.
If only I hadn't made that mistake I wouldn't be in this position.
3 I'm very unhappy that I have to get up early every morning.
If only I didn't have to get up early every morning!
4 I'm going to that conference next weekend, which I really don't want to do.
If only I wasn't going to that conference next weekend!
5 I can't find a job that I enjoy and I'd really like to.
If only I could find a job that I enjoy!

C **Complete the second sentence so that it means the same as the first, using *regret*.**

1 I wish I hadn't spent all that money.
I regret spending all that money.
2 One day you'll wish you'd studied.
One day you'll regret not studying.
3 Later, Georgia wished she hadn't said it.
Later, Georgia regretted saying it.
4 He wishes he hadn't treated her so badly.
He regrets treating her so badly.
5 We are sorry to say that the train has been cancelled.
We regret to say (that) the train has been cancelled.

→ Glossary p218

9.4 Size

A **Read the text about London and underline the correct word 1–20.**

LONDON

There is a 1 wide / high variety of things that visitors to London can do. There is a 2 big / large number of theatres, for example, where you can see performers of 3 great / large talent and skill. Some ticket prices are 4 high / big , especially for shows that are in 5 wide / great demand, but it is possible to see many shows at comparatively 6 small / low cost without 7 large / great difficulty.

Transport can be a 8 big / high problem and some people complain that the public transport system is of a 9 little / low standard. They feel that this is a subject of 10 great / wide importance and that it is a 11 high / big mistake to ignore it. They say that a 12 large / wide amount of money should be spent to improve the system and that this would make a 13 high / big difference to life in the city. Many cars go into the city every day but drivers experience 14 great / big frustration because the traffic moves so slowly and there are a relatively 15 little / small number of parking places.

However, these are 16 small / low problems of 17 little / large interest to most visitors. They enjoy going to the 18 wide / high range of shops in the centre, take 19 big / great pleasure in visiting the famous places and leave with a 20 large / high opinion of the city.

B **Fill in the gaps using one of the words below.**

high little low small large

1 He made a few ....small......... mistakes but no serious errors.

2 Everyone complains about paying income tax, especially if taxes are ....high.............. but even in places with comparatively ....low........... taxes.

3 I have ....little.............. sympathy with him – his problems are his own fault.

4 If you buy goods of such ....low........... quality, you can't expect them to last for long.

5 Life is hard for people on ....low........... incomes.

6 A test on an athlete showed a ....large.......... quantity of an illegal drug, so he was disqualified.

7 The workers are well paid, so the cost of production is ....high.............. .

8 All of our furniture is made to a very ....high........... standard.

→ Glossary p218

9.5 Word focus

Phrasal verbs: *give* & *let*

A Match the phrasal verbs in italics with the list of meanings A–D.

A stop trying B distribute C admit defeat D provide without charge

1 The teacher asked her to *give out* the books to the rest of the class. ....B........
2 They put her under so much pressure that she had to *give in*. ....C........
3 They're going to *give away* a calendar in next month's magazine. ....D........
4 He refused to *give up* until he had achieved his ambition. ....A........

B Complete these sentences with the correct particle below.

down off on out

1 She let .....out...... a loud cry of pain.
2 The judge let him .....off...... with a fine rather than sending him to prison.
3 Sara is very unreliable and keeps letting me ...down..... .
4 He never let .....on...... that he was planning to leave the country.

Word formation: noun suffixes

C Complete this text by forming nouns using the word in capitals at the end of each line and the suffixes below. You may need to make more than one change to the word given to form the correct noun.

-ance -ation -ee -ence -ion -ing -ise -ity -ment

Training manager – restaurant chain

This post involves 1 ......responsibility..... for staff training at our fast-food RESPONSIBLE
takeaway restaurants. We stress the 2 ....importance....... of training so that IMPORTANT
all our staff are able to demonstrate 3 ....expertise......... with the state-of- EXPERT
the-art 4 ....equipment..... we use and are also fully aware of what is EQUIP
required in their 5 ....dealings......... with customers. You will be involved in DEAL
the 6 ....preparation...... of a series of training courses for both managers PREPARE
and 7 ....employees........ and you will also be expected to provide advice and EMPLOY
8 ....guidance........ on a variety of staff issues. For this post, we have a GUIDE
9 ....preference........ for candidates with experience of the fast-food business PREFER
but our 10 ....selection......... procedure will take other relevant experience SELECT
into account.

→ Glossary p219

Collocations

D Fill the gaps in this text with the correct forms of the appropriate verbs below.

cause have make take

My Uncle Tony

My Uncle Tony is someone I really admire and he's quite a character! As a young man, he 1 ....had.......... lots of adventures and 2 ....made.......... journeys all over the world, long before it was common for people to travel much. He was never afraid to 3 ....take.......... risks and sometimes this attitude 4 ....caused.......... him problems. For example, he 5 ....took.......... part in what are now called 'adventure sports' before any of them were at all well-known. Needless to say, he 6 ....had.......... lots of accidents, including one time when he injured himself badly doing a bungee jump. He had to 7 ....have.......... several operations on his back after that, but he 8 ....made.......... a full recovery and carried on 9 ....taking.......... chances and doing dangerous things.

Uncle Tony is much older now but he still doesn't 10 ....take.......... life too seriously. He says that if he hadn't 11 ....made.......... the choice to enjoy life all the time, he could have 12 ....made.......... a fortune in business, but he doesn't care about that - he thinks that his approach to life has 13 ....had.......... a good result for him. He hasn't 14 ....made.......... much money in his life but he doesn't 15 ....have.......... a high opinion of people who care about money a lot. He thinks too many people 16 ....make.......... a fuss about things that don't really matter - if something goes wrong, he prefers to 17 ....make.......... jokes about it. Recently, I had to 18 ....make.......... a speech about Uncle Tony at a party to celebrate his 70th birthday. While I was preparing it, I 19 ....made.......... an interesting discovery about him. Apparently, he appeared in several well-known films when he was a young man, but he's never 20 ....made.......... any mention of that to me.

Word sets

E Complete each sentence with one of the words below.

united combined attached associated

1 Research has shown that pollution is ....associated.......... with various diseases.
2 This wire should be ....attached.......... to this plug.
3 She ....combined.......... her career with a very busy private life.
4 As a leader, he ....united.......... the whole country.

pointed indicated presented exhibited

1 Suddenly, she ....pointed.......... at someone on the other side of the road.
2 He ....indicated.......... that he wanted me to follow him.
3 It was important that I ....presented.......... myself well at the interview.
4 She ....exhibited.......... a complete lack of interest in what was happening.

pouring leaking flowing splashing

1 The children were ....splashing.......... each other with water.
2 Outside it was ....pouring.......... with rain.
3 The river was ....flowing.......... so quickly that it was hard to control the boat.
4 The roof was ....leaking.......... and water was coming into the kitchen.

ECCE Practice 9

Grammar

1 Debbie won't be able to understand the speakers __c__ there is an interpreter.
- a if
- b if only
- **c** unless
- d provided

2 Will you be home to let them in, just in case I __a__ late?
- **a** am
- b was
- c were
- d will be

3 John left without a word. If only he __a__ something.
- **a** had said
- b says
- c was saying
- d to say

4 I would have cooked something special if I __d__ you were coming.
- a knew
- b know
- c have known
- **d** had known

5 It has been raining for days now. I wish it __b__ soon.
- a will stop
- **b** would stop
- c stops
- d had stopped

6 Beth was very surprised to see us there. I wish I __d__ her face.
- a have seen
- b saw
- c would have seen
- **d** could have seen

7 If I __b__ to the store later, I'll get you some milk.
- a will go
- **b** go
- c went
- d was going

8 We'll be late for the lesson, __d__ we run.
- a even though
- b even
- c even without
- **d** even if

Vocabulary

9 I'm having __a__ difficulty understanding what he means.
- **a** great
- b broad
- c large
- d full

10 It wasn't me who stole the jewels. You've made a __a__ mistake.
- **a** big
- b large
- c great
- d high

11 Watch out! The ink from your pen is __c__ .
- a dripping
- b trickling
- **c** leaking
- d slipping

12 I wasn't impressed with the exhibition – most of the paintings were of a very __d__ standard.
- a little
- b small
- c narrow
- **d** low

13 I've given __c__ all my old books. We just didn't have enough space in the apartment.
- a out
- b in
- **c** away
- d up

14 I need you to give 100% effort out there – so don't __b__ me down.
- a put
- **b** let
- c sit
- d have

15 Ron __b__ a business trip to Italy with a visit to his uncle in Venice.
- a attached
- **b** combined
- c joined
- d united

16 'Don't __c__ at people – it's rude.'
- a show
- b indicate
- **c** point
- d aim

Exam techniques
→ p223

FCE Practice 9

Part 2

For Questions **1–15**, read the text below and think of the word which best fits each space. Use only **one** word in each space.

THE SCHOOLGIRL MODEL

A sixteen-year-old model who is determined to stay **(1)** .....at....... school against her father's advice has won a cosmetic modelling contract. Sarah Thomas, **(2)** ....who...... earned £6,500 a day last autumn during her school holidays modelling at shows in New York, has been chosen **(3)** .....as....... this year's model for Cover Girl, the international cosmetics firm. She beat thousands of other models to win the contract, worth **(4)** ....a....... great deal of money, and will fly to Miami and New York to film television commercials to **(5)** .....be....... screened worldwide.

She had refused to fly to New York earlier **(6)** .....to........ audition at the firm's request, saying that she thought she had absolutely **(7)** ......no...... chance of getting the job. 'I thought **(8)** ......it....... was going to be a wasted journey, so I was amazed when I got it. I still can't believe they chose me,' she said yesterday. 'I don't know at **(9)** ......this.... stage exactly **(10)** ....how..... much money I will be getting as it is still under negotiation, but I do know that it will be very lucrative.' **(11)** ...Instead.. of travelling to New York, Sarah was interviewed in London and a video of her performance was sent to New York.

Her father, Peter Thomas, who runs a motor repair business and petrol station, has urged her to leave school **(12)** ......so...... that she can take full advantage of her earning power. But she has refused to stop studying for her exams. She added: 'I should be able to fit most of the filming around my holidays, so hopefully I won't need to take too **(13)** ...much.... time off school. I am finding all this fuss a little embarrassing. All I really want to do **(14)** .....is....... get on with my schoolwork. Passing my exams is going to give me more satisfaction **(15)** ....than..... any modelling assignment.'

Unit 10 The passive

Grammar
10.1 The passive
10.2 *Have / get something done*
10.3 Received information

Vocabulary
10.4 Amount & number
10.5 Word focus

10.1 The passive

Stop & check

Look at these pairs of sentences. Tick (✓) the correct sentence in each pair.

1 A The idea is being considered by the committee at the moment. ✓
  B The idea is considered by the committee at the moment. ......
2 A The parcel should have been delivered last Friday. ✓
  B The parcel should be delivered a week ago. ......
3 A This job needs be done immediately. ......
  B This job needs to be done immediately. ✓
4 A The event is going to hold next month. ......
  B The event is going to be held next month. ✓

Active	Passive
present simple *They collect the rubbish every Monday.*	***am / is / are*** **+ past participle** *The rubbish is collected every Monday.*
present continuous *They are building a road.*	***am / is / are*** **+** ***being*** **+ past participle** *A road is being built.*
past simple *Someone stole the money.*	***was / were*** **+ past participle** *The money was stolen.*
past continuous *They were repairing the road.*	***was / were*** **+** ***being*** **+ past participle** *The road was being repaired.*
present perfect *Someone has changed the arrangements.*	***has / have*** **+** ***been*** **+ past participle** *The arrangements have been changed.*
past perfect *Someone had invited me.*	***had*** **+** ***been*** **+ past participle** *I had been invited.*
will *They will publish the book next year.*	***will*** **+** ***be*** **+ past participle** *The book will be published next year.*
going to *They are going to hold a meeting tomorrow.*	***going to*** **+** ***be*** **+ past participle** *A meeting is going to be held tomorrow.*
present modals *You can change the date of your journey.*	**modal +** ***be*** **+ past participle** *The date of your journey can be changed.*
past modals *You should have done this yesterday.*	**modal +** ***have been*** **+ past participle** *This should have been done yesterday.*
-ing *I don't remember anyone telling me this.*	***being*** **+ past participle** *I don't remember being told this.*

infinitive *He wanted people to like him.*	***to be* + past participle** *He wanted to be liked.*
perfect infinitive *Someone seems to have made a mistake.*	***to have been* + past participle** *A mistake seems to have been made.*

▶ note: Passive forms of the present perfect continuous, past perfect continuous, future continuous or continuous infinitives are not normally used.

Using the passive

- use the passive when the object of the verb is more important than the subject
- Look at these sentences:

> Charles Dickens wrote the novel 'Great Expectations'.
> The novel 'Great Expectations' was written by Charles Dickens.

In the first sentence, Charles Dickens, who is the subject of the verb *write*, is the main topic of the sentence. Therefore the verb *write* is in the active form.
In the second sentence, the novel '*Great Expectations*', which is the object of the verb *write*, is the main topic. Therefore the verb *write* is in the passive form.

- the passive is often used in formal or fairly formal contexts, for example, in media reports, public information material (rules, brochures, signs, etc.), formal letters, factual reports, etc.
- the agent in a passive pattern is the person or thing that did the action. For example, in the sentence *The novel 'Great Expectations' was written by Charles Dickens,* Charles Dickens is the agent. If the verb was active, the agent would be the subject.
- use *by* after the passive verb and before the agent
- use the agent if it is essential to the meaning of the sentence or if it adds important or interesting information. The second sentence would have no real meaning without the agent. The sentence *The novel 'Great Expectations' was written in 1861 by Charles Dickens* makes perfect sense without the agent, but the agent adds important information.

Verbs with two objects

- there are several common verbs which can have two objects in the active form. These verbs are connected with the idea of 'doing something for somebody', for example *give / bring / buy / take / lend / send / show / sell*
- in the active, these verbs can be used with both a direct object (the thing that the subject gives, lends, etc.) and an indirect object (the person who 'receives' the direct object) in these two patterns:
  A friend gave / lent / bought me this book.
  A friend gave / lent / bought this book to / for me.

- in the passive, the direct object or the indirect object can be used as the subject of the sentence
  This book was given to me by a friend. OR
  I was given this book by a friend.

A **Complete this text by putting in the correct passive forms of the verbs in brackets.**

Rugby Union

Rugby is a team game that 1 ....has been played.......... (play) in Britain since the middle of the 19th century. According to legend, it 2 ....was invented.......... (invent) at Rugby School in England in 1823 by a boy who 3 ....was called.......... (call) William Webb Ellis. A game of football 4 ....was being played.......... (play) at the school when Webb Ellis suddenly picked up the ball and ran with it. This story might 5 ....have been made up.......... (make up) but it 6 ....is told.......... (tell) whenever the history of the game 7 ....is explained.......... (explain).

Towards the end of the 19th century, official rules for the game 8 ....were written.......... (write) and it began 9 ....to be played/being played.... (play) in more and more countries, such as France, Australia, New Zealand and South Africa. International matches and tours 10 ....have been organized.......... (organize) since the beginning of the 20th century and since 1987 a World Cup tournament 11 ....has been held.......... (hold). At present, more and more countries 12 ....are being added.......... (add) to the list of those that take part in the tournament. Television audiences for international matches are high and it is hoped that the game 13 .will be watched/is going to be watched. (watch) by even more people in the future.

Until 1995, Rugby Union was an amateur game but the top players said that they were in favour of 14 ....being paid.......... (pay) to play and that the sport should 15 ....be turned into.......... (turn into) a professional one. Despite various problems, this seems 16 ....to have been done.......... (do) successfully and the sport is growing in popularity, with spectator numbers rising in Britain and elsewhere.

In Rugby Union, there are 15 players in each team and different skills 17 ....are required.......... (require) in each position. People of all shapes and sizes 18 ....are attracted.......... (attract) to the game because some positions 19 ....are suited.......... (suit) to very big people while others can 20 ....be filled.......... (fill) by smaller people.

B **Complete the second sentence so that it means the same as the first.**

1 My parents lent me the money.
The money was lent to me by my parents...........

2 They gave her a special prize at the ceremony.
She was given a special prize at the ceremony...........

3 The company sent me these brochures.
I was sent these brochures by the company...........

4 My girlfriend bought me this watch.
This watch was bought for me by my girlfriend...........

5 The salesman showed me various kinds of hi-fi system.
I was shown various kinds of hi-fi system by the salesman.

6 A neighbour sold the car to her.
The car was sold to her by a neighbour...........

C **Rewrite this newspaper report, changing all the verbs from active to passive forms and including an agent where necessary.**

Agreement on New Football Stadium

The local authority announced yesterday it has agreed that the Earlsdon Rangers Football Club can build a new football stadium on the outskirts of the city. The club has done a great deal of research and has found a suitable site. It seems that the planners have solved problems concerning transport to and from the site – the plans are going to include a new railway station and special train service. They also had to consider environmental issues and the opinions of local residents, who say that they are not opposed to the club building the stadium. Builders will start work on the new stadium next year and they should complete it within 18 months. The club is planning a special match to celebrate the opening of the stadium and they will give details of this when they have finalized them.

Yesterday it 1 ....was announced by the local authority.... that it 2 ....has been agreed.... that a new stadium 3 ....can be built by Earlsdon Rangers Football Club.... on the outskirts of the city. A great deal of research 4 ....has been done by the club.... and a suitable site 5 ....has been found.... . Problems concerning transport to and from the site seem 6 ....to have been solved.... – a new railway station and train service 7 ....are going to be included.... in the plans. Environmental issues and the opinions of local residents also had to 8 ....be considered.... and the local residents say that they are not opposed to the stadium 9 ....being built.... . Work 10 ....will be started.... next year and it 11 ....should be completed.... within 18 months. A special match to celebrate the opening of the stadium 12 ....is being planned.... and details of this 13 ....will be given.... when they 14 ....have been finalized.... .

D **Complete the second sentence so that it means the same as the first, using passive forms.**

1 Police discovered that the thieves had stolen over £1 million from the bank.
It ....was discovered that thieves.... had stolen over £1 million from the bank.

2 John doesn't like other people telling him what to do at work.
John doesn't like ....being told what to do.... at work.

3 Someone should have dealt with this problem a long time ago.
This problem ....should have been dealt with.... a long time ago.

4 People felt that the government wasn't spending enough money on this issue.
It ....was felt that not enough money.... was being spent by the government on this issue.

5 I think that he could have written this letter more politely.
I think that this letter ....could have been written.... more politely.

6 Helen expects other people to praise her all the time.
Helen expects ....to be praised.... all the time.

7 Applicants must return this form by 21st March.
This form ....must be returned.... by 21st March.

8 Heavy traffic delayed him and that's why he was late.
He ....was delayed by heavy traffic.... and that's why he was late.

9 They had closed the road and the emergency services were treating the injured.
The road ....had been closed and.... the emergency services were treating the injured.

10 The judge is considering the case and he will give his decision tomorrow.
The case ....is being considered.... and the judge will give his decision tomorrow.

10.2 *Have / get something done*

Use	Example
***have / get* + object + past participle** this pattern is a mixture of active and passive; use *get* if the subject causes the action to be done. Both *have* and *get something done* can be used to express the following ideas:	
• when the subject of *have / get* does not do the action; someone else (usually someone who is paid to do it) does the action for the subject	*I'm going to have / get my hair cut tomorrow.* *I'm having / getting my car repaired at the moment.* *You should have / get your eyes tested.*
• to say that something unpleasant happened to the subject; more usual to use *have* in this pattern	*She had her bag stolen last week.* *He had his leg broken in the accident.*
• to say that the subject completes an action rather than leaving it in the middle or leaving it until later; more usual to use *get* in this pattern	*I must get this job done today.* *Let's get the house tidied and then we can go out.*

A Rewrite these sentences using the correct form of *have* and *get* and the correct form of the verb in brackets. In some answers, both *have* and *get* can be used; in others, only one of them is possible.

1 Workers collect our rubbish twice a week. (collect)
We have/get our rubbish collected twice a week.

2 If you finish all your work early, you can go home early. (finish)
If you get all your work finished early, you can go home early.

3 The airline changed my flight for me yesterday. (change)
I had/got my flight changed yesterday.

4 We will have to arrange for someone to replace that broken window. (replace)
We will have to have/get that broken window replaced.

5 An engineer repaired my computer a couple of weeks ago. (repair)
I had/got my computer repaired a couple of weeks ago.

6 A well-known designer made the dress for her. (make)
She had/got the dress made by a well-known designer.

7 A professional cleaner cleans their house for them. (clean)
They have/get their house cleaned by a professional cleaner.

8 A local hairdresser does her hair once a month. (do)
She has/gets her hair done by a local hairdresser once a month.

9 My passport will expire soon. (renew)
I'll have to have/get my passport renewed soon.

10 I solved the problem as quickly as I could. (solve)
I got the problem solved as quickly as I could.

11 Someone broke into his car last week. (break into)
He had his car broken into last week.

12 A national newspaper published his letter. (publish)
He had/got his letter published in a national newspaper.

13 A company is going to develop these photographs for me next week. (develop)
I'm going to have/get these photographs developed next week.

14 Let's do the washing-up now. (do)
Let's get the washing up done now.

10.3 Received information

Use *said / reported / believed / understood / thought / known*

- when talking about information that has been received, we often use these verbs in the passive form because it is not known who provided the information or because it is the information, and not the person who provided it, that is important
- these verbs can be used to report information in these patterns:

***It* + *be* + *said*, etc. (+ *that*) + subject + active verb**

It is said that this area gets crowded in the summer.
It was reported / understood that he was living in another country.
It is believed / known that he has resigned.
It is thought that she has been doing her job very badly.

Subject + *be* + *said*, etc. + appropriate form of infinitive with *to*

This area is said to get crowded in the summer.
He was reported / understood to be living in another country.
He is believed / known to have resigned.

→ ExA p171

Use subject + *be* + *supposed* + the appropriate form of the infinitive with *to*

- to talk about what people say about something or what you have heard about something
  It's supposed to be a good film. (= the critics, friends, etc. say that it is a good film)
  He's supposed to have been making a lot of money. (= people say he's been making a lot of money)

→ ExB p172

A Rewrite these sentences in two different ways, using the verb in brackets.

1 Some people say that this is a dangerous area. (said)
It is said that this is a dangerous area.
This area is said to be dangerous.

2 The company is certainly making a big profit. (known)
It is known that the company is making a big profit.
The company is known to be making a big profit.

3 Reporters say that she has resigned from her post as minister. (reported)
It is reported that she has resigned from her post as minister.
She is reported to have resigned from her post as minister.

4 The club has apparently been planning these changes for some time. (understood)
It is understood that the club has been planning these changes for some time.
The club is understood to have been planning these changes for some time.

5 The police know that the man is using a false name. (known)
It is known that the man is using a false name.
The man is known to be using a false name.

6 Reports suggest that he has been ill for some time. (believed)
It is believed that he has been ill for some time.
He is believed to have been ill for some time.

7 It seems likely that the suspects escaped in a stolen car. (thought)
It is thought that the suspects escaped in a stolen car.
The suspects are thought to have escaped in a stolen car.

8 Insiders say that she earns £10 million per film. (believed)
It is believed that she earns £10 million per film.
She is believed to earn £10 million per film.

9 Reporters say that an agreement has been reached. (**thought**)
It is thought that an agreement has been reached.
An agreement is thought to have been reached.

10 The newspapers say that the economy is getting better. (**reported**)
It is reported that the economy is getting better.
The economy is reported to be getting better.

11 Apparently, five people were injured in the accident. (**understood**)
It is understood that five people were injured in the accident.
Five people are understood to have been injured in the accident.

12 Insiders say that he is planning a comeback to the stage. (**said**)
It is said that he is planning a comeback to the stage.
He is said to be planning a comeback to the stage.

13 Some people think that she is one of the richest people in the world. (**thought**)
It is thought that she is one of the richest people in the world.
She is thought to be one of the richest people in the world.

14 People know that he has a very bad temper. (**known**)
It is known that he has a very bad temper.
He is known to have a very bad temper.

15 In court he was accused of committing several crimes. (**said**)
In court it was said that he had committed several crimes.
In court he was said to have committed several crimes.

B **Rewrite these sentences using *be supposed to*.**

1 I've heard that they're moving house soon.
They're supposed to be moving house soon.

2 People have told me that it was a fantastic party.
It's/was supposed to have been a fantastic party.

3 I've heard that they've been having money problems recently.
They're supposed to have been having money problems recently.

4 People say that it's a very interesting place.
It's supposed to be a very interesting place.

5 I've heard that James is an expert on this subject.
James is supposed to be an expert on this subject.

6 People say that it was the best game of the season.
It's supposed to have been the best game of the season.

7 I've been told that Alice is leaving the country next week.
Alice is supposed to be leaving the country next week.

8 People say that he committed some terrible crimes.
He is supposed to have committed some terrible crimes.

➔ Glossary p219

10.4 Amount & number

A **Complete the second sentence so that it means the same as the first, using the word given.**

1 I've done quite a lot of work today. (**fair**)
I've done ......a fair amount of work...... today.

2 Unfortunately, most people at the meeting disagreed with me. (**majority**)
Unfortunately, ...the majority of people...... at the meeting disagreed with me.

3 She doesn't have many friends in this town. (**large**)
She doesn't have ......a large number of friends...... in this town.

4 I can't pay more than €100. (**maximum**)
I can pay ......a maximum of...... €100.

5 Your mistake caused me a lot of trouble, you know. (**deal**)
Your mistake caused me ......a great deal of trouble...... , you know.

6 There was a lot of traffic on the roads. (**large**)
There was ......a large amount of traffic...... on the roads.

7 Allow at least three weeks for delivery of the goods. (**minimum**)
Allow ......a minimum of three weeks...... for delivery of the goods.

8 Only a few fans cause violence at football matches, in my view. (**minority**)
Violence at football matches is caused by ......a minority of fans...... , in my view.

9 There were lots of complaints about the programme. (**great**)
There were ......a great many/a great deal of complaints...... about the programme.

10 Next, add a little water to the mixture. (**amount**)
Next, add ......a small amount of water...... to the mixture.

11 I have no interest in this subject. (**slightest**)
I haven't got ......the slightest interest...... in this subject.

12 It won't take you longer than three hours to get there. (**most**)
It will take you ......at most three hours/three hours at most...... to get there.

13 I cannot afford more than £20. (**maximum**)
£20 ......is the maximum (that)...... I can afford.

14 We worked quite hard last week. (**quite**)
We did ......quite a lot of work...... last week.

15 I won't be able to finish this in less than two hours. (**least**)
I will need ......at least two hours/two hours at least...... to finish this.

16 Not many buses run on Sundays here. (**number**)
Only ......a small number of buses...... run on Sundays here.

17 She had no difficulty in passing her driving test first time. (**least**)
She passed her driving test first time without ......the least difficulty...... .

18 Each customer must pay at least £5 in this restaurant. (**minimum**)
In this restaurant, ...the minimum (that)...... each customer must pay is £5.

→ Glossary p219–20

10.5 Word focus

Phrasal verbs: *look* & *pay*

A Complete the second sentence so that it means the same as the first, using the correct form of one of the phrasal verbs with *look* below.

look after look back on look down on look forward to look into look out for look up look up to

1 I'm excited about seeing them play live in concert next week.
I'm ......looking forward to...... seeing them play live in concert next week.
2 David has always respected his parents.
David has always ......looked up to...... his parents.
3 Police are currently investigating the matter.
Police are currently ......looking into...... the matter.
4 You should always take care of your books.
You should always ......look after...... your books.
5 You may need to find this word in a dictionary.
You may need to ......look up...... this word in a dictionary.
6 Try to find the market when you're in that part of the city.
......Look out for...... the market when you're in that part of the city.
7 When you think about this event in the future, you'll be glad it happened.
When you ......look back on...... this event in the future, you'll be glad it happened.
8 Teresa thinks she is superior to me.
Teresa ......looks down on...... me.

B Complete each sentence with one of the words below.

back off out

1 I lent him some money weeks ago but he still hasn't paid me ......back...... .
2 They took a risk but it paid ......off...... because they're now very successful.
3 I had to pay ......out...... a lot of money to get the car repaired.
4 I'm going to pay them ......back...... for treating me so badly!

Collocations

C Fill the gaps in these sentences with the correct forms of the appropriate verbs below.

come do keep take put

1 It's hard to ......keep...... track of all the changes that happen in this place.
2 The idea ......came...... to nothing because I couldn't afford to do it.
3 Could you ......do...... me a favour? I need a lift tonight.
4 He ......keeps/has kept...... a record of all the work he has done in a special file.

→ Glossary p220

5 I don't know whether we'll be able to ....put............ this theory into practice.
6 She has ....come............ to the conclusion that she's in the wrong job.
7 If you ....did............ a bit more exercise, you'd be be fitter.
8 You don't ....take............other people's feelings into account enough.

Word formation: prefixes & suffixes

D Complete this text by forming new words using the words in capitals at the end of each line and the prefixes / suffixes below. You may need to make more than one change to the word given to form the correct word.

prefixes: dis- in- mis- un-

suffixes: -able -action -ed -ing -ity -ment -y

Singer dismissed

The music business may be highly 1 ....unpredictable..... but for singer Lance Dean, his sacking from the group Topnotch was totally 2 ....unexpected.... . Fellow band members say, however, that it was 3 ....unavoidable.... and they refer to 4 ....dissatisfaction.... within the group which has been going on for some time. They say that Lance has shown an 5 ....inability.... to put the interests of the group before his own and describe as 6 ....unacceptable.... various recent incidents involving him. Lance is now facing 7 ....unemployment.... and considers himself extremely 8 ....unlucky.... . He says that the decision to sack him is 9 ....unbelievable.... and that he has always done his best for the group. He thinks that the whole situation is simply a 10 ....misunderstanding.. that can easily be resolved.

PREDICT
EXPECT
AVOID
SATISFY
ABLE
ACCEPT
EMPLOY
LUCK
BELIEVE
UNDERSTAND

Prepositional phrases with two prepositions

E Complete these sentences with the correct preposition below.

in of on to with

1 I have a lot ....in............ common ....with............ her, and that's why we're such good friends.
2 He did the work ....to............ the best ....of............ his ability.
3 I am writing this letter ....on............ behalf ....of............ the manager.
4 They're ....in............ competition ....with............ several other companies.
5 They're quite rich ....in............ comparison ....with............ my family.
6 I was ....in............ the middle ....of............ cooking the meal when they arrived.
7 She was ....on............ the way ....to............ school when she met him.
8 I spoke to her ....in............ the hope ....of............ getting her to change her mind.
9 I'm injured so someone else will have to play ....in............ place ....of............ me.
10 I am replying ....with............ regard ....to............ your recent enquiry.

ECCE Practice 10

Grammar

1 'Who wrote this poem?' 'It is said __b__ written by one of the Brontë sisters.'
- a to be
- **b** to have been
- c to being
- d to having been

2 'Do you know who composed Carmen?' 'I think it __c__ composed by Bizet.'
- a is
- b has been
- **c** was
- d was being

3 I'm surprised, she __b__ her husband to do the washing up.
- a has
- **b** got
- c made
- d had

4 'What happened to his face?' 'He __d__ his nose broken in a fight.'
- a have
- b has
- c made
- **d** had

5 'Where's your car?' 'It __c__ repaired at the moment.'
- a was being
- b has been
- **c** is being
- d is to be

6 'I don't know why you're doing that now. You know it __d__ finished yesterday.'
- a should be
- b should been
- c should have being
- **d** should have been

7 The marathon is __c__ to be a very physically demanding race.
- a knowing
- b know
- **c** known
- d knew

8 'When's the cinema closing?' 'Tomorrow, I think – it's __a__ knocked down next week.'
- **a** going to be
- b going to
- c having
- d having been

Vocabulary

9 'Were you chosen for the team?' 'No, I'm too small – the __b__ height required is six foot two.'
- a maximum
- **b** minimum
- c tallest
- d shortest

10 'How was the first night of the play?' 'Oh pretty good – there were a __c__ amount of people there.'
- a full
- b big
- **c** fair
- d great

11 My younger sister read the whole book without the __d__ difficulty.
- a most
- b minimum
- c large
- **d** least

12 It shouldn't cost more than $100 at the very __a__ .
- **a** most
- b greatest
- c largest
- d biggest

13 If you don't __a__ that bike, it won't last very long.
- **a** look after
- b look out for
- c look into
- d look over

14 I've borrowed the money from the bank, but I have to pay it __b__ by the end of the year.
- a out
- **b** back
- c up
- d down

15 Rex and Sabine had always planned to open a restaurant, but it __d__ to nothing.
- a got
- b went
- c resulted
- **d** came

16 John and Lisa have a lot in __c__ with each other.
- a regard
- b competition
- **c** common
- d similar

Exam techniques
→ p223

FCE Practice 10

Part 1

For Questions **1–15**, read the text below and decide which answer **A**, **B**, **C** or **D** best fits each space.

WAKE UP!

Do you **(1)** .B. yourself going into work later and later every day just to sleep a little longer? Do you **(2)** .A. asleep in the cinema, wake up and laugh at the wrong moments? Do you spend half the weekend asleep and love it? **(3)** .B. you're a sleepaholic.

Someone somewhere **(4)** .A. said that the average amount of sleep the average person wants is five minutes longer than they **(5)** .B. . Being a sleepaholic is about wanting five hours longer. But sleepaholics can find that their habit gets them **(6)** .D. deep trouble with colleagues and friends. Being late for work because of oversleeping is a pretty poor story if you're **(7)** .C. about a career. Friends can get **(8)** .C. offended if you leave them early to get some sleep.

Throughout history, ambitious people have often **(9)** .D. their enormous energy with a lack of need for sleep. It's easy to see how this can **(10)** .A. people a competitive advantage. So if you want to **(11)** .D. advantage of career opportunities, or if you've just been criticized once too often about sleeping **(12)** .B. the best bit of a party, what's the **(13)** .B. ? A psychiatrist studied sleep needs and over time he claimed to **(14)** .D. his own daily sleep from a standard eight hours to two, saying he experienced no bad reactions.

But if you really can't **(15)** .C. without sleep and don't want to lose your job, become so irreplaceable in it that you can be openly lazy, like the US President Calvin Coolidge, who slept for about 13 hours a day.

	A	B	C	D
1	realize	find	remark	occur
2	fall	go	become	drop
3	Just as	Then	In case	Such
4	once	ago	past	prior
5	win	get	last	keep
6	at	for	down	into
7	keen	fond	serious	eager
8	largely	fully	quite	plenty
9	joined	united	attached	linked
10	give	make	let	turn
11	have	come	hold	take
12	across	through	along	upon
13	resolution	cure	correction	repair
14	subtract	descend	sink	reduce
15	stand	deal	do	put

Unit 11

Relative clauses & participles

Grammar
11.1 Relative clauses
11.2 Participles

Vocabulary
11.3 Trying, succeeding & failing
11.4 Word focus

11.1 Relative clauses

Stop & check

Tick (✓) the correct sentences and correct the errors.

1 My parents don't like some of the music that I listen to. ✓..........................
2 I told him about something which ~~it~~ happened last week. ....which happened....
3 My colleague, who I told you about ~~him~~ recently, came with me. ....about recently....
4 Mike, whose sister lives in Rome, is going to Italy. ✓..........................
5 The club where we go ~~there~~ most often is in the city centre. ....go most....
6 He is the person that I spend most of my time with. ✓..........................

Use	Example
defining relative clauses	
• ***which*** or ***that*** to refer to things	
• ***who*** or ***that*** to refer to people	
• a defining relative clause is used because the sentence would not make sense without it. It gives essential information that identifies or specifies which person or thing is being talked about.	*The kind of music which/that my group plays is hard to describe.* (without the clause *which / that my group plays*, we do not know which music is being referred to and the sentence has no clear meaning)
• the relative pronoun *which*, *that* or *who* can be left out of the relative clause if the relative clause contains a second subject that is different from the subject of the whole sentence	*The kind of music (which / that) my group plays is hard to describe.* (the main subject of the sentence is *the kind of music* and a different subject, *my group*, is the subject of the relative clause and the verb *plays*)
non-defining relative clauses	
• ***which*** to refer to things	*My car, which I only bought two months ago, has broken down.*
• ***who*** to refer to people	
• a non-defining relative clause gives additional or interesting information about people or things. This information is not essential and the sentence has a clear meaning without the relative clause.	*My brother, who knows a lot about this sort of thing, told me what I should do.* (without the relative clauses the meaning of each sentence is clear, but the relative clauses give relevant information)
• usually put a comma both before and after a non-defining relative clause	
▶ note: The relative pronoun *which* or *who* cannot be left out of a non-defining relative clause.	
▶ note: Do not use *that* to refer to people or things in a non-defining relative clause.	NOT ~~*My brother, that knows a lot ...*~~
which **for facts, situations and actions**	
• *which* can be used to link a whole sentence describing a fact, situation or action with a comment on that fact, situation or action	*They lost the game, which disappointed their supporters.* (They lost the game is a full sentence; the relative clause refers to it and comments on it)

Use	Example
where • to refer to places in both defining and non-defining relative clauses • *where* cannot be left out	*In the part of the city where I live, nothing interesting ever happens.* (defining) *The hotel, where I had stayed previously, was excellent.* (non-defining)
when • to refer to times in both defining and non-defining relative clauses • it is possible to leave *when* out of a defining relative clause but do not leave it out of a non-defining relative clause	*This is the time of year (when) the tourists start to arrive.* (defining) *At this time of year, when the tourists have left, this place is lovely.* (non-defining)
***whose* + noun** • use as a possessive form in both defining and non-defining relative clauses	*She is a writer whose books I always like to read.* (= I like to read her books) (defining) *Rachel, whose address I don't know, lives somewhere outside the city centre.* (= I don't know her address) (non-defining)

▶ note: Do not use an object pronoun after a subject in a relative clause.
It is not correct to say ~~*My car, which I only bought it two months ago*~~ ...
It is not correct to use *it* here.

▶ note: Do not use a subject pronoun to refer for a second time to the subject at the beginning of a relative clause.
It is not correct to say ~~*Most of the people who they go to this club*~~ ...
It is not correct to use *they* here.

▶ note: Do not use *there* after *where* in a relative clause.
It is not correct to say ~~*The hotel, where I had stayed there previously*~~ ...

A Complete this text by filling the gaps with one suitable word.

Steven Spielberg

Steven Spielberg is an American film director 1 ....whose......... films have been very successful. They include *Jaws,* 2 ....which.......... he made in 1975, and 3 ....which........... was about a shark 4 ....which/that....... attacked people on a beach. In 1982 he made *ET,* 5 ....which.......... is about a creature from space 6 ......which/that........ has been left on earth by mistake and 7 ....which/that....... is protected by three children until it can go back to its own planet. Spielberg was probably the most well-known film director in the world in the 1980s, 8 ....when........... he made a series of Indiana Jones films, 9 ....which............ were about an archaeologist 10 ....who/that.......... often got into dangerous situations. *Schindler's List,* 11 ....which........... won seven Oscars, came out in 1993 and was about a real German man 12 ....who/that......... saved the lives of Jews 13 ....who/that......... had been sent to work in his factory during World War II. Most of the films 14 ....which/that....... Spielberg has made have been enormously popular all over the world.

B **Complete this text by filling each gap with one suitable word. If it is not necessary to put a word into a gap, leave it blank (–).**

QUENTIN TARANTINO

Quentin Tarantino, 1 ....who............ was born in the US in 1963, is a film director, writer and actor, and the films 2 ......–/which/that...... he made in the 1990s caused a sensation. Many of the characters 3 ......–/which/that..... he put into his films were violent people and many of the scenes 4 ......–/which/that...... he included shocked audiences. At the time 5 ....–/when............ films such as *Reservoir Dogs* and *Pulp Fiction* came out, they attracted criticism from people 6 ....who/that.......... regarded them as too violent but they were also widely admired by people 7 ....who................ thought that they represented a new and exciting style of film-making. John Travolta, 8 ....who............... had been extremely famous in the 1970s for films such as *Saturday Night Fever* and *Grease*, starred in *Pulp Fiction* and the film was a huge success, 9 ....which........... was very good for his career. Tarantino, 10 ....who.............. has always been a controversial figure in the film world, also wrote *Natural Born Killers*, 11 ....which.......... was a very violent film about a young couple travelling around America, 12 ....where........... they commit several murders. In some places 13 ....where............ the authorities considered it too violent, the film was banned, 14 ....which.......... created a lot of publicity for it.

C **Some lines in this text contain an extra word which should not be there. Write this word in the appropriate space next to the question number. Some lines are correct. For these, put a tick (✓) in the appropriate space.**

~ *Alfred Hitchcock* ~

1 ....he..........	Alfred Hitchcock was an English film director who ~~he~~ was best known for the
2 ....✓..........	thrillers and horror films that he made during his long career. In the 1930s
3 ....they..........	he became very famous in Britain, where his most successful films ~~they~~ were
4 ....✓..........	*The Thirty-Nine Steps* and *The Lady Vanishes*, which were both based on
5 ....there..........	novels. In 1940, he moved to the US, where he had even more success ~~there~~.
6 ....it..........	Perhaps his best-known film is *Psycho*, which ~~it~~ is about a man who owns a
7 ....he..........	hotel and who ~~he~~ kills all his visiting guests. One scene in the film,
8 ....✓..........	which shows this man, whose name is Norman Bates, killing a woman in a
9 ....✓..........	shower, is considered to be one of the most frightening scenes that has ever
10 ....it..........	appeared in a film. *Psycho*, which he made ~~it~~ in 1963, is still regarded as
11 ....✓..........	one of the best films of its kind ever made. Other famous films which he
12 ....✓..........	directed include *North by Northwest*, which has a very famous scene in a field
13 ....✓..........	of crops, where the main character is being chased by people in an aeroplane
14 ....there..........	~~there~~, and *The Birds*, which is about people being attacked by large groups of birds.

D **Decide whether these sentences are correct or not. Correct those which are incorrect.**

1. Francis Ford Coppola, ~~that~~ made the Godfather films, is a very well-known director. ....who..........
2. The Godfather films are about a Mafia family ⋀ live and operate in the US. ....who/that..........
3. The Godfather films, which Coppola based on a novel by Mario Puzo, were a huge success. ....correct..........
4. The first two Godfather films, which Coppola made ~~them~~ in the 1970s, are considered classics. ....made in..........
5. The Godfather films, which ~~they~~ starred Al Pacino, follow the history of the fictional Corleone family. ....which starred..........
6. Coppola also made the film *Apocalypse Now*, ⋀ ~~that~~ was set in the Vietnam War. ....which..........
7. *Apocalypse Now* was filmed in the Philippines, where Coppola had a lot of problems. ....correct..........
8. *Apocalypse Now*, which cost more money than it was supposed to, was a big success. ....correct..........

11.2 Participles

Use	Example
the present participle *(doing / not doing)*	
• can be used instead of repeating a subject to talk about two things happening at the same time	*She stood there wondering what to do next.* (= and she was wondering …)
• can be used instead of *while / when* + subject + continuous verb to talk about one thing happening during the same period as another	*I began to feel ill getting off the plane.* (= while / when I was getting off …)
• can be used after *while / when* instead of subject + *be*	*I found this while looking through a magazine.* (= while I was looking …)
• the subject of a participle must always be the same as the subject of the main verb in a sentence	*Coming out of the house, I saw an accident.* (= I saw an accident when I was coming out of the house; *I* is the subject of both *coming* and *saw*. It is not correct to say *Coming out of the house, an accident happened* because *an accident* is not the subject of *coming*.)
the past participle *(done)*	
• can be used instead of *and* + subject + passive verb to give a first piece of information about someone or something, which is then followed by another piece of information	*Built in 1927, this is one of the finest cinemas in London.* (= this is one of the finest cinemas in London and it was built in 1927)
• can be used to give a reason instead of *because* + subject + passive verb	*Forced to save money, she stopped buying expensive clothes.* (= because she was forced to save …)
***get* + past participle**	
• use as a passive pattern instead of *be + past participle* to say that something unpleasant or undesirable happens to the subject	*She got injured in the accident.*
• also used in certain common phrases, such as these: *get married / get divorced / get dressed / get changed / get started*	*When are they getting married?* *I went into my room and got dressed quickly.* *There's a lot to do so let's get started.*

A **Decide whether these sentences are correct or not. Correct those which are incorrect.**

1 She ~~was~~ got married last month. ....She got ....
2 ~~Walking~~ down the street, the wind was blowing very hard. ....While/When I was walking........
3 Being made by hand, this furniture is quite original. ....correct........
4 Feeling nervous, ~~his speech began~~. ....he began his speech........
5 I usually watch TV while ~~I~~ doing the ironing. ....… while doing …........

B **Rewrite the sentences, using participles.**

1 I asked a lot of questions. I was trying to find out what had really happened.
I asked a lot of questions, trying to find out what really happened./Trying to find out what really happened, I asked a lot of questions.

2 We met. We were working in the same office.
We met (while) working in the same office together.

3 The Tate Modern is a huge art gallery in London. It was opened in 2000.
Opened in 2000, the Tate Modern is a huge art gallery in London.

4 This novel was written over 100 years ago. It is still relevant today.
Written over 100 years ago, this novel is still relevant today.

5 The storm damaged several buildings.
Several buildings got damaged in the storm.

6 I must change my clothes for the party.
I must get changed for the party.

7 The managers are running the company. They are making a lot of mistakes.
The managers running the company are making a lot of mistakes.

8 I was coming into the room. I realized that something was wrong.
(While/When) Coming into the room, I realized that something was wrong.

9 There's not much time left, so let's begin now.
There's not much time left so let's get started.

10 There is a big tourist attraction in London. It is known as The London Eye.
There is a big tourist attraction in London known as The London Eye.

→ Glossary p220

11.3 *Trying, succeeding & failing*

A Complete the second sentence so that it means the same as the first, using the word in brackets.

1 He tried unsuccessfully to persuade her to change her mind. (attempt)
He failed ......in his attempt...... to persuade her to change her mind.

2 After a while, we were able to repair the car. (succeeded)
After a while, ...we succeeded in repairing...... the car.

3 He finished all his work on time. (managed)
He ......managed to finish...... all his work on time.

4 She didn't try to help me at all. (effort)
She ......made no effort to help...... me at all.

5 She couldn't do everything that she was supposed to do. (failed)
She ......failed to do...... everything that she was supposed to do.

6 I have never done any acting in public before this. (attempt)
This is ......my first attempt to act/at acting...... in public.

7 I tried to repair it myself but I couldn't. (efforts)
My ......efforts to repair it myself...... were unsuccessful.

8 I stood between them, trying to stop them fighting. (attempted)
I stood between them ......and attempted to stop...... them fighting.

9 We put the cupboard in a different place to see what it looked like. (tried)
We ......tried putting the cupboard...... in a different place to see what it looked like.

10 The problem was impossible for me to solve. (effort)
I ......made an effort to solve...... the problem, but couldn't.

B Complete these book titles by choosing A, B or C.

1 How to ......C...... your ambitions at work
A succeed B manage **C** achieve

2 How to ......A...... your own expectations of yourself
A fulfil B succeed C manage

3 How to ......C...... without really trying
A achieve B fulfil **C** succeed

C Complete this review by forming a word from the word in capitals.

Hill makes a comeback

For many years, the director Alan Hill had a highly 1 ......successful...... career and it seemed that he could do no wrong. Then he tried 2 ......unsuccessfully...... to move into musicals, none of which were a 3 ......success...... . Now, several years later, it seems that these 4 ......failures...... are behind him, for his latest movie is a magnificent 5 ......achievement...... .

SUCCEED
SUCCEED
SUCCEED
FAIL
ACHIEVE

→ Glossary p220–21

11.4 Word focus

Phrasal verbs: various

A Complete each sentence with the correct form of one of the phrasal verbs below. The meaning of each phrasal verb is given in brackets.

back up call off clear up hang on hold up pull up see to stand for stick to throw away

1 Don't change your mind – ....stick to.......... what you've already agreed. (keep to a decision)
2 A car ....pulled up.......... outside and three men got out. (stopped)
3 There was only one assistant to ....see to.......... all the customers. (deal with)
4 You can recycle newspapers now instead of just ....throwing.......... them ....away.......... . (getting rid of as rubbish)
5 We'll have to ....call off.......... the meeting because nobody can attend. (cancel)
6 Could you ....hang on.......... for a moment – I'll be right back. (wait)
7 We were ....held up.......... on the journey by a problem with the train. (delayed)
8 I'll ....back.......... you ....up.......... if anyone says you're not telling the truth. (support)
9 The initials UN ....stand for.......... United Nations. (represent the words)
10 I must ....clear up.......... the kitchen, it's in a terrible mess. (tidy)

Word formation: various

B Read this film review and fill the gaps by forming a word from the word given in capitals at the end of each line.

Sounds In The Dark

Horror film fans will find this movie highly 1 ....enjoyable.......... . The plot centres on ENJOY
Harry, a man who seems perfectly normal and even rather 2 ....boring.......... most BORE
of the time but who turns into something truly 3 ....scary.......... whenever it rains, SCARE
and it rains a lot in this movie. The special effects are very 4 ....impressive.......... IMPRESS
and some scenes are very 5 ....frightening.......... , even for committed horror film fans. FRIGHTEN
The ending, in particular, will come as an enormous 6 ....shock.......... . I won't spoil SHOCKED
things by saying what happens but it certainly gave me a 7 ....fright.......... ! So, if FRIGHTEN
you're 8 ....enthusiastic.......... about horror films and you want to see something that is ENTHUSE
full of 9 ....surprises.......... , this could be the film for you. But beware! You'll come SURPRISED
out of the cinema totally 10 ....exhausted.......... after you've seen it! EXHAUST

→ Glossary p221

C Read this advertisement and fill the gaps by forming a word from the word given in capitals at the end of each line.

The Computer User's Friend

It's a common situation: much to your 1 ....annoyance....... , you can't work out how	ANNOY
to do something simple on your computer and after hours of 2 ....frustration........ ,	FRUSTRATE
you still can't do it. Your computer manual only causes more 3 ....confusion......... and	CONFUSE
you get the 4 ....impression....... that it was written for experts only. If all this sounds	IMPRESS
familiar, The Computer User's Friend will be of enormous 5 ....interest.......... to you.	INTERESTED
With its simple solutions to common problems and 6 ....attractive......... presentation, it	ATTRACT
will give you a lot more 7 ....confidence........ when using your computer and show you	CONFIDENT
how you can even get a lot of 8 ....pleasure.......... out of it. The Computer User's	PLEASE
Friend is already being used by many thousands of 9 ....satisfied.......... customers	SATISFY
and, as they will tell you, it takes the 10 ....worry........... out of using your computer.	WORRIED

Word sets

D The underlined words do not fit correctly in the sentences in which they appear. Put each one into the sentence in which it does fit correctly.

right valid proper precise

1 I didn't make a <u>right</u> speech, I just said a few words. ....proper............

2 She didn't want to cause a problem, she wanted to do the <u>precise</u> thing. ....right..............

3 Your card is no longer <u>proper</u>, it's out of date. ....valid..............

4 I know it's going to happen next year but I don't know the <u>valid</u> date. ....precise...........

fit suited convenient relevant

1 We can meet at any time that's <u>suited</u> for you. ....convenient........

2 The food was so badly cooked that it wasn't <u>relevant</u> to eat. ....fit..............

3 He's not really <u>fit</u> to this type of work. ....suited............

4 What you're saying isn't really <u>convenient</u> to the situation. ....relevant..........

set pack flock bunch

1 There was a <u>set</u> of sheep on the hillside. ....flock..............

2 He bought a <u>pack</u> of flowers and gave them to her when he arrived. ....bunch............

3 There's a <u>flock</u> of instructions on that piece of paper. ....set..............

4 She took out a <u>bunch</u> of cards and suggested that we play a game. ....pack............

ECCE Practice 11

Grammar

1 'Who's Winnie?' 'She's the girl __b__ father won millions of dollars in the lottery.'
 a who's
 b whose
 c in which her
 d to which her

2 You should stop seeing Susan. __c__ involved with her means trouble.
 a Living
 b Having lived
 c Getting
 d Having got

3 'Football's so boring?' 'No way – I think __a__ a good match is the best thing ever.'
 a watching
 b to watch
 c having watched
 d to have watched

4 The book, __b__ I only bought last week, is falling apart already.
 a what
 b which
 c who
 d that

5 I love the spring, __d__ the flowers all begin to appear.
 a where
 b that
 c what
 d when

6 You shouldn't borrow my clothes without __b__ .
 a ask
 b asking
 c to ask
 d you ask

7 'You know the man __c__ the roof left his ladder behind?' 'It's OK – he'll be back tomorrow.'
 a fixed
 b fix
 c fixing
 d who fixing

8 Dan always left the milk out of the fridge, __c__ really annoyed her.
 a that
 b what
 c which
 d where

Vocabulary

9 You can only drive if you've got a __b__ license.
 a right
 b valid
 c precise
 d correct

10 What you're saying isn't at all __d__ to what we're talking about.
 a relation
 b fit
 c suitable
 d relevant

11 What does D.C. __b__ in Washington D.C?
 a means
 b stand for
 c stand by
 d represents

12 Your room is in a mess! Do a bit of __b__ up, will you?
 a washing
 b clearing
 c fixing
 d sorting

13 It's Winnie's graduation tomorrow. She has finally __c__ her dreams.
 a managed
 b succeeded
 c fulfilled
 d obtained

14 Winning that prize was one of the greatest __d__ of my life.
 a efforts
 b attempts
 c manages
 d achievements

15 'Hurry up!' '__c__ a minute – I'm just coming.'
 a Hold up
 b Back up
 c Hang on
 d Hold off

16 Much to his __a__ , Dirk couldn't find the house in the dark.
 a annoyance
 b interest
 c enthusiasm
 d worry

Exam techniques
➔ p223

FCE Practice 11

Part 5

For Questions **1–10**, read the text below and use the word given in capitals at the end of each line to form a word that fits in the space in the same line.

BEING A PRIVATE DETECTIVE

Private detectives are employed by **(1)** ....lawyers.... , businesses and ordinary	**LAW**
members of the public. They need to have a detailed **(2)** ...knowledge.. of the	**KNOW**
law and be good at blending into a crowd without attracting **(3)** ...attention....	**ATTEND**
The hours are long and very **(4)** unpredictable – every day is different.	**PREDICT**
Ken Lodge runs his own detective **(5)** ....agency..... in London. He has been	**AGENT**
working as a private detective now for 30 years. 'We **(6)** ...generally.... take	**GENERAL**
on all sorts of work,' he explains. 'A client might ask us for **(7)** ....evidence...	**EVIDENT**
that someone is breaking the law or to find a **(8)** ...missing..... member	**MISS**
of their family. Some companies even ask us to check their **(9)** ....security.....	**SECURE**
by breaking into their offices.' But is the job as **(10)** ..glamorous... as it seems	**GLAMOUR**
on TV? 'You can spend 12 hours in a car, waiting for someone!'	

Unit 12

Comparison & degree

Grammar
12.1 Comparisons
12.2 *So, such & too*
12.3 *Enough*

Vocabulary
12.4 Degree
12.5 Word focus

12.1 Comparisons

Stop & check

Tick (✓) the correct sentences and correct the errors.

1 Felicity is a much better musician than I am. ✓
2 Your idea is a better one ~~that~~ mine. than
3 I find tennis much more interesting ~~as~~ football. than
4 The weather is getting ~~worser~~ all the time. worse
5 This book is not as good ~~than~~ his last one. as
6 She takes life less seriously than I do. ✓
7 She understood more quickly than I did. ✓
8 You haven't got as many problems as she has. ✓

Comparative adjectives

adjectives of one syllable • add *-er* • if the adjective ends with *-e*, add *-r* • if the adjective ends with a single vowel and a single consonant, double the consonant and add *-er* • if the adjective ends with *-ed*, use the pattern *more / less* + adjective	 *smaller, older* *nicer, larger* *bigger, hotter* *more tired, less worried*
better / worse / further • the comparative form of *good* is *better* • the comparative form of *bad* is *worse* • the comparative form of *far* is *further*	 *better weather* *worse luck* *travel further*
adjectives of two syllables • the pattern *more / less* + adjective is usually used • if the adjective ends with *-y*, use a comparative ending *-ier* or *less* + adjective • with certain adjectives, *-er* is usually added (instead of using *more* + adjective)	 *more common, less useful* *prettier, less happy* *cleverer, quieter, simpler*
adjectives of three or more syllables always use the pattern *more / less* + adjective	 *more interesting, less expensive*

Comparative adverbs

adverbs ending with *-ly* • use the pattern *more / less* + adverb • use *more / less* with often ▶ note: do not use this pattern with *early*; say *earlier*	 *work more quickly, drive less carefully* *visit more often* *get up earlier*
fast / hard / soon / early / late / near add *-er*	 *work harder, drive faster*
well / badly • the comparative form of *well* is *better* • the comparative form of *badly* is *worse*	 *play better* *play worse*

→ ExA p190

as ... as

Use these patterns to talk about two things or people that are equal or not equal in some way:

(not)* be + *as* + adjective + *as **(negative) verb + *as* + adverb + *as***	*He is / isn't as tall as his brother.* *I walked / didn't walk as quickly as I could.*
verb + *as much* + uncountable noun + *as* **verb + *as many* + plural noun + *as*** **verb + *as much / as many* + *as*** can be used when the noun is understood	*I need as much help as I can get.* *I haven't got as many books as you.* *I don't earn as much* (= money) *as you.* *I've got a lot of books but I haven't got as many* (= books) *as you.*
half / twice / three times*, etc. + *as* + adjective / adverb / *much / many* + *as	*This one is twice as expensive as that one.* *I earn half as much as him.*
... *as* + object	*You don't work as hard as me. / ... as hard as I do.*
... *as* + subject + *be* / auxiliary either of these patterns can be used at the end of a comparison of this kind	*They've got a smaller flat than us. / ... a smaller flat than we have.*

→ ExB p191

... than

Use these patterns to compare two things or people and to say that they are different in some way:

verb + comparative adjective + *than* **verb + comparative adjective + noun + *than***	*She's taller than me.* *This is a better film than his previous one.*
verb + *more* + uncountable / plural noun + *than* **verb + *less* + uncountable noun + *than*** **verb + *fewer* + plural noun + *than*** **verb + *more / less* + *than*** use this pattern when the noun is understood	*You've got more confidence than me.* *I've got less confidence than her.* *You've got fewer problems than I have.* *She earns more / less* (= money) *than me.*
verb + comparative adverb + *than* **... *than* + object ... / *than* + subject + auxiliary** either of these patterns can be used at the end of comparisons of this kind	*She works harder than me.* *I earn less than her. / ... less than she does.*

Superlative adjectives

→ ExC p191

adjectives of one syllable • add *-est* • if the adjective ends with *-e*, add *-st* • if the adjective ends with a single vowel and a single consonant, double the consonant and add *-est* • if the adjective ends *-ed*, use the pattern *most / least* + adjective	 *the smallest / oldest building* *the nicest meal* *the biggest book* *the most shocked person* *the least worried person*
best / worst the superlative form of *good* is *best* the superlative form of *bad* is *worst*	 *his best idea* *the worst player*
adjectives of two syllables • the pattern *most / least* + adjective is usually used • if the adjective ends with *-y*, use a superlative ending *-iest* or *least* + adjective • with certain adjectives, *-est* is usually added (instead of using *most* + adjective)	 *the most common name* *the least useful advice* *the prettiest baby* *the least happy person* *the cleverest boy* *the simplest story*
adjectives of three or more syllables always use the pattern *most / least* + adjective	 *the most interesting film*

Superlative adverbs

adverbs ending *-ly* use the pattern *most / least* + adverb	*the most carefully* *the least impressively*
fast / hard add *-est*	*work the hardest / fastest*
well / badly the superlative form of *well* is *the best*; the superlative form of *badly* is *the worst*	*perform the best / the worst*

→ ExD+E p192

A **Complete these sentences with the correct comparative form of the words in brackets.**

1 Let's talk about something ......less serious....... – this subject is depressing. (**serious**)
2 The experience left him ....sadder........... but ....wiser........... . (**sad; wise**)
3 He likes his new job because it's ......more varied...... than his previous one. (**varied**)
4 Mary's feeling much ....better........... now. (**good**)
5 He made the wrong decision and so the situation is now even ....worse........... . (**bad**)
6 The students are working ....harder........... than ever. (**hard**)
7 I think you should be .....more honest...... and say exactly what you think. (**honest**)
8 We did it because we couldn't think of anything ....better........... to do. (**good**)
9 Let's hope it's ....sunnier........... tomorrow – I want to go to the beach. (**sunny**)
10 The situation is .more complicated.. now and there isn't an easy solution. (**complicated**)
11 We don't work together any more so I see him ....less frequently..... than I used to. (**frequently**)
12 Don't drive any ....faster............. – there's a speed limit here. (**fast**)

B **Complete the second sentence so that it means the same as the first, using *as*.**

1 Tom is keener on football than I am.
I'm not as keen on football as Tom (is).

2 I've eaten more than you.
You haven't eaten as much as me/as I have.

3 Will is a better guitar player than me.
I can't play (the) guitar as well as Will (can)/(does).

4 They have won more games than the other teams.
The other teams haven't won as many games as them/as they have.

5 His first and second film were equally successful.
His second film was as successful as his first (film) (was).

6 You've got more confidence than I have.
I haven't got/don't have as much confidence as you (have).

7 John and his boss work equally hard.
John works as hard as his boss (does).

8 You've seen more films than I have.
I haven't seen as many films as you (have).

9 Helen's salary is double mine.
Helen earns twice as much (money) as me/as I do.

10 The factory used to make double the number of cars it now makes.
The factory now makes half as many cars as it used to.

C **Complete the second sentence so that it means the same as the first, using *than*.**

1 His previous CD wasn't as good as this one.
This CD is better than his previous one/CD (was).

2 You haven't got as much experience of this kind of thing as I have.
You've got less experience of this kind of thing than I have/than me.

3 My car didn't cost as much as yours.
Your car cost more than mine (did).

4 I don't learn things as quickly as you do.
You learn things more quickly than me/than I do.

5 My job isn't as interesting as yours.
You have a more interesting job than me/than I have.

6 I haven't got as much interest in politics as you have.
You've got more interest in politics than me/than I have.

7 She didn't react as enthusiastically as I did.
She reacted less enthusiastically than me/than I did.

8 Your life isn't as complicated as mine.
You lead a less complicated life than me/than I do.

9 I haven't got as many hobbies as you have.
You've got more hobbies than me/than I have.

10 I haven't been to as many countries as you have.
I've been to fewer countries than you (have).

D **Complete these sentences with the correct superlative form of the adjectives in brackets.**

1 April is often ......the wettest....... month of the year – it rains all the time then. (wet)
2 It's a very boring film; in fact it's ..the least exciting... film I've seen for ages. (exciting)
3 It was a wonderful day; in fact it was ......the happiest...... day of my life. (happy)
4 She's so famous that she's one of the most well-known. people in the whole country. (well-known)
5 Nobody likes him and he's ..the least popular... politician in the country. (popular)
6 Sometimes .....the cleverest..... ideas are also ......the simplest...... ones. (clever; simple)
7 I was really ill – it was ....the worst......... I've ever felt. (bad)
8 She sat there calmly – she was ..the least worried... person in the room. (worried)
9 As a company, we aim to provide ....the best.......... possible service. (good)
10 Jones is a very good player, in fact he's ....the most skilful.... player in the team. (skilful)

E **Complete the second sentence so that it means the same as the first, using superlative forms.**

1 I've seen more exciting films than this one.
This isn't the most exciting film I've ever seen.
2 I have never met a kinder person than Eric.
Eric is the kindest person I've ever met.
3 I've never had a less enjoyable journey than that one.
That was the least enjoyable journey I've ever had.
4 I've never met people who are more pleasant than them.
They are the most pleasant people I've ever met.
5 Nobody in my class is stranger than William.
William is the strangest person in my class.
6 He has never given a more impressive performance than that one.
That is the most impressive performance he has ever given.

12.2 *So, such & too*

so with all these patterns, ... *that* is used to talk about the effect or result	
***so* + adjective**	*She's so impatient (that) she can't wait for anything.*
***so* + adverb**	*He drove so fast (that) I was frightened.*
so much	*I've eaten so much (that) I can't eat any more.*
***so much* (+ adjective) + uncountable noun**	*We've done so much (hard) work today that we're exhausted.*
so many	*There were so many (that) I didn't know which one to choose.*
***so many* (+ adjective) + plural noun**	*You've made so many (careless) mistakes (that) you'll have to do it all again.*
such with all these patterns, ... *that* is used to talk about the effect or result	
***such a* + singular noun**	*The noise was such a nuisance (that) we had to leave.*
***such a* + adjective + singular noun**	*It was such a wonderful day (that) I'll never forget it.*
***such* (+ adjective) + uncountable noun**	*I felt such terrible embarrassment (that) I had to leave.*
***such* (+ adjective) + plural noun**	*They're such (total) idiots (that) everyone laughs at them.*
such a lot	*We did such a lot during the trip (that) we were very tired by the end of it.*
***such a lot of* (+ adjective) + uncountable noun**	*We've done such a lot of (hard) work today (that) we're exhausted.*
***such a lot of* (+ adjective) + plural noun**	*You've made such a lot of (careless) mistakes (that) you'll have to do it all again.*

Compare

so* and *such

- do not use *so* + adjective + noun.
  NOT ~~*They were so unpleasant people*~~ or ~~*It was so lovely countryside*~~.
  Instead, use *such*:
  They were such unpleasant people.
  It was such lovely countryside.

- do not use *a so* + adjective + noun or *so a* + adjective + noun.
  NOT ~~*It was a so terrible day*~~ or ~~*It was so a terrible day.*~~
  Instead, use *such*:
  It was such a terrible day.

- to talk about a large amount or number, both *so much / many* and *such a lot of* can be used with the same meaning
  so much (hard) work = such a lot of (hard) work
  so many (careless) mistakes = such a lot of (careless) mistakes

too use *too*, *too much* and *too many* for expressing the idea 'more than is suitable', 'more than is wanted' or 'more than enough'	
***too* + adjective**	*You've been working too hard.*
***too* + adverb**	*You take everything too seriously.*
too much	*Don't spend too much.*
***too much* (+ adjective) + uncountable noun**	*You eat too much unhealthy food.*
too many	*I like peas but don't give me too many.*
***too many* (+ adjective) + plural noun**	*He makes too many (stupid) mistakes.*
• + *for* somebody / something can be used after all the above patterns • an infinitive with *to* can be used after all the above patterns to talk about a result or effect, with the meaning that something is impossible	*The job is too hard for him.* *She spoke too quickly for me.* *It was too cold (for us) to go outside.* *She spoke too quickly for me to follow what she said.*
▶ note: Do not use *too* + adjective + noun.	NOT ~~*They are too young people to vote.*~~ Instead, say *They are too young to vote*: *too* can be followed by an adjective but not by an adjective and a noun.
▶ note: Do not use *too much* + adjective.	NOT ~~*He was too much rude.*~~ Instead, say *He was too rude*: *too much* can be followed by a noun but not by an adjective alone.

Compare

so, *such* and *too*

- these examples show how the same idea can be expressed in different ways
  She's so impatient that she can't wait for anything.
  She's such an impatient person that she can't wait for anything.
  She's too impatient to wait for anything.

A **Fill the gaps in this text with one of the words or phrases below.**

so　so much　so many　such　too　too many

The Beatles

The Beatles were 1 ....so.......... famous in the 1960s that millions of people throughout the world knew who they were. They had 2 ....such.......... enormous fame that they were among the most well-known people in the world. For one or two of them, this all happened 3 ....too.......... quickly for them to be able to cope with it, and they had personal problems. Many people say that The Beatles had 4 ....so much.......... influence on popular music that they changed it for ever. They wrote 5 ....so many.......... famous songs that most people would recognize at least one of them. Some people believe that they were 6 ....such.......... brilliant songwriters that nobody else has been as good as them. However, it was all 7 ....too.......... good to last for long. After a few years, they decided that their fans behaved 8 ....so.......... hysterically that they couldn't perform in public any more, because it was 9 ....too.......... dangerous for them to do so. There were 10 ....too many.......... problems for them to go on tour again.

The Beatles wrote 11 ....too many.......... memorable songs for people to forget them. They were 12 ....such.......... an important group that their songs are still played throughout the world today.

B **These sentences are all incorrect. Rewrite them correctly.**

1 I'm too very busy to get bored.
I'm too busy to get bored.

2 She had such much bad publicity, she stopped being popular.
She had so much bad publicity, she stopped being popular.

3 They're having much fun to want to leave now.
They're having too much fun to want to leave now.

4 He has a such strong opinions that nobody can make him change his mind.
He has such strong opinions that nobody can make him change his mind.

5 We eat too much sweet things – it's not good for our teeth.
We eat too many sweet things – it's not good for our teeth.

C **Complete the second sentence so that it means the same as the first, using the word given.**

1 This food is very good. I'm going to have some more.
such
This ...is such good food that... I'm going to have some more.

2 She spoke very quietly. Nobody could hear her.
so
She ...spoke so quietly that... nobody could hear her.

3 This film is very complicated. I can't follow it.
too
This film ...is too complicated for me... to follow.

4 He made a lot of mistakes. He lost the job.
so
He made ...so many mistakes that... he lost the job.

5 This is a very exciting city. I'd like to stay here longer.
such
This is ...such an exciting city that... I'd like to stay here longer.

6 I am very hungry. I could eat anything.
so
I am ...so hungry that I could... eat anything.

7 I was very tired last night. I didn't go out.
too
I ...was too tired to go... out last night.

8 She was very good at the job. She was promoted quickly.
so
She was ...so good at the job that... she was promoted quickly.

9 He's got a lot of money. He doesn't know what to do with it all.
so
He's got ...so much money that... he doesn't know what to do with it all.

10 She's got a lot of friends. She doesn't get lonely.

too

She's got too many friends to get lonely.

11 He was very rude. He offended everyone at the party.

so

He was so rude that he offended everyone at the party.

12 They're very nice people. I'd like to spend more time with them.

such

They're such nice people that I'd like to spend more time with them.

13 It happened very quickly. I couldn't react in time.

too

It happened too quickly for me to react in time.

14 This restaurant is very expensive. Most people can't afford it.

too

This restaurant is too expensive for most people to afford.

15 He bought lots of new clothes. He had no money left.

such

He bought such a lot of new clothes that he had no money left.

16 My car is in very bad condition. It won't last much longer.

such

My car is in such bad condition that it won't last much longer.

12.3 *Enough*

enough = as much / many as is required or suitable	
adjective + *enough*	*I won't win, I'm not lucky enough.*
***a / an* + adjective + *enough* + singular noun**	*This isn't a big enough bag.*
adverb + *enough*	*You didn't do it carefully enough.*
***enough* + plural noun**	*We haven't got enough potatoes.*
***enough* + uncountable noun**	*We haven't got enough rice.*
***enough of* + determiner + plural noun**	*She answered enough of the questions correctly.*
***enough of* + determiner + uncountable noun**	*We've spent enough of our time discussing this.*
***enough of* + determiner + singular noun**	*We've seen enough of this city.*
***enough of* + pronoun**	*The food was good but there wasn't enough of it.*
verb + *enough*	*I haven't improved because I haven't practised enough.*
enough • pronoun • + *for* somebody / something can be used after all the above patterns • use an infinitive with *to* after all the above patterns to talk about the result or effect	 *That's enough. Let's stop now.* *He isn't good enough for the team.* *This isn't a big enough bag for all my clothes.* *He isn't good enough to play in the team.* *This isn't a big enough bag for me to put all my clothes into it.*

→ ExA p197–8

***plenty of* + noun** determiner	 *She has plenty of friends.* *I don't play very well, although I do plenty of practice.*
▶ note: Do not use *it* / subject + *be* + *plenty of* ...	NOT ~~*The party was plenty of people*~~. Instead say *There were plenty of people at the party* OR *Plenty of people were at the party.*
plenty • pronoun • = enough or more than enough; a lot	 *I don't want any more to eat, thanks, I've had plenty.*

→ ExB p198

A Complete the second sentence so it means the same as the first, using the word in brackets and *enough*.

1. I can't vote yet because I'm too young. (**old**)
   I'm ......not old enough to vote...... yet.
2. I didn't say what I thought because I was too frightened. (**courage**)
   I didn't have ......enough courage to say...... what I thought.
3. She didn't understand me. I didn't explain very clearly. (**clearly**)
   I didn't explain ......clearly enough for her to...... understand me.
4. The hotel was fairly cheap. We could stay there for a few days. (**cheap**)
   The hotel ......was cheap enough for us...... to stay there for a few days.
5. There was quite a lot of food. Everyone would be able to eat well. (**food**)
   There was ......enough food for everyone...... to eat well.
6. He earns a reasonable amount of money. He can pay his bills. (**money**)
   He earns ......enough money to pay...... his bills.
7. She won't become a star. She doesn't have the necessary talent. (**talent**)
   She doesn't have ......enough talent to become...... a star.

8 He's quite young. He can start a new career. (**young**)

He's ....young enough to start........ a new career.

9 She's quite a good player. She should be in the national team. (**player**)

She's a ....a good enough player to be........ in the national team.

10 I can't do crosswords. I'm not that clever. (**clever**)

I'm not ....clever enough to do........ crosswords.

11 I answered many of the questions. I passed the test. (**questions**)

I answered ....enough (of the) questions to pass........ the test.

12 I know some of the grammar. I can speak the language quite well. (**grammar**)

I know ....enough (of the) grammar to speak........ the language quite well.

13 It's a big car. Five people can fit into it comfortably. (**car**)

It's ....a big enough car for........ five people to fit into it comfortably.

14 I heard some of their conversation. I found out what they were discussing. (**conversation**)

I heard ....enough of their conversation........ to find out what they were discussing.

15 I only saw a bit of the city. I didn't get to know it well. (**it**)

I saw a bit of the city but I didn't ....see enough (of it) to........ get to know it well.

16 She has a lot of qualifications. She can get a good job. (**qualifications**)

She has ....enough qualifications to get........ a good job.

17 It's not a very big stadium. It's not possible for all the fans to go to the game. (**stadium**)

It's ....not a big enough stadium........ for all the fans to go to the game.

18 I don't know him well. I have no opinion of him. (**him**)

I don't know ....enough about him to have........ an opinion of him.

19 I've done this journey many times. I can find the way without a map. (**times**)

I've done this journey ....enough times to (be able to) find........ the way without a map.

20 He answered many questions correctly. He passed with Grade B. (**questions**)

He answered ....enough (of the) questions correctly........ to pass with Grade B.

B Complete the second sentence so that it means the same as the first, using the word *plenty*.

1 Don't worry – we've got more than enough time to get to the airport.

Don't worry – ....we've got plenty of time to get........ to the airport.

2 When we arrived, there were a lot of seats still available.

When we arrived, ...there were plenty of seats........ still available.

3 Don't worry about money, I've brought more than enough with me.

Don't worry about money, ...I've brought plenty........ with me.

4 The shop was full of interesting souvenirs.

There ....were plenty of interesting souvenirs........ in the shop.

→ Glossary p221–22

12.4 Degree

A **Decide which word (A, B, C or D) best fits each space.**

Arrival in New York

Sam was feeling 1 ..B.. nervous as he left the airport. This was 2 ..C.. because the flight had not been good, but also because he had never been to New York before. He took a taxi into the city. It was 3 ..A.. a hot day and he looked in 4 ..D.. amazement at all the traffic. It was 5 ..A.. different from the small town he came from – there was 6 ..A.. more noise and 7 ..B.. more people and all the buildings were 8 ..A.. bigger.

He checked into his hotel and went to his room. It was 9 ..B.. small but it was 10 ..B.. comfortable. Before unpacking, he lay on the bed and after a while he started to feel 11 ..B.. better. Suddenly, there was an 12 ..B.. loud knock at the door. Sam was 13 ..D.. frightened and did not want to answer the door. 'Who's there?' he called out, nervously. 'My name's Robertson,' said a male voice. He sounded 14 ..C.. embarrassed. 'I sat next to you on the plane today. I'm afraid I accidentally took one of your bags with me. It's 15 ..D.. my fault.' Still feeling nervous Sam made his way towards the door.

1	A partly	**B** rather	C considerably	D far
2	A rather	B quite	**C** partly	D a bit
3	**A** quite	B fairly	C complete	D slightly
4	A far	B rather	C quite	**D** absolute
5	**A** rather	B total	C utter	D lot
6	**A** far	B absolutely	C totally	D quite
7	A absolutely	**B** a lot	C quite	D utterly
8	**A** considerably	B terribly	C utterly	D absolutely
9	A bit	**B** fairly	C partly	D considerably
10	A slightly	**B** reasonably	C utterly	D partly
11	A fairly	**B** slightly	C partly	D reasonably
12	A utterly	**B** extremely	C absolutely	D a lot
13	A much	B considerably	C a lot	**D** terribly
14	A partly	B bit	**C** slightly	D reasonably
15	A extremely	B quite	C far	**D** completely

→ Glossary p221–22

B **Complete the second sentence so that it means the same as the first, using the word given.**

1 I was extremely disappointed by the film.
terribly
The film was ....terribly disappointing.......... in my opinion.

2 I thought he was a slightly strange person when I first met him.
quite
I thought he was ....quite a strange person.......... when I first met him.

3 I was extremely annoyed and I couldn't be polite.
far
I was ....far too annoyed.......... to be polite.

4 I was expecting Venice to be slightly bigger.
little
Venice was ....a little smaller.......... than I was expecting.

5 The water was rather cold so I didn't go swimming.
bit
The water was ....a bit too cold.......... for me to go swimming.

6 It was much too expensive for me.
considerably
It ....was considerably more than.......... I could afford.

7 She was extremely unhappy and she couldn't smile.
much
She was ....much too unhappy.......... to smile.

8 The other students in her class aren't quite as intelligent as her.
bit
She is ....a bit more intelligent.......... than the other students in her class.

→ Glossary p222

12.5 Word focus

Phrasal verbs: various

A Complete each sentence with the correct form of one of the phrasal verbs below.

carry out check in count on hand in knock down live up to pick up show off wear out work out

1 I've worn these shoes for years and they're beginning to ......wear out...... .
2 You can always ......count on...... Paul to keep his promises.
3 A survey has been ......carried out...... to find out people's views on this subject.
4 I couldn't ......work out...... what he was trying to tell me.
5 We ......checked in...... at reception in the hotel and then we went to our rooms.
6 My teacher wasn't pleased when I ......handed...... my work ......in...... late.
7 Claudia is always ......showing off...... because she likes to be the centre of attention.
8 They've ......knocked down...... the old library and built a supermarket where it was.
9 I ......picked up...... how to cook from watching other people when I was younger.
10 Did London ......live up to...... your expectations of how exciting it would be?

Word formation: various

B Complete this newspaper article by forming words from the words given in capitals at the end of each line.

Happy At Work?

A survey this week reveals that a 1 ......surprising...... number of people are not SURPRISE
gaining enough 2 ......satisfaction...... from their work. More than a quarter of those SATISFY
interviewed said that 3 ......boredom...... was the biggest factor in why they disliked BORE
work, while 10% said their initial 4 ......enthusiasm...... for their jobs had quickly ENTHUSE
been replaced by a strong sense of 5 ......disappointment...... . Many people questioned DISAPPOINT
commented on how 6 ......tiring...... they found their jobs, with longer hours TIRE
and more and more pressure resulting in feelings of constant 7 ......anxiety...... . ANXIOUS
Experts have described the findings of this survey as 'very 8 ......worrying...... for WORRY
all employers'. However they also believe that the 9 ......solution...... could be fairly SOLVE
simple. Employers would see great 10 ......improvements...... if they valued their workers IMPROVE
more and created a relaxed and happy environment for people to work in.

→ Glossary p222

C Complete these sentences, which are all from newspaper articles and reviews, by forming a word from the word given in capitals.

1	*Chez Bert* is a ......delightful...... new restaurant in the city centre.	DELIGHT
2	Workers reacted with ......anger...... to the news of job losses.	ANGRY
3	Family and friends said that they were ......saddened...... by his death.	SAD
4	This scandal has caused great ...embarrassment... to the government.	EMBARRASS
5	A report out this week shows that ......tiredness...... is the cause of a great many road accidents.	TIRED
6	Much to everybody's ......amazement...... , she came back to win the game.	AMAZE
7	These statistics are likely to ......please...... the education authorities.	PLEASED
8	Although ......amusing...... in parts, this book is unlikely to be a best seller.	AMUSE
9	The coach admitted that his tactics had been an ....embarrassing.... failure.	EMBARRASS
10	This is a ......fascinating...... and highly original new book.	FASCINATE
11	His speech caused great ......amusement...... among the audience.	AMUSE
12	This is just the place for a ......relaxing...... weekend break.	RELAX
13	If it's ......excitement...... that you want, this is just the place for you.	EXCITED
14	The report says that the economic outlook is not as ......depressing...... as some experts have been predicting.	DEPRESS
15	A spokesman said that she had cancelled the show because she was suffering from ......exhaustion...... .	EXHAUSTED
16	The terrible news was greeted with ......sadness...... throughout the country.	SAD
17	Nobody had been expecting this ......shocking...... new development.	SHOCK
18	Fans of her work may find this latest novel rather ......disappointing...... .	DISAPPOINT
19	......Relaxation...... is more important than sleep, according to a new survey.	RELAX
20	It was clear that .nervousness/nerves. affected the performance of both players.	NERVOUS

Prepositional phrases : various

D Fill the gap in each sentence using one of the prepositions below.

at by in of on to

1 According ......to...... an article I read, this is a big problem.
2 ......To...... my amazement, I actually won the game.
3 She does all her work ......at...... a very fast pace.
4 There was nothing ......at...... all that I could do about it.
5 How much sleep do you get ......on...... average?
6 Does this bag belong ......to...... you?
7 I went to the shops ......in...... search ......of...... a new coat.
8 All these goods are made ......by...... hand.
9 The weather wasn't very nice but ......at...... least it didn't rain.
10 ......In...... the light ......of...... what's just happened, I'll have to change my plans.

ECCE Practice 12

Grammar

1 'Do you like this sweater?' 'Yes, but it's __c__ expensive for me to buy.'
- a more
- b so
- **c** too
- d such

2 Since we moved house, I have to get up __d__ for school than before.
- a early
- b earliest
- c more early
- **d** earlier

3 'What happened at the meeting?' 'There was __c__ fuss about nothing really.'
- a so many
- b as much as
- **c** such a lot of
- d very much

4 This is __b__ composition I've ever read! It won't pass the exam.
- a worse
- **b** the worst
- c the worse
- d worst

5 Christina is a __a__ driver than I thought.
- **a** better
- b the best
- c very good
- d more good

6 'You look tired today.' 'The dog made __c__ much noise that I could hardly sleep.'
- a too
- b such
- **c** so
- d such a

7 I haven't got as many CDs __d__ you.
- a such
- b than
- c to
- **d** as

8 We had lots of people over to lunch yesterday, but there was __c__ food for everybody.
- a enough of
- b plenty
- **c** plenty of
- d too much

Vocabulary

9 'Are we going to the movies tonight?' 'Not today, I'm __a__ tired.'
- **a** rather
- b reasonably
- c partly
- d far

10 You really need some new tires for your car – those ones are __a__ .
- **a** worn out
- b burned down
- c worn off
- d put off

11 Sally's really __a__ – she makes everyone laugh all the time.
- **a** amusing
- b pleasure
- c amusement
- d pleases

12 Come on! Don't be such a __b__ – let's go out and have some fun!
- a bother
- **b** bore
- c dull
- d pester

13 The __a__ city was without electricity last night – it was chaotic.
- **a** entire
- b complete
- c total
- d impaired

14 'I'm not __d__ interested in old buildings, I'm afraid.'
- a considerably
- b a lot
- c reasonably
- **d** terribly

15 You can __c__ Rita to be late! She never gets anywhere on time.
- a depend
- b rely
- **c** count on
- d look to

16 Everybody was staring and laughing at her – she felt so __c__ .
- a excited
- b exhausted
- **c** embarrassed
- d amused

FCE Use of English Practice Test

PART 1

For Questions **1–15**, read the text below and decide which answer **A**, **B**, **C** or **D** best fits each space.

THE TOUR GUIDE

I'm a tour guide at the Tower of London, one of the city's principal tourist attractions. When you **(1)** .A. the public for your first guided tour, 'terrifying' is the word that springs to mind. I'm quite sociable, but having 300 or **(2)** .B. visitors in front of you is quite daunting.

Of course, visitors **(3)** .D. you to know the answers to every question. If someone asks you something **(4)** .C. which you don't know the answer, it's mighty embarrassing. You always get the history experts. They are the visitors who have **(5)** .B. an age at home or in a library researching a **(6)** .A. subject. When they visit the Tower, already knowing the answers, they will ask their question in the **(7)** .D. of catching us out. We don't try **(8)** .B. to know the answer; if we don't know, we **(9)** .A. it and ask a colleague.

The most irritating people are those who ask really stupid questions while their friends video our reactions. We get asked all **(10)** .C. of things, the most common being 'Where's the lavatory?' We have a book in which we **(11)** .C. the silliest questions we've been asked. Often, people just don't **(12)** .C. before they speak.

You always get the odd person who's in a bad **(13)** .A. and is determined to spoil your day. We just stand there and take it. We never **(14)** .B. our tempers, it's not what we're here for. We want visitors to **(15)** .D. a nice time and there's nothing better than when someone says, 'Great, it's been a wonderful day'.

1	**A** face	**B** cope	**C** bear	**D** oppose
2	**A** further	**B** so	**C** other	**D** even
3	**A** predict	**B** foresee	**C** suppose	**D** expect
4	**A** that	**B** of	**C** to	**D** such
5	**A** afforded	**B** spent	**C** concentrated	**D** lasted
6	**A** pet	**B** liked	**C** precious	**D** close
7	**A** wish	**B** desire	**C** aim	**D** hope
8	**A** lying	**B** pretending	**C** acting	**D** deceiving
9	**A** admit	**B** tolerate	**C** let	**D** cooperate
10	**A** forms	**B** orders	**C** sorts	**D** cases
11	**A** enrol	**B** commit	**C** enter	**D** compose
12	**A** judge	**B** attend	**C** think	**D** examine
13	**A** mood	**B** feeling	**C** emotion	**D** nature
14	**A** fail	**B** lose	**C** forget	**D** miss
15	**A** gain	**B** make	**C** take	**D** have

PART 2

For Questions **16–30**, read the text below and think of the word which best fits each space. Use only **one** word in each space.

A MUM'S OWN ADVENTURE STORY

What do you do if you can't find anything suitable **(16)** ......for...... your sons to read? Easy: publish something yourself. **(17)** ......At...... least, that was Christine Cubitt's response when she found herself searching **(18)** ...without... success for a magazine that would bridge the gap **(19)** ..between.. children's comics and football magazines. Two months ago, she realized her dream with the launch of *Boys 1st*, **(20)** ......a....... monthly mix of facts and fun for 8- to 13-year-olds. **(21)** ....It....... contains science, dinosaurs and cars, a comic strip and star interviews. 'The aim is **(22)** ......to...... entertain, inform and stimulate,' Christine explains. And it seems to **(23)** ......be...... catching on. Issue One has **(24)** ....been.... reprinted and the demand for the second edition has led to the number being printed increasing from 10,000 to 30,000. 'Interest from readers and shops proves that **(25)** ....there.... is a market for it,' she says.

Christine, 39, **(26)** .....was..... for nine years a full-time mum to her three sons. 'When my youngest went to school, I felt I wanted to go back to work,' she says. Which is exactly **(27)** ....what.... she did, as a secretary. But she felt restless: 'I realized I really wanted to work for myself.' Doing what, she wasn't sure, until she started to wonder **(28)** ....about.... the absence of what **(29)** .....she..... calls the 'right' material for her sons to read. 'I began to research the market **(30)** .....and..... found there was a gap that could be filled,' she says.

PART 3

For Questions **31–40**, complete the second sentence so that it has the same meaning as the first sentence, using the word given. **Do not change the word given.** You must use between **two** and **five** words, including the word given.

31 It's a pity I can't go to the game next Saturday.

wish

I ....wish I could go.................... to the game next Saturday.

32 Dave couldn't drive well enough to pass his driving test.

enough

Dave wasn't a ....good enough driver............ to pass his driving test.

33 In spite of losing his job, he remained cheerful.

even

He remained cheerful ....even though he (had) lost........ his job.

34 Do I have to fill in any forms?

necessary

Is ....it necessary for.................... me to fill in any forms?

35 This machine is so noisy that you can hear it in the street.

noise

This machine .....makes so much noise..... that you can hear it in the street.

36 I had difficulty understanding her accent.

found

I ....found it difficult to................ understand her accent.

37 I'll try to contact Christine when I go to Paris.

touch

I'll try to ....get in touch with............. Christine when I go to Paris.

38 Because the Managing Director was ill, he cancelled the meeting.

caused

The Managing Director's ..illness caused him to cancel.. the meeting.

39 I only found out the truth because I heard the two of them talking.

found

If I hadn't heard the two of them talking, I .wouldn't/would not have found out. the truth.

40 Two brothers started the business in the US in the 1950s.

set

The business ....was set up by............. two brothers in the US in the 1950s.

PART 4

For Questions **41–55**, read the text below and look carefully at each line. Some of the lines are correct and some have a word which should not be there. If a line is correct, put a tick (✓) in the space next to the number of the line. If a line has a word which should **not** be there, put that word in the space next to the number of the line.

SIGHTSEEING IN LONDON

41 ....✓.... Last weekend all of the students in my class went on a trip to London

42 ....of.... to do some ~~of~~ sightseeing. We left very early in the morning so that

43 .places. we would be able to see as much ~~places~~ as possible. After getting off

44 .which. the coach somewhere ~~which~~ in the centre, the first place that we visited

45 ....it.... ~~it~~ was Buckingham Palace. As everyone knows, that is the place where

46 ....in.... the Queen lives ~~in~~. Despite the fact that there were loads of tourists

47 ....✓.... taking photographs there, I enjoyed seeing this famous building. Next

48 ..one... we went to the Houses of Parliament, which is another ~~one~~ impressive

49 ....to.... place. Unfortunately, visitors couldn't go ~~to~~ inside that day. After that,

50 ....✓.... we saw Downing Street, where the Prime Minister's house is. Then we

51 ....at.... sat and had our lunch in a very nice park ~~at~~ nearby. Then it was time

52 ..and... to visit an art gallery called the Tate, ~~and~~ which had modern art in it.

53 ....✓.... When we came out of there, our coach was waiting to take us back. I

54 ....✓.... was tired by then because London is a rather noisy place. But I want

55 ...for.... to go back – there are lots of other famous places ~~for~~ to see there.

PART 5

For Questions **56–65**, read the text below. Use the word given in capitals at the end of each line to form a word that fits in the space in the same line.

THE BRITISH AND QUEUING

'All things come to those who wait.' It's a **(56)** ...traditional... phrase that has	**TRADITION**
kept the British patiently in line for years. For **(57)** .generations.. , we've	**GENERATE**
been waiting our turn. This may sometimes have led to **(58)** .....anger......	**ANGRY**
abroad, when **(59)** ..foreigners... haven't always respected the rules of the	**FOREIGN**
orderly queue. But at home we have **(60)** ....secretly..... enjoyed our reputation.	**SECRET**
It's rather **(61)** .unfashionable.. , though, isn't it? Today's highly developed culture	**FASHION**
of **(62)** ....service..... to the public seems to have more in common with the	**SERVE**
American 'I want it and I want it now' philosophy. But our **(63)** ...patience....	**PATIENT**
seems to be growing. We may wait with less **(64)** ..politeness... than we used	**POLITE**
to – you only have to observe the **(65)** ...frustrated... shoppers in a	**FRUSTRATE**
supermarket queue. But wait we still do.	

Glossary

Unit 1

Frequency (p9)

invariably always or almost always *She invariably arrives late for class.*
time after time many times *I've told you time after time not to do that!*
time and (time) again too many times *You make the same mistake time and (time) again.*
over and over again repeatedly *He said the same thing over and over again.*
as a rule usually or habitually *As a rule we eat at 7.30pm.*
as often as not very frequently *The trains are cancelled as often as not on a Sunday.*
generally usually *We don't generally go out in the evening.*
most of the time usually *Most of the time we eat together.*
normally usually *I don't normally watch much TV.*
all the time very often *He criticizes me all the time.*
constantly all the time *She constantly changes her mind.*
continually all the time *They argue continually.*
frequently often *His car frequently breaks down.*
regularly often *Do you eat in restaurants regularly?*
periodically at intervals *It's usually quiet at work, but periodically it gets very busy.*
every so often occasionally *They don't travel much, but every so often they have a holiday abroad.*
from time to time sometimes *I'm not very interested in politics but I read about it from time to time.*
now and again sometimes *I go away for the weekend now and again.*
now and then occasionally *We invite our friends round for a barbecue now and then.*
occasionally at times *You can occasionally see rare birds around here.*
once in a while almost never but occasionally *He hardly ever reads books but once in a while he reads a novel.*
rarely almost never *I've rarely had much money.*
seldom almost never *Paul seldom writes letters to people.*
hardly ever almost never *He used to be a good friend but now I hardly ever see him.*
in a while in a moment *I'm just off to the shops – I'll be back in a while.*
usually normally *She usually goes to bed at 11pm.*

Word focus (p10–11)

Phrasal Verbs

be away go to another town, country *I'll be away for the week on a business trip.*
be on be shown - film, programme, etc *What time is the news on tonight?*
be out of sth not have any more of something *I'm out of biscuits so I can't offer you any.*
be over be finished *This programme will be over in ten minutes.*
be up be a problem *What's up? You look worried. / He looked worried. I think something's up.*
be up to s.o. be someone's choice or decision *I don't mind where we go tonight, it's up to you.*
do away with cause something to stop existing or being used *They should do away with these silly rules.*
do up repair and decorate a house, apartment, etc *They're currently doing up their new apartment.*
do with need (used with could, want or need) *I could do with something to eat.*
do without manage, despite not having something *There's no coffee left, so we'll have to do without it until the shops open.*

Word formation

Noun	Verb	Adjective
memory	–	memorable
person	–	personal
use	use	useful
history	–	historic = important in history historical = that really lived or happened
addition	add	additional
culture	–	cultural
–	miss	missing
marvel	marvel	marvellous
peace	–	peaceful
energy	–	energetic

Collocations

cause confusion create a situation of not understanding *All these different rules simply cause confusion.*
cause (s.o.) trouble create an unpleasant situation *He's always causing trouble at school.*
do work use your body or mind on a task *It's time you did some work.*
have a/the feeling sense sth *I have a feeling that he isn't telling the truth.*
have a relationship (with s.o) associate with s.o. *He has a good relationship with his employees.*
have sympathy with/for feel pity for / feel sorry for s.o. *have a great deal of sympathy with you.*
make an assumption believe sth is true without any proof *You're making assumptions without checking the facts.*
make a comment give an opinion;say sth *She made a rude comment about his clothes.*
make a contribution to sth do something that helps towards a result *Everyone makes a contribution to the company's success.*
make a decision decide, reach a conclusion *You'll have to make a decision soon.*
make an excuse give a false reason *I didn't want to go out with him so I made an excuse.*
make a mess create an untidy state *You've made a mess in this room - tidy it up.*
do something very badly *I made a mess of the dinner – everything was overcooked.*
make a mistake do sth wrong *I think you're making a terrible mistake.*
make a profit/a loss make or lose money *The company made a small profit/loss last year.*
make a statement give an account of facts / officially inform *The minister will make an official statement tomorrow.*
make a suggestion put forward an idea *Could I make a suggestion?*

make certain check sth is true or sth happens *Make certain that you sign the form at the bottom.*
take place happen (of an event) *When will the next meeting take place?*
take (sth) seriously believe that something is important *He takes games very seriously and always wants to win.*
take (the) time require a period of time *It will take some time to save up the money.* give your time for something *He took the time to make sure I was OK.*

Word sets

contain have inside *This book contains 12 units.*
consist of have as the parts of something *A football team consists of 11 players.*
involve have as a necessary or important part *Her job involves meeting a lot of people.*
include have as one of a number of parts *The price includes service and tax.*

particular one, and not others *Is there any particular film you'd like to see?*
single one and only one *The whole job was done by one single person.*
unique completely unlike any other *I had a unique opportunity to travel the world.*
individual being a separate one, not part of a group *Let's deal with each individual problem, one at a time.*

win be the person who is the most successful in a game, competition, etc *John won first prize in the competition.*
gain obtain or get more of something *I've been gaining weight recently.*
earn get money for work *She earned a fortune in that job.*
achieve succeed in getting something that is aimed for *He achieved a lot of success in his career.*

Unit 2

Periods of Time 2 (p25)

ages a very long time (informal) *I haven't seen George for/in ages.*
years a very long time *She's been working there for years.*
period a particular length of time *This has been a good period for the tourist industry.*
term a fixed or limited period of time *US presidents are in power for a four-year term.*
period of the academic year in Britain *The winter term ends on 21st December.*
stage a period of time in the development of sth *This kind of technology is still in the early stages. We don't know how things are going to turn out at this stage.*
era a period in history *The early 20th century was an exciting era for inventions.*
while a fairly long time *We had to wait for a while until a bus came.*
some time a fairly long time *It will be some time before I find out whether I got the job.*
(the) whole (time/day) a complete period of time *I spent the whole day sitting at home and watching TV.*
all the time constantly *He talks about himself all the time.*
forever for a period without end *You're having a terrible time but it won't last forever.*
long a long time *Will this take long? It wasn't long before I found out. I haven't been waiting for long.*
for the time being temporarily *We're just living here for the time being, until we find somewhere better.*
permanently for a long time that is not planned to end *I like it here so much, I've decided to stay permanently.*
in the long term/run for a period in the future *I think my decision is the best one in the long term.*
at a time a long way into the future *You might regret this decision in the long run.*
long-term lasting or having an effect for a long time *Consider the long-term damage this will do to your career.*
in the short term for a short period in the future *It's a good plan in the short term but you may have to change it soon.*
short-term lasting or having an effect for a short time *This is only a short-term solution.*
at short notice done only a short time before sth is planned to happen *The meeting was arranged at short notice, so a lot of people couldn't attend.*
in advance before sth that is planned is going to happen *If you buy tickets in advance, they're a bit cheaper.*
in good time a long enough time before sth is planned to happen *If you let me know in good time when you're coming, I'll cook you a meal.*
in time + infinitive with to not late *I set off late but I arrived in time to catch the plane.*
in time + infinitive for sth with enough time to do sth *I got to the hotel in time for dinner.*
note: Do not confuse *in time* with *on time. The bus arrived on time.*
in time = not late; before sth happens
on time = at exactly the arranged time

Word focus (p26–7)

Phrasal Verbs

bring about cause to happen *What brought about this situation? / The new law brought about a lot of changes.*
bring in introduce a new law or rule *New parking restrictions have been brought in.*
bring out to make available to be bought – a new product *They are going to bring out their new CD later.*
bring s.o. up care for a child, especially as a parent, often passive *The way you are brought up has a big influence on you in later life.*
take after be similar in a way to an older member of the family, especially parents *He takes after his father – he's always in a bad mood.*
take off remove clothes *It was quite warm so I took off my jacket.*
take over take control of *Another firm has taken over the company where I work.*
take to like immediately; feel comfortable with *A lot of children take to the water when they're very young.*
take up start a hobby or activity for pleasure *James has taken up photography and he's doing a course on it.*
take up occupy or use time or space *He doesn't have much of a social life - his job takes up all his time.*

Word Formation

Adjective	Verb	Noun
entertaining	entertain	entertainment
existing	exist	existence
popular	–	popularity
–	behave	behaviour
various	vary	variety
competitive	compete	competition/competitor
–	react	reaction
strange	–	stranger
public	publicise	publicity= in the media public=people
starring	star	stardom = fame star = famous person

Collocations

do damage to do sth bad to; cause sth to be in a less good condition *You have done a lot of damage to your reputation.*

have a problem -ing *I had a problem/problems understanding the instructions.*

have a reason for -ing *I have a very good reason for asking this question.*

make a/no reference to mention/not mention *He made no reference to our previous conversation.*

make sense to be possible to understand *This article makes no sense/doesn't make sense to me.*

take care of *I'll take care of all the arrangements.*

take notice of *She took no notice/didn't take any notice of my advice.*

lose your temper show that you are angry *I got very angry and lost my temper with him.*

Prepositional phrases

in fact really, and/but the truth is *I thought it would take two hours but in fact it only took one.*

in return as a reaction to sth done *I helped him and he bought me a present in return.*

in a state in the condition described *He was in an awful state when we found him.*

in writing in the form of a letter *Put your application in writing.*

in particular more than anything else; special *Is there anyone in particular you'd like me to invite?*

on sale available to be bought *This record is not on sale yet.*

on a trip travelling; on a journey *We went on a two-week trip to Africa.*

on the whole in general *There were some problems, but on the whole it was a successful project.*

on an occasion at a particular time when sth happens *We've met on several previous occasions.*

on fire burning *Part of the forest was on fire.*

Unit 3

Time adverbs and prepositions 3 (p40)

in + period of time in the specified amount of time from now *I'll see you in half an hour.* the length of time sth takes *The job will be finished in three days.*

in + possessive period + time in the specified amount of time from now *What will you be doing in five years' time?*

within + period of time inside a period of time but not after it ends *I'll be there within an hour.*
the latest time in the future when sth will/can happen *You must reply within seven days.*

by + point in time on or before that time but not later than it *I'll let you know the result by the end of the week.*
at that time but probably before it *He was a big success by the age of 21.*

by now now but probably before now *You should know how to do this by now.*

by then at that time in the past but probably before it *She rang him eventually but he'd gone home by then.*

next + day/week/month/year, etc the day/week/month/year etc after this one *Call me next Wednesday.*

last + day/week/month/year, etc the day/week/month/year, etc before this one *It happened last year.*

the following/the next + day/week/month/year, etc the day/week/month/year, etc after the one mentioned already or understood *I wrote to him and he replied the following/the next week.*

the previous + day/week/month/year, etc the day/week/month/year etc before the one already mentioned or understood *The same thing had happened the previous week.*

some time / one day at an unknown or unspecified time in the future *I'm sure I'll see you again some time / one day.*

in future / from now on starting now and continuing in the future *I'll try to do better in future / from now on.*

from then on starting at that point in time and continuing *From then on, life was never quite the same.*

from ... until/to ... to talk about the beginning and end of a period of time *I lived there from June until/to November.*

between ... and ... *I lived there between June and November.*

Word Focus (p41–2)

Phrasal verbs

come about be caused to happen *How did this situation come about?*

come across find by accident; find when not actually looking for *I came across this article in a magazine.*

come out become available (a new product) *Their new CD comes out next week.*

come up happen unexpectedly *I'm going to be late – something's come up.*

come up with produce an idea *I thought about the problem but I couldn't come up with a solution.*

go away go to another town, country, etc for more than one day *'Did you have a holiday this year?' 'Yes, I went away for two weeks in July.'*

go off sth stop liking sth *I was keen last week but I've gone off the idea now.*

go on happen *The whole situation is confusing – I don't know what's going on.*

go out leave home/office etc for a short time *'Did you go out last night?' 'Yes, I met some friends at a club.'*

go through experience a bad period, suffer *Considering the terrible things she's been through, she's very cheerful.*

Collocations

do my/your, etc best try as hard as possible *He did his best but he didn't win the game.*

do well/badly *I think I did well in the interview.*

make progress improve; advance towards a better or finished state *She's been making progress since she started taking the course.*
make up your mind decide *When I've made up my mind, I'll let you know what my decision is.*
tell a story *A friend told me this story last week.*
put into words explain *She couldn't put her feelings into words.*
give an answer *I asked several questions but she didn't give me any answers.*
give pleasure to make s.o. happy *Sport gives pleasure to millions.*
come to an end finish *When the party came to an end, everyone went home.*
come as a surprise be unexpected *The result came as a surprise to everyone.*
keep a promise do sth that you said you would do *He kept his promise to buy her a new car.*
keep a secret not tell anyone else *I've got something to tell you, if you can keep a secret.*

Word formation

Noun	Verb	Adjective	Adverb
origin	originate	original	originally
joint	join	joint	jointly
music	–	musical	musically
fortune	–	fortunate	fortunately
truth	–	true	truly
care	care	careful	carefully
remark	remark	remarkable	remarkably
surprise	surprise	surprising	surprisingly
–	suit	suitable	suitably
hope	hope	hopeful	hopefully

Word sets

bit a small quantity of *Let me give you a bit of advice.*
part one, when there are others that make the whole thing *Part of the company is based in Italy.*
piece an amount of sth separated from the rest *He took a large piece of meat.*
share an amount when sth is divided between people *We all got our share of the profit.*
advantage gain from; use *You should take advantage of every opportunity you have.*
benefit the useful effect or result that sth has *Local people will get the benefit of the new arts centre.*
profit receiving more than it cost *He sold the car at a profit.*
reward sth given because s.o. has done sth good or worked hard *All the staff got a bonus as a reward for their hard work.*
aspect one part of a situation, problem or idea *We thought about the financial aspect of the proposal.*
case particular situation or example *This theory can't be applied in every case.*
matter issue, aspect; in this expression (matter of time) it means that sth will certainly happen but when it will happen is not certain *With your lifestyle, it's a matter of time before you damage your health.*
point the most important thing/part of the subject is *The point is that the mistake shouldn't have happened at all.*

Unit 4

Intention & purpose (p59–60)

intend (v) + infinitive with to have in your mind as a future action *What are you intending to do next? Did you intend to spend so much?*
be intended for + s.o./sth be produced, done, created etc for a particular type of person or thing *I'm sure this programme is intended for adults only.*
intention (n) + infinitive with to *Her intention is to become rich.*
have no intention of + -ing *I have no intention of agreeing.*
with the intention of + -ing *I stood up with the intention of leaving.*
intentional/unintentional *It was an intentional/unintentional criticism.*
intentionally/unintentionally *He hurt her intentionally/unintentionally.*
aim (v) + infinitive with to have as sth you want to achieve *He's aiming to become famous.*
aimed at + s.o./sth intended to be useful or attractive to s.o. *That advert is aimed at families.*
aim (n) + infinitive with to *My aim is to get promoted soon.*
aimless having nothing that you want to achieve in life *He's lazy and aimless.*
plan (v) + infinitive with to make a decision to do sth *I'm not planning to go out tonight.*
plan on + -ing plan and expect to do sth *Do you plan on getting married?*
plan + object + for + noun/time plan to do sth at a particular time or for a particular person *What are you planning for today? We're planning a party for him.*
plan (n) + infinitive with to *My plan is to buy a car soon.*
plan for + noun/time *I have no plans for the weekend.*
mean + infinitive with to do sth intentionally *I didn't mean to spend so much.*
be meant for + s.o./sth be aimed at s.o./sth *This leaflet is meant for tourists.*
deliberate intentional *a deliberate foul in a football match*
deliberately intentionally *injure s.o. deliberately*
on purpose intentionally *He charged me too much on purpose.*
accidental not intentional *There's been an accidental collision.*
accidentally *hit sth accidentally*
by accident not intentionally *Sorry, I broke this by accident.*
ambition + infinitive with to sth that you really want to achieve *My ambition is to be a great player.*
ambitious *an ambitious politician*
determined + infinitive with to having a strong intention to do sth *He's determined to succeed.*
determination + infinitive with to *They always play with great determination to win.*
goal (n) + infinitive with to ambition *It is my goal to be a millionaire.*
reach a goal *After years of hard work, he reached his goal.*
target a level, amount etc that you want to achieve *Her target is to learn 20 new words a week.*

Word focus (p61–2)

Phrasal verbs

break down stop working – machines *My car broke down on the motorway.*

break in/into enter a building by force to steal *Burglars broke in while we were away. / Thieves broke into the office.*
break out start happening - violence or disease *Fighting broke out at the demonstration.*
break up end a relationship, (also split up) *They've broken up and they're going to get divorced.*
fall apart break into pieces *The chair fell apart when I sat on it.*
fall for believe sth untrue and therefore be tricked *I fell for his story and gave him some money.*
fall out (with) stop being friends with s.o. because of a disagreement *We fell out (with each other) and I never see him now.*
fall over fall onto the ground *She fell over and hurt her leg.*
fall through fail to happen *My plans for the weekend fell through so I had nothing to do.*

Prepositional phrases

familiar with known to s.o. *I'm not familiar with this part of the city.*
proud of feeling pleased and satisfied about *She's proud of her work.*
aware of knowing that sth exists *I wasn't aware of the problem.*
high in of food - containing a lot of *These drinks are high in sugar.*
tired of not wishing to do any more; having become bored with *I'm tired of living here, I think I'll move.*
well-known for famous for *He's well-known for his generosity.*
committed to + *-ing* having promised to do and determined to do *He was committed to helping the poor.*
full of containing as much or as many as possible *The wardrobe was full of clothes.*
kind to s.o. pleasant, friendly and polite *People here have been very kind to me.*
equal to being the same amount as sth else *My income is now equal to his.*

Collocations

put pressure on try to force s.o. to do sth *Her boss is putting pressure on her at work.*
put a stop to force sth undesirable to stop *The authorities would like to put a stop to the use of cars in this area.*
give help *His family gave him a lot of help in his career.*
come first/second, etc. finish in first/second, etc. place *She won't come first in the race but she might come second or third.*
come to power become in political control *This government came to power three years ago.*
keep s.o. company be or go with s.o. so that they are not alone *I went with her to keep her company on the journey.*
keep an eye on watch s.o./sth so that they are safe *Could you keep an eye on my bags while I go to the shop?*
keep s.o. waiting force s.o. to wait *I'm sorry to keep you waiting - I'll be able to see you in about ten minutes.*
catch a cold become ill with a cold *Temperatures were freezing and I caught a bad cold.*
catch fire start to burn *Nobody knows how the building caught fire.*

Word formation

Base word	Verb
emphasis	emphasize
broad	broaden
able	enable
clear	clarify
understand	misunderstand
sure	ensure
simple	simplify
rise	arise (=appear)
advantage	disadvantage
courage	discouraged

Unit 5

Speech (p74–5)

accusation a statement saying that a person has done sth bad *This accusation has upset me a lot.*
make an accusation (against s.o.) *Make sure you're right before you make such serious accusations against her.*
with/without s.o.'s agreement (not) arranged with s.o. else *He borrowed the book without my agreement.*
reach/come to/make an agreement *We reached/came to/made an agreement not to discuss/that we wouldn't discuss it again.*
apologetic feeling or saying sorry for doing sth wrong *He was very apologetic and promised not to do it again.*
offer / make an apology (for + noun / *-ing*) tell s.o. you regret or are sorry for sth *My bank offered their apologies for the mistake.*
owe s.o. an apology need to say sorry to s.o. *You have been dishonest and you owe her an apology.*
have an argument (with s.o.) (about + noun/*-ing*) *I had an argument with her about politics.*
blame accuse s.o. of being responsible for sth *I didn't blame you for doing it.*
be to blame (for sth) be responsible for sth bad *They say she was to blame for the accident.*
get the blame (for + noun/*-ing*) be accused of doing sth bad *I didn't break the window but I got the blame.*
complaint a statement saying you are annoyed or not satisifed *She has to deal with complaints from customers in her job.*
make a complaint (to s.o.) (about + noun) *They made several complaints to the manager about the service.*
conversation a talk especially an informal one about everyday matters *I enjoyed our conversation.*
have a conversation (with s.o.) (about + noun) *I had a short conversation with her about the news.*
convincing causing or likely to cause s.o. to be convinced *He was a convincing liar.*
critical (of + noun) indicating the faults in sth *She was very critical of his behaviour.*
a criticism a remark that indicates the faults *I became tired of the constant criticisms.*
make a criticism (of + noun) *She made a criticism of my behaviour at the party.*
demand (for + noun) a very determined request *The company tries to respond to customers' demands for better service.*
denial (of + noun) a statement that sth is not true *I couldn't believe his denial of the accusation.*

discussion the process of talking about sth with s.o. *After our discussion I changed my decision.*
have a discussion (with s.o.) (about + noun) *I had a long discussion with her about the situation at work.*
encouragement the action of giving s.o. support *Without her parents' encouragement, she wouldn't have succeeded.*
give s.o. encouragement *My teachers gave me a lot of encouragement.*
encouraging *His results in the test were very encouraging.*
explanation the action of giving s.o. a reason for sth *I went to the manager and demanded an explanation.*
give (s.o.) an explanation (for + noun/-*ing*) *He gave (me) no explanation for his late arrival/for arriving late.*
insistent (that) (+ reported speech) not allowing refusal or opposition *He is insistent (that) he has done nothing wrong.*
insistence (on + -*ing*) / (that ...) *Her insistence on coming with me/that she come with me irritated me.*
persuasive able to convince *He is a very persuasive salesman*
persuasion *It took a lot of persuasion before she agreed.*
promise (n) a declaration that you will definitely do sth *I'll see you tomorrow and that's a promise.*
promise (v) say you'll definitely do sth *He promised to love her forever.*
make (s.o.) a promise (+ infinitive with to) / (that) + reported speech *She made a promise to pay him back. I made (her) a promise that I would lend her money.*
protest an expression of opposition *Despite my protests, she made me do the washing-up.*
make a protest *We made a protest about the size of the bill.*
refusal (+ infinitive with to) a statement that you will not do sth you have been asked or told to do *The shop's refusal to give me my money back annoyed me.*
threaten make a threat against s.o. *I don't like you threatening me like that.*
threat a statement that you will do sth bad to s.o. *My threats had no effect on him.*
make a threat (against so) *When I refused to leave, he started to make threats against me.*

Word focus (p76–7)

Phrasal verbs

run after run and try to catch *I ran after him but he was too fast for me.*
run into meet s.o. by chance *I ran into a friend of mine while I was shopping.*
run out (of) use all of sth, with the result that none is left *I've run out of money - could you lend me some?*
run over hit s.o. who is walking while driving a vehicle *A car ran him over when he ran into the road.*
catch on become popular *Mobile phones caught on in the 1990s.*
catch up (with) reach the same level as s.o./sth else *I couldn't go to lessons for a while and when I went back it took me some time to catch up with the others.*

Collocations

do s.o. good *It will do her good to get away for a while*
have difficulty (in) + -*ing* *I had difficulty (in) understanding the instructions.*
have an/no effect on *The weather has an effect on my mood.*
have trouble + -*ing* *I had trouble understanding the instructions.*
make contact with *I tried to make contact with him but he was away.*
make sure/certain *Make sure/certain (that) you sign the form at the bottom.*
make use of *Guests can make use of all the hotel's facilities.*
take advantage of *People take advantage of him because he's so generous.*
pay attention to *I wish you'd pay attention to what I'm saying.*

Word Formation

Noun	Verb	Person
editing	edit	editor
read	read	reader
politics	politicize	politician
law	–	lawyer
journal	–	journalist
creation	create	creator
music	–	musician
assistance	assist	assistant
instruction	instruct	instructor
participation	participate	participant

Word Sets

the cause of why sth happens *What's the cause of this disease?*
the reason why what causes sth *Could you tell me the reason why you're late?*
on the grounds that for the reason that *She was chosen on the grounds that she was the best candidate.*
the influence of the power that sth/s.o. has to cause sth *The influence of his friends is clear in the way he behaves.*
be required to do sth be expected to do sth; be forced to do sth because of rules *In my job, I am required to dress smartly.*
call for need; require *This problem calls for immediate action.*
demand sth need, in order to be done successfully *The work demanded all his concentration.*
insist on say forcefully that sth must happen or be done *She insisted on a full apology.*
maintain keep the same amount or level *I found it hard to maintain my interest.*
can't stand + -*ing* dislike very much doing *Tony can't stand working for that company.*
support agree with; be in favour of *Not many people supported my proposal.*
cope (with) be able to deal with successfully *She has so much work to do that she can't cope (with it).*

Unit 6

Like & dislike (p94–5)

keen + infinitive with to wanting to do sth very much *Joan was keen to impress her employers.*
keen on + object/-*ing* liking very much or very interested in sth *Alan is keen on photography. Sue is not very keen on working there.*

fond of + object/-*ing* liking very much and with strong emotion *I'm very fond of you.*
liking very much to do sth *Harry is fond of playing tricks on people.*
eager + infinitive with to wanting to do sth very much *Rachel is eager to succeed in her career.*
feel like + object/-*ing* want to do sth at a particular time *Do you feel like a game of chess this evening? I don't feel like working now.*
fancy + object/-*ing* want sth or to do sth *I don't fancy a meal at the moment. Do you fancy seeing that film?*
in the mood + for + object / + infinitive with to feeling that you would like sth or to do sth *I'm in the mood for some fun. She wasn't in the mood to dance.*
desperate + for + object / + infinitive with to wanting sth or to do sth very much *They are desperate for money. She is desperate to get another job.*
have a desire + for + object / + infinitive with to the feeling of wanting sth *I had a strong desire for some chocolate / to eat some chocolate.*
desirable being sth that s.o. would like *This isn't a very desirable situation.*
appeal to + object cause s.o. to like or be interested in *The idea of living in another country appeals to me.*
appealing causing s.o. to like or be interested in *I find the idea of living in another country appealing.*
appeal the quality of causing s.o. to like or be interested in *I can't understand what the appeal of this music is.*
attract s.o. to + object cause s.o. to like or want sth *The idea of living there doesn't attract me. They are keen to attract tourists to the place.*
attractive to s.o. causing s.o. to like or want *The idea of living there isn't very attractive to me.*
attraction sth people can go to visit for enjoyment/interest *The Parthenon is an important tourist attraction.*
attraction of + object/-*ing* the quality of causing s.o. to like or want *I can't see the attraction of living there.*
approve of + object like or agree with an idea or action *I don't approve of violence.*
approve of s.o. + -*ing* / of + object *I don't approve of anyone using violence.*
approval the act or feeling of liking or agreeing with an idea or action *He left school without his parents' approval.*
disapprove of (+ s.o.) + -*ing* dislike or disagree with an idea or action *She disapproves of me doing this.*
disapproval *He showed his disapproval by walking out of the room.*
dislike + object/-*ing* not like *I dislike him very much. I disliked living in that part of the city.*
dislike for + object the feeling of not liking *He showed his dislike for me by being rude to me.*
have a dislike for + object dislike sth *I have a strong dislike for that kind of music.*
detest + object/-*ing* dislike very much *I really detest that man. She detests working in that office.*
hatred of +object/-*ing* the feeling of hating *They are enemies and they have a strong hatred of each other.*
enjoyment of + object the feeling of enjoying sth *The audience's enjoyment of the play was obvious.*
get enjoyment out of / from + object feel enjoyment because of *She gets a lot of enjoyment out of / from her hobbies.*
enjoyable causing a feeling of enjoyment *It was a very enjoyable evening.*
pleasure enjoyment *There is not a lot of pleasure in his job.*
get pleasure out of / from + object enjoy *She gets a lot of pleasure out of / from her hobbies.*
fun enjoyment *The holiday was a lot of fun.*
have fun enjoy yourself *We had a lot of fun on holiday.*
have a good time enjoy yourself *I hope you have a good time on your holiday.*
object to sth/-*ing* say that you dislike or disagree with sth *Lots of people objected to the plan. I object to doing other people's work for them.*
objection to sth/-*ing* feeling of, statement of or reason for *What is your objection to the idea? There were many objections to building the new road there.*
have an/no objection to sth/-*ing* not dislike or disagree with *Do you have an objection to the plan? I have no objection to waiting a bit longer.*
oppose sth dislike or disagree with *Many people opposed the new law.*
be opposed to sth/-*ing* oppose *Many people were opposed to the new law. We are opposed to paying this tax.*
opposition to sth/-*ing* the feeling or action of opposing *There was a lot of opposition to the new law. There was a lot of opposition to paying the new tax.*

Word focus (p96–7)

Phrasal verbs

keep out of not get involved in *I kept out of their argument – it was nothing to do with me.*
keep to not change from *You've made a promise and you must keep to it.*
keep up with follow at the same speed as s.o./sth *He spoke so fast that I couldn't keep up with him.*
keep up maintain *I found it difficult to keep up my concentration.*
put away put sth into the place where it is kept *Don't leave your clothes on the floor, put them away.*
put s.o. off stop s.o. from concentrating *The noise outside put me off while I was working.*
put sth off delay doing sth until later *Could we put off our meeting until next week?*
put s.o. off sth cause s.o. not to want to do sth *That bad experience has put me off going there again.*
put on put clothes onto your body *I'd better put on a suit for the interview.*
put s.o. through to s.o. connect s.o. with s.o. on the phone *Could you put me through to the manager, please?*
put s.o. up give s.o. a place to sleep *Don't worry about getting home, we can put you up for the night.*
put up with tolerate *I'm not going to put up with your rudeness any more.*

Collocations

make an appointment *I'd like to make an appointment with the manager, please.*
make friends with s.o. become s.o.'s friend *I've made friends with several people on my course.*
take into consideration/account think about before making a decision or forming an opinion *Have you taken into consideration/account how much this is likely to cost you?*
pay a visit to *Pay a visit to the museum, it's really good.*
put emphasis on *At school, they put a lot of emphasis on discipline.*
reach a level *After a few years, her income reached a high level.*

change your mind change a decision *I've changed my mind - I'm not going to go to that concert next week.*
keep in touch with remain in contact with *I'll keep in touch with you while I'm away.*

Word formation

Adjective (positive)	Adjective (negtive)
aware	unaware
efficient	inefficient
correct	incorrect
honest	dishonest
legal	illegal
capable	incapable
polite	impolite
willing	unwilling
wise	unwise
fair	unfair

Prepositional phrases

adapt to change in order to deal with new circumstances *He had to adapt to the new way of working.*
apply to concern, relate, be true for *My criticism doesn't apply to you.*
concentrate on using all possible mental power for *He was concentrating on his work.*
congratulate s.o. on tell s.o. they have done very well or that you are very pleased for them *He congratulated her on her exam results.*
depend on vary according to *How much tax you pay depends on how much you earn.*
divide sth into separate to form different parts or groups *He divided the class into small groups.*
exchange sth for give sth back and receive a different one instead *I had to exchange the coat for a bigger one.*
limit sth to make sure that the number of sth is not greater than a fixed maximum *She had to limit her spending to £50 a week.*
receive sth with react to sth in a particular way *The public received the news with disbelief.*
treat s.o. to buy sth for s.o. as a special action *He was so pleased that he treated all his friends to a meal.*

Unit 7

Worth & no point (p122)

not worth to say that an action is a waste of time because it will not produce anything or will not produce the desired result
It is used in the following structures:
it + be + not worth + *-ing* *It's not worth applying for that job because I won't get it. It wasn't worth going there because I didn't enjoy myself.*
note: We can use *it* instead of the verb if the verb is understood. *I'm not going to apply for the job because it isn't worth it.* (= applying)
note: Do not end a sentence like this with *worth.* It is not correct to say ~~*I'm not going to apply for the job because it isn't worth*~~.
subject + be + not worth + *-ing* *This film isn't worth seeing, it's very boring. The course wasn't worth taking because I didn't learn much.*
note: We can use *it* to refer to an understood subject. *A friend of mine has seen that film and he says it's* (= the film is) *not worth seeing.*
worth can be used in a positive form with all the above patterns to say that sth is not a waste of time because it does or might produce a positive result *It's worth applying because I might get the job.*
The film is worth seeing because it's quite entertaining.
At that price I think it's worth the money.
The party went well so it was worth the effort.
You can form questions with all the above patterns:
Is it worth applying?
Is the film worth seeing?
Was it worth the money?
Was it worth the trouble?
there + be + no point + in + *-ing* to say that an action is a waste of time because it won't produce the desired result or change the situation *There's no point in asking her because she won't agree. There was no point in saying anything because nobody was listening.*
what's the point + in + -ing? to make an emphatic statement meaning 'there is no point' *What's the point in continuing? We're not making any progress.*
it + be + no use / pointless / useless / no good + *-ing* = it's not worth / there's no point *It's no use apologizing now, it's too late.*
It's pointless asking me again, I've already given you my answer.
It was useless talking to him, he couldn't help me.
It's no good shouting, I can't hear you.
there's no sense + in + *-ing* to say that an action is not a good idea because it may make the situation worse or produce a bad result *There's no sense in causing even more trouble.*
what's/where's the sense + in + *-ing*? to make an emphatic statement meaning 'there is no sense' *What's the sense in starting an argument?*
there's no harm + in + *-ing* to say that, although an action may not produce a good result, it certainly won't produce a bad result *There's no harm in asking her to lend you the money, I'm sure she won't get angry.*

Word focus (p123–4)

Phrasal verbs

get away with sth do sth bad and not be punished *They shouldn't get away with charging such high prices.*
get s.o. down make s.o. unhappy *This terrible weather gets me down.*
get on with sth make progress with/ concentrate on *I'm not going out tonight - I want to get on with some work.*
get on well with s.o. have a good relationship with *I get on well with the other people at work.*
get over recover from *It took her a long time to get over the shock.*
get sth over with do or finish sth unpleasant as quickly as possible *I just want to get this over with because it's really boring.*
get round to *-ing* find the time to do sth *I haven't got round to replying to their letter yet.*
get to arrive at/reach *I got to the office 20 minutes late.*
set about start doing a difficult task *The flat was a complete mess so I set about cleaning it.*
set off/out start a journey *I don't know why I'm late, I set off/out at the usual time.*
set out + infinitive intend from the beginning *She didn't set out to be famous, it just happened to her.*

set up start an organization, a company, etc *They're going to set up their own company.*

Collocations

tell apart be able to see the different between things/people *Jack and his brother look very similar and I can't tell them apart.*
tell the difference between *I can't tell the difference between these two makes of car.*
tell a lie *Don't trust him, he tells lies.*
tell the truth *If you tell the truth, everything will be fine.*
give advice *I'm not sure what to do – could you give me some advice?*
give a description of *He gave me a description of his office.*
give an explanation for *They gave no explanation for the delay to the train.*
give s.o. a hand help s.o. *Shall I give you a hand with those bags?*
give s.o. a fright/shock *A sudden loud noise gave me a fright.*
give a reason for *Has he given a reason for his strange behaviour?*

Word formation

Adjective	Verb	Noun
famous	–	fame
–	lend	loan
–	believe	belief
lost	lose	loss
–	choose	choice
nervous	–	nerve = courage
–	contain	contents
wealthy	–	wealth
proud	–	pride
–	prove	proof

Word sets

like similar to *His personality is like mine.*
similar to *Your opinions are similar to mine.*
the same as *Your course isn't the same as mine.*
alike very similar to each other *These two makes of car are alike.*
imagine create a mental picture of *I tried to imagine what the place would look like.*
think of bring into your mind *I couldn't think of any more ideas.*
bear in mind think about, remember or consider sth so that it has an influence on a decision, opinion, etc *If you bear in mind how young he is, he's doing very well.*
consider think about before acting, deciding, etc *Consider all the facts before you decide.*
at fault responsible for sth bad *Nobody was at fault, it was a complete accident.*
get the blame for be considered responsible for sth bad *I always get the blame for other people's mistakes.*
hold s.o. responsible for believe or say that s.o. is responsible for sth bad *I don't hold you responsible for this disaster.*
guilty of responsible for sth bad *He was guilty of cheating in the game.*

Unit 8

Chance & possibility (p149)

chance/possibilty to talk about whether you think sth will happen or not or whether you think sth is true or not
It is used in the following structures: note: *possibility* cannot be used in some of these patterns.
there's a chance/possibility of + object + *-ing*
There's a chance/possibility of them offering me the job.
there's a chance/possibility that + subject + verb, etc
There's a chance that they will offer me the job.
is there any chance/possibility of + object + *-ing*?
Is there any chance of them offering you the job?
is there any chance/possibility that + subject + verb, etc?
Is there any possibility that they could tell me today?
what are the chances of + object + *-ing*?
What are the chances of them offering you the job?
what are the chances that + subject + verb etc?
What are the chances that they will offer you the job?
no chance/possibility to say that sth will certainly not happen or is certainly not true *I've got no money so there's no chance/possibility of me buying a car.*
a slight chance/possibility to express a hopeful idea that, although sth is unlikely to happen or be true, it might happen or be true *There's a slight chance/possibility that I'll be able to buy a car soon.*
not much chance/possibility little chance/possibility to express a negative idea that sth is unlikely to happen or be true *There's not much/little chance/possibility of me being able to afford a car.*
a good chance/possibility to say that sth is likely to happen or be true *There's a good chance/possibility of you succeeding.*
the chances are that + subject + verb etc to say that sth is likely to happen or be true *The chances are that things will get better soon.*
have a chance of + *-ing* to talk about whether it is possible for the subject to do sth *I have a chance of getting that job.*
what are + possessive + chances of + *-ing*? to ask whether it is possible for the subject to do sth *What are your chances of getting the job?*
note: It is not correct to say *have the/a possibility to do sth.* To express the idea that s.o. is able to do sth because circumstances or someone else make it possible for them to do it, use *have a/the chance + infinitive with to* OR *have an/the opportunity to do / of doing.*
I haven't had a/the chance to read the paper today.
I have an/the opportunity to travel around Europe this summer. (NOT ~~*I have the possiblity to travel*~~ …)

Word focus (p150–1)

Phrasal verbs

turn s.o. away refuse to allow s.o. to enter somewhere *People without tickets will be turned away.*
turn down say 'no' to an offer *She turned down the job because the salary wasn't high enough.*
turn into become sth completely different *Since he became successful, he's turned into a very arrogant man.*
turn up arrive *They turned up half an hour late.*
turn up attend an event *About a hundred people turned up for the concert.*
make for go in the direction of *When we left the airport, we made for the city centre.*

make out pretend *He made out that he couldn't remember agreeing to pay me.*
make out understand/see/hear/read clearly (used with can/can't) *I can't make out why she left so suddenly. / I can't make out what that sign says. / I can't make out what you're saying. / I can't make out the signature on this letter.*
make up invent *She's always making up stories.*
make up for compensate for, balance *I'll have to do some extra work tomorrow to make up for not doing any today.*

Word formation

Base word	Adjective
comfort	comfortable
reason	reasonable
profession	professional
help	helpful
except	exceptional
count	countless
surround	surrounding
tradition	traditional
number	numerous
day	daily

Collocations

do s.o. harm be bad for s.o. *A bit of hard work wouldn't do you any harm.*
do research (into) *A lot of research has been done into that disease.*
have an/no influence on *His teachers had a big influence on his choice of career.*
make a/no difference to *Fame made a/no difference to his personality.*
make a/no mention of *He made no mention of our previous conversation.*
make s.o. an offer *I made them an offer but they didn't accept it.*
take advice *I'm glad that I took your advice.*
take part in *She didn't take part in the game, she just watched it.*
lose interest in *He seems to have lost interest in the idea.*
lose touch with *I've lost touch with him since we left school.*

Prepositional phrases

attitude to/towards way of thinking about *He has a terrible attitude to work.*
confidence in belief in the qualities of sth; feeling of certainty about *Team members need to have confidence in each other.*
demand for people wishing to buy sth *There was huge demand for tickets for the game.*
fear of being afraid of *Do you have a fear of heights?*
involvement in being involved in *When did your involvement in the sport begin?*
one in + number used for giving percentages or statistics *In that place, one in ten people is out of work.*
play a part in be involved in *I played a part in the organization of the event.*
recollection of memory of; ability to remember *I have no recollection of meeting you before.*
retirement from act of giving up work or an activity, especially because of age *His retirement from football came at the age of 38.*
revenge for act of doing sth bad to s.o. who has done sth bad to you *She wants revenge for the way she was treated.*
talent for special ability at sth *He's always had a talent for music.*
way of method or style *She has an unusual way of walking.*

Unit 9

Size (p161)

big: problem, mistake, difference
small: number, amount, quantity, problem, mistake
large: number, amount, quantity
great: talent, skill, demand, difficulty, importance,
little: talent, skill, demand, difficulty, importance, cost,
low: cost, standard, tax, quality, income, price, opinion
high: cost, standard, tax, quality, income, price, opinion
wide: variety, range

note: *great* and *little* can be used with any noun describing a feeling. For example, *frustration*, *pleasure*, *interest*, *sympathy*.

Word Focus (p162–3)

Phrasal verbs

give away give without charge, give free *I gave away a lot of my old clothes.*
give in agree as a result of pressure after at first disagreeing *Eventually I gave in and did what they wanted.*
give out distribute; give sth to a number of people *Someone was giving out leaflets at the entrance to the shop.*
give up stop trying to do sth; or stop a habit *She wanted to be a dancer but after several attempts she gave up trying.*
let s.o. down disappoint s.o. by failing to do sth you had agreed to do *She promised to help me but she let me down at the last moment.*
let s.o. off not punish s.o. for sth bad they have done *The teacher was in a good mood and let him off.*
let on tell s.o. sth that is secret *He wouldn't let on what his plans for the future were.*
let out make a loud noise through the mouth *The animal let out a roar.*

Word formation

Base word	Noun
responsible	responsibility
important	importance
expert	expertise
equip	equipment
deal	dealing
prepare	preparation
employ	employees
guide	guidance
prefer	preference
select	selection

Collocations

have an accident *Lots of people have accidents in the home.*
have an adventure *They had lots of exciting adventures during their trip.*
have an operation *She had a minor operation in the local hospital.*
have an opinion *I don't have any strong opinions on this subject.*
have a result *Your actions are unlikely to have a good result.*
make a choice *It's important that you make the right choice.*
make a discovery *Scientists have made an important discovery.*
make a fortune *They made a fortune and bought a huge house.*
make a fuss create an unnecessary problem or complication *Don't make such a fuss about such a silly little problem.*
make a joke *I made a joke but nobody was amused.*
make a journey *He has made several journeys overseas.*
make money *He works hard but he doesn't make much money.*
make a/no mention of *He made no mention of our previous conversation.*
make a recovery *She is going to make a full recovery from the illness.*
make a speech *I have to make a speech at the conference.*
take a risk/chance + -*ing* *You took a risk/chance investing all that money in a new company.*
take sth seriously *He takes games very seriously and always wants to win.*
take part in *She didn't take part in the game, she just watched it.*
cause s.o. a problem *I don't want to cause you any problems.*

Word sets

unite join people together so that they are in agreement *Local people united to fight the council's plans.*
combine with join things together; do more than one thing at the same time *During the trip, he combined business with tourism.*
attach to join one thing to another physically *We attached the rope to the tree.*
associate with connect one thing with another in the mind *In some countries, football is associated with violence.*
point at indicate sth with a finger in the direction of it *He pointed at a picture on the wall.*
indicate show or suggest sth in words or action *She indicated that she wanted to leave by standing up and putting her coat on.*
present appear in a particular way *The company decided to present a new image.*
exhibit show a particular feeling *He tried not to exhibit his anger.*
pour (with rain) rain heavily *It was pouring with rain when I went out.*
leak of liquid, to come through a hole that should not be there *Oil was leaking out of the pipe.*
flow of liquid, to move along *Water flows through the pipes and out of the taps.*
splash s.o. make s.o. wet by causing drops of liquid to fly onto them *His friends were splashing him in the swimming pool.*

Unit 10

Amount & number (p173)

a fair amount of + uncountable noun a fairly large amount of *Doctors earn a fair amount of money.*
quite a lot of + uncountable noun / plural noun a fairly large *Doctors earn quite a lot of money. They have had quite a lot of problems with their house.*
the majority of + uncountable noun / plural noun / singular noun = most of *You've eaten the majority of the bread. He thinks that the majority of jobs are boring. He ate the majority of his meal.*
a/the minority of + plural noun *Only a minority of young people commit crimes.*
a large number of + plural noun *She tends to make a large number of phone calls.*
a small number of + plural noun *I live in a village with a small number of shops.*
a large amount of + uncountable noun *They've done a large amount of damage.*
a small amount of + uncountable noun not much, a little *We try to save a small amount of money every month.*
a great many + plural noun a lot of *Mary's visited a great many countries.*
a great deal of + uncountable noun a lot of *I feel a great deal of anger about it.*
a maximum of + a number or amount no more than *Luggage can weigh a maximum of 40 kilos.*
the maximum the largest number or amount possible pronoun *What's the maximum you can afford?*
maximum (adjective) *Do you know what this car's maximum speed is?*
a minimum of + a number or amount not less than *The journey will take a minimum of 3 hours.*
the minimum the smallest amount or number possible *What's the minimum it will cost?*
minimum (adjective) *We'll do it with the minimum effort.*
the slightest (with negative verbs + uncountable noun) the smallest amount of *I didn't have the slightest difficulty finding it.*
the least (with negative verbs + uncountable noun) the smallest amount of *I haven't got the least interest in this subject.*
at least a minimum of *It will cost at least £50.*
at most a maximum of *It will take at most two hours to repair this.*

Word focus (p174–5)

Phrasal verbs

look after take care of *You should look after your health.*
look back on think about sth in the distant past *When she looks back on her childhood, she has good memories.*
look down on feel superior to *She looks down on people who are less intelligent than her.*
look forward to + -*ing* feel excited about or keen on the idea of sth in the future *I'm looking forward to going on holiday next month.*
look into investigate, find out details about *The manager said that he would look into my complaint.*
look out for be careful to notice; try to find *Look out for thieves if you're in that part of the city. She's looking out for a new job.*
look up look for information in a book *I looked up their address in my diary.*

look up to respect *He looks up to his older brother.*
pay back return money that was borrowed *If you lend me the money, I'll pay you back next week.*
pay s.o. back do sth bad to s.o. in return for sth bad they have done to you *He insulted me and I'll pay him back one day!*
pay off result in a benefit *His hard work paid off because he got promoted.*
pay out spend what you regard as a large sum of money *We had to pay out a fortune to get these tickets!*

Collocations

do exercise *You should do more exercise.*
do s.o. a favour do sth helpful to s.o. when you do not have to do it *Could you do me a favour? I need to borrow some money.*
take sth into consideration/account consider sth before making a decision or forming an opinion *Have you taken into consideration/account how much this is likely to cost you?*
put sth into practice actually do sth that was previously only an idea or a theory *It will be hard to put this idea into practice.*
come to the conclusion that decide after much thought *He's come to the conclusion that there's more to life than money.*
come to nothing fail to happen *Unfortunately, my holiday plans came to nothing.*
keep a record of *He kept a record of all the money he spent.*
keep track of keep up to date with, follow sth that changes or develops a lot *I can't keep track of all the developments in her life.*

Word formation

Base word	Adjective or noun
predict	predictable/unpredictable
expect	expected/unexpected
avoid	avoidable/unavoidable
satisfy	satisfaction/dissatisfaction
able	ability/inability
accept	acceptable/unacceptable
employ	employment/unemployment
luck	lucky/unlucky
believe	believable/unbelievable
understand	understanding/misunderstanding

Prepositional phrases

in common with having similar personalities, interests, opinions, etc *We get on well because I have a lot in common with him.*
in comparison with when compared to *In comparison with some people, you're quite rich.*
in competition with competing with *He was in competition with three other people for the job.*
in the hope of hoping to *I went back to the shop in the hope of getting my money back.*
in the middle of busy doing sth; in the act of doing *He was in the middle of doing his homework when the phone rang.*
in place of instead of; as a substitute for *My friend couldn't go so I went in place of him.*
on behalf of instead of s.o. and representing them *Parents have to sign this form on behalf of their children.*
on the way to travelling to *While I was on my way to the airport, I got stuck in traffic.*
to the best of + s.o.'s + ability/knowledge as far as my ability/knowledge goes *To the best of my knowledge, he's an honest person.*
with regard to on the subject of; concerning; regarding *I am writing with regard to my recent stay at your hotel.*

Unit 11

Trying, succeeding & failing (p183)

try + infinitive with *to* make an effort / attempt to do sth *I tried to talk to Judy but she wasn't there.*
try + *-ing* make an experiment / do sth to see what will happen *I tried talking to Judy but she couldn't help me.*
attempt + infinitive with to try to do sth but not necessarily succeed *He attempted to apologize but she ignored him.*
an attempt + infinitive with to / an attempt at + noun/*-ing* *This is my first attempt to cook/at cooking this.*
an effort + infinitive with to the use of mental or physical energy in order to do sth *My efforts to learn Spanish proved unsuccessful.*
make an/no attempt/effort + infinitive with to (not) try to do *They made an/no attempt/effort to be friendly.*
in an attempt/effort + infinitive with to *She ran as fast as she could in an attempt/effort to get there on time.*
succeed in + *-ing* do sth which you try to do *Eventually she succeeded in finding a job.*
success the achievement of a desired aim *He had great success in business.*
(un) successful (not) having success *My brother is now a successful lawyer. All her efforts to find a job were unsuccessful.*
(un) successfully *The doctors operated successfully. She has been trying unsuccessfully to find a job.*
manage + infinitive with to try to do and succeed *Eventually she managed to find a good job.*
achieve + noun succeed in doing sth after a long effort *It took him years to achieve any success.*
achievement sth which s.o. has succeeded in doing *List all your achievements on your CV.*
fulfil + noun achieve an aim, ambition, etc; do what is expected *Having fulfilled all his ambitions, he retired. He couldn't fulfil his family's expectations.*
fail + infinitive with to try but not succeed *I failed to finish all my work on time.*
failure *The film was a failure despite the publicity.*

Word focus (p184–5)

Phrasal Verbs

back up support s.o. in an argument, discussion, etc *Will you back me up in the meeting tomorrow?*
call off cancel *The game was called off because of the terrible weather.*
clear up tidy sth *It took ages to clear up after the party.*
hang on wait, usually for a short time *Could you hang on for a minute - I won't be long?*
hold up delay *I was held up in a traffic jam on my way there.*
pull up of a vehicle or driver slow down and stop *I pulled up at the traffic lights.*
see to deal with or try to arrange *If you get the food for the party, I'll see to the drinks.*

stand for of initials, letters, etc represent a certain word or phrase *BBC stands for the British Broadcasting Corporation.*
stick to not to change a decision, opinion, etc *I'll stick to my original choice.*
throw away/out remove sth unwanted so that it can be collected as rubbish *You should throw away/out those awful old clothes.*

Word Formation

Adjective (feeling)	Adjective (cause)	Verb	Noun
annoyed	annoying	annoy	annoyance
attracted	attractive	attract	attraction
bored	boring	bore	boredom
confident	–	–	confidence
confused	confusing	confuse	confusion
–	enjoyable	enjoy	enjoyment
enthusiastic	–	enthuse	enthusiasm
exhausted	exhausting	exhaust	exhaustion
frightened	frightening	frighten	fright
frustrated	frustrating	frustrate	frustration
impressed	impressive	impress	impression
interested	interesting	interest	interest
pleased	pleasing	please	pleasure
satisfied	satisfying	satisfy	satisfaction
scared	scary	scare	scare
shocked	shocking	shock	shock
surprised	surprising	surprise	surprise
worried	worrying	worry	worry

note: adjectives ending with *-ed* describe feelings that people have
I'm extremely tired. / I'm getting bored with this film. / We got excited during the game.
adjectives ending with *-ing* describe the causes of feelings
I've had a tiring day. / This is a boring film. / It was an exciting game.

Word sets

right correct morally *You were right to tell the truth.*
valid legally or officially acceptable *You'll need a valid passport.*
proper real, what is normally expected or understood *I've only had a snack, I haven't had a proper meal.*
precise exact, not approximate *I don't know what the precise cost will be.*
fit + infinitive with to of a good enough quality *The apartment wasn't fit to live in.*
suited to having the appropriate qualities for *They aren't suited to life in the city.*
convenient for at a good time or place for *Would 3 o'clock be convenient for you?*
relevant to connected with the subject *I have some information that's relevant to this matter.*
set a group of things that form one whole thing when together *I've got a complete set of the group's CDs.*
pack a complete set of playing cards *I've brought a pack of cards in case we get bored.*
flock a group of certain animals or birds *A flock of birds passed overhead.*
bunch a group of flowers or certain kinds of fruit, fastened together *He gave her a bunch of grapes when he visited her in hospital.*

Unit 12

Degree (p199–200)

Adverbs

fairly/quite/rather/reasonably + adjective/adverb = to some extent but not very; can be used for describing good, bad or neutral feelings, actions, facts and situations *The film was fairly exciting. I was quite upset. He's rather tall. He played reasonably well. They drove fairly quickly.*
note: *reasonably* is usually used for good feelings, actions, facts and situations. *It was a reasonably pleasant day.*
partly = to some extent but not completely *She left the country partly because she was unhappy there and partly because she was offered another job.*
slightly + adjective = to some extent but not very; often used with feelings *I'm slightly confused – could you explain again?*
extremely + adjective = to a very great extent; very, very *It was an extremely serious problem.*
terribly + adjective/adverb can be used to describe both good and bad feelings, actions, facts and situations *She's terribly worried. I'm terribly happy. He played terribly well.*
far / much / a lot / considerably + comparative = very much; to a very great extent *My idea was far better than hers. He's much older than her. He's got a lot more money than me. Their next flat was considerably larger.*
far / much / a lot / considerably + too + adjective/adverb = very much; to a very great extent; for emphasis *It's far too expensive for me. He spoke far too quickly. The meal was much too spicy for me. You're driving much too fast.*
note: The pattern far + too much/many can also be used. *I've got far too much work/too many things to do.*
rather / a little / a (little) bit / slightly + comparative = to some/a small extent but not very *She's rather more intelligent than him. She is a little older than me. I feel a (little) bit better today. This one is slightly cheaper.*
rather / a little / a (little) bit / slightly + too + adjective/adverb *He's rather too confident. She said it rather too rudely. The music was a little too loud for me. You're driving a little too fast. The film was a (little) bit too long in my opinion. I did it a (little) bit too carelessly. It's slightly too far to walk.*

Adjectives and adverbs

complete/total/absolute/utter
= as much as possible; can be used before a singular or plural noun *He is a complete idiot! The party was a total success. They're absolute fools! She's an utter genius.* can also be used before an uncountable noun *She does everything with complete confidence. He behaved with total stupidity. She reacted with absolute amazement. You're talking utter nonsense.*
completely/totally/absolutely/utterly = to an extent that is as great as possible; can be used before an adjective *The operation was completely successful. You're totally wrong. You're absolutely right! That's utterly ridiculous!* can be used before the verb, at the end of the sentence or between the auxiliary verb and the main verb *The plan failed completely. You've totally ruined my day. It absolutely confused me. The news thrilled me utterly.*
note: These adverbs are not used to express weak or neutral feelings or opinions, they are used with adjectives

that express strong feelings or opinions. For example, do not say ~~*It is absolutely nice*~~ or ~~*I was totally angry*~~. Instead, say *It was absolutely wonderful* or *I was totally furious*. With weaker adjectives, use *very*. *It was very nice. I was very angry.*

quite = completely; can be used before an adjective *You're quite right! Are you quite sure?* can be used before the verb or between the auxiliary verb and the main verb, but not after the verb *I quite agree with you. I don't quite agree with you.*

Word focus (p201–2)

Phrasal verbs

carry out sth do a task *They carried out an investigation into the problem.*

check in go to the desk to register when arriving at a hotel, airport, etc *You should check in two hours before your flight.*

count on rely on, depend on *She can always count on her friends when she has problems.*

hand in give a piece of work, a document, etc to a person in authority *All course work must be handed in on time.*

knock down destroy a building, often in order to build sth new *They knocked down the houses and built a new road there.*

live up to be as good as expected *Did the holiday live up to your expectations?*

pick up learn, usually by watching or listening rather than by having lessons *I picked up the language simply by living in the place.*

show off try to attract attention by behaving in a way that in fact annoys others *He was showing off about how much money he has.*

wear out become useless because of being used a lot or for a long time *These shoes shouldn't wear out for years.*

work out find or try to find a solution to sth *I couldn't work out what to do next.*

Word formation (see also Glossary 11)

Adjective (feeling)	Adjective (cause)	Verb	Noun
amazed	amazing	amaze	amazement
amused	amusing	amuse	amusement
angry	–	anger	anger
anxious	–	–	anxiety
delighted	delightful	delight	delight
depressed	depressing	depress	depression
disappointed	disappointing	disappoint	disappointment
embarrassed	embarrassing	embarrass	embarrassment
excited	exciting	excite	excitement
fascinated	fascinating	fascinate	fascination
nervous	–	–	nervousness
relaxed	relaxing	relax	relaxation
sad	sad	sadden	sadness
tired	tiring	tire	tiredness
Also:			
improved	improving	improve	improvement
–	–	solve	solution

Prepositional phrases

according to as said by s.o. or stated in sth *According to John, the game was fantastic.*

at all used for emphasis in a negative statement *I know nothing at all about this.*

at least used for saying that there is sth positive in a situation which is generally negative *We lost the game but at least we scored one goal.*

at a pace at a specified speed *She walked at a leisurely pace.*

belong to be owned by *That camera belongs to me.*

by hand not made by machine; made by people using their hands *These clothes were made by hand.*

in search of looking for *I went in search of a place to stay.*

in the light of as a result of; after learning about or considering *In the light of recent events, a change of plan is required.*

on average being the usual amount or level *He works 40 hours a week on average.*

to + noun describing feeling causing the feeling *To my surprise, she agreed.*

Exam techniques for FCE Paper 3

Part 1

- Read the title and the text quickly for a general understanding.
- Read the text more slowly stopping at each gap to choose an answer.
- Remember to look at the whole sentence where the gap appears.
- If you know the answer, try all the other options to make sure they don't fit.
- If you are unsure of the answer, try to eliminate three choices.
- Think about grammar as well as vocabulary. Some options may have the correct meaning but not be grammatically correct.
- If you are still not sure, make a sensible guess. Don't leave any questions unanswered.

Part 2

- Read the title and the text quickly for a general understanding.
- Read the text more slowly, one sentence (not line) at a time.
- Use the words before and after the gap to help you decide what kind of word is missing, e.g. article, auxiliary verb, preposition or pronoun.
- Complete any gaps you are confident about.
- Read the text again to complete the remaining gaps. The gaps that you have already completed may help you to find the answers this time.
- If you are still not sure, make a sensible guess. Don't leave any questions unanswered.
- Check your completed text by reading for overall sense.
- Remember you must spell the word correctly to get a mark.

Part 3

- Think carefully about the meaning of the first sentence and underline any key structures.
- Think carefully about the key word and how it should be used grammatically in the gapped sentence.
- Ask yourself if the key word needs a preposition, if you need to change the form of another word, or if the second sentence should be active or passive.
- Count the words in your answer. Remember that contractions, like *didn't*, count as two words, not one.
- Don't change the key word and don't leave out any information in the first sentence.
- If you are still not sure, make a sensible guess. Don't leave any questions unanswered. Each answer is worth two marks, so it's possible to get one mark, even if you don't get everything right.
- Read the new sentence again to make sure it means the same as the first one and to make sure your answer fits grammatically.

Part 4

- Read the title and the text quickly for a general understanding.
- Read the text more slowly, one sentence (not line) at a time.
- Look for possible extra words and underline them.
- Common extra words are auxiliary verbs, pronouns and prepositions after verbs to make them look like phrasal verbs.
- Reread the whole sentence without the possible word to check that it still makes sense.
- Check the possible extra word does not refer to something else in the sentence.
- Remember there is never more than one extra word in a line.
- There are usually about five correct lines.
- Read the whole text once more to check that it makes sense.

Part 5

- Read the title and the text quickly for a general understanding.
- Read the text more slowly, one sentence (not line) at a time to identify the parts of speech needed.
- Change the word into the word you need by adding a prefix or suffix, or by making some other change, e.g. adding an adjective ending (*-y*, *-able*, *-ing*, *-ed*).
- Some words may need to be turned into the negative form, plural form (with a change of spelling) or may need another word adding, e.g. *rain* + *drop* = *raindrop*.
- If you are still not sure, make a sensible guess. Don't leave any questions unanswered.
- Read the whole text once more to check that it makes sense.
- Remember you must spell the word correctly to get a mark.

OXFORD
UNIVERSITY PRESS
Great Clarendon Street, Oxford OX2 6DP
Oxford University Press is a department of the University of Oxford.
It furthers the University's objective of excellence in research, scholarship, and education by publishing worldwide in
Oxford New York
Auckland Bangkok Buenos Aires Cape Town Chennai
Dar es Salaam Delhi Hong Kong Istanbul Karachi Kolkata
Kuala Lumpur Madrid Melbourne Mexico City Mumbai
Nairobi São Paulo Shanghai Taipei Tokyo Toronto
OXFORD and OXFORD ENGLISH are registered trade marks of Oxford University Press in the UK and in certain other countries

First published 2004
2008 2007 2006 2005 2004
10 9 8 7 6 5 4 3 2 1

ISBN 0 19 453371 9

Typeset by Oxford University Press in Arial MT

Printed in Spain by Unigraf S. L.

ACKNOWLEDGEMENTS

Illustrations by: Roger Penwill

The publisher would like to thank Takis Loulakis at Omiros Institutes of Foreign Languages for his contributions